# Reproductive Tourism in the United States

This book examines the United States as a destination for international consumers of assisted fertility services, including egg donation, surrogacy, and sex selection. Based on interviews conducted with fertility industry insiders who market their services to an international clientele in three of the largest American hubs of the global fertility marketplace—New York City, Los Angeles, and San Francisco—and focusing on the providers rather than the consumers of assisted fertility services, the book shines a light on how professional ethics and norms, in addition to personal moralities, shape the practice of reproductive tourism.

**Lauren Jade Martin** is Assistant Professor of sociology at Pennsylvania State University, Berks.

# Routledge Advances in Sociology

*For a full list of titles in this series, please visit www.routledge.com*

# Reproductive Tourism in the United States

## Creating Family in the Mother Country

**Lauren Jade Martin**

Routledge
Taylor & Francis Group

LONDON AND NEW YORK

First published 2015
by Routledge

2 Park Square, Milton Park, Abingdon, Oxfordshire OX14 4RN
52 Vanderbilt Avenue, New York, NY 10017

*Routledge is an imprint of the Taylor & Francis Group, an informa business*

First issued in paperback 2020

*Library of Congress Cataloging-in-Publication Data*
Reproductive tourism in the United States : creating family in the mother
    country / by Lauren Jade Martin.
      pages cm. — (Routledge advances in sociology ; 142)
    Includes bibliographical references and index.
  1. Human reproductive technology—Social aspects—United
States.   2. Medical tourism—United States.   3. Fertility
clinics—United States.   4. Reproductive health services—United
States.   I. Title.
    RG133.5.M3825  2015
    304.6′320973—dc23
    2014035556

ISBN: 978-1-138-80984-0 (hbk)
ISBN: 978-0-367-59997-3 (pbk)

Typeset in Sabon
by Apex CoVantage, LLC

In memory of my grandmothers, Eva Martin and
Chui Sun Ng Moy

# Contents

# Tables

# Acknowledgments

The research and writing of this book was made possible by funding from the Graduate Center of the City University of New York, including a Provost's Fellowship, Writing Fellowship, Doctoral Student Research Grant, and the Women's Studies Certificate Program Nina Fortin Dissertation Proposal Award. Additional funding from Penn State University Berks Research Development Grants provided time and resources towards the completion of the manuscript.

This book would not have been possible without the generosity of the physicians, lawyers, egg and surrogate brokers, and other fertility industry professionals who took time out of their very busy schedules to meet with me to discuss their work. They let me come into their places of work and have a glimpse of their world, offered up their opinions, and told fascinating stories about helping people achieve their dreams of bringing home a child. I hope that I have accurately and respectfully recorded and portrayed their views and words.

Thank you to my editor, Max Novick, and to senior editorial assistant Jennifer Morrow for guiding the publication of this book. Thanks also to the anonymous peer reviewers for their critical feedback.

Innumerable faculty at the CUNY Graduate Center generously gave their support, guidance, and mentorship. Barbara Katz Rothman has been an advisor, mentor, friend, and colleague who always brings equal measure expertise, outrage, and humor into any discussion of the brave new world of reproductive technology. Hester Eisenstein, Frances Fox Piven, Setha Low, Victoria Pitts-Taylor, and Juan Battle all played significant roles in the development of this work.

My colleagues at Penn State Berks helped me transform this project from a dissertation into a book with advice about publishing, providing invaluable feedback on chapters, and creating a nurturing environment that encouraged enthusiasm for teaching and scholarship. Thank you to Kirk Shaffer, Belén Rodriguez-Mourelo, Radhica Ganapathy, Nathan Greenauer, Heidi Mau, Edwin Murillo, Randy Newnham, Cheryl Nicholas, Michele Ramsey, Toby Rider, Holly Ryan, Jessica Schocker, and Kesha Morant Williams. I also owe a great deal of thanks to my students, who have asked me important questions about this research that pushed me in new directions. Thank you to Niema Elliott for research assistance.

Jeannine Gailey and Denise Coppelton deserve big thanks for advice and feedback on the manuscript. I benefitted immensely from conversations about fertility and reproductive technology with Daisy Deomampo, Larry Greil, Marcia Inhorn, Katie Johnson, Susan Markens, Lisa Rubin, Sharmila Rudrappa, Ayo Wahlberg, and Catherine Waldby. *Globalizations* editor Mark Amen and *Science, Technology & Human Values* editor Ed Hackett, along with those journals' anonymous reviewers, were instrumental in shaping earlier versions of chapters.

Many, many thanks for the support, conversations, and collaborations from my CUNY GC Sociology family, including Nazreen Bacchus, Wilma Borrelli, Carlene Buchanan, Erynn Massi de Casanova, Kim Cunningham, Karen Gregory, Patrick Inglis, Danielle Jackson, Kate Jenkins, Mike Jolley, Yvonne Liu, Jeff London, Justin Myers, Soniya Munshi, Julie Netherland, Mitra Rasteger, Diana Rickard, Gina-Louise Sciarra, Marcos Tejeda, and Craig Willse.

My friends and family cheered me along the way. Thank you to Andy and Irene Martin, Ezra Martin, Joshua Howard, Rana Boland, Keight Bergmann, Miramar Dichoso, Brian Ford, Danielle Latman, Adrienna Moy, Lisa Thompson, Christina Varner, and Eleanor Whitney for your love and support.

# Introduction
## Procreative Outlaws

The husband and wife were from Japan where, like most countries, surrogacy is not formally recognized as a legitimate means of family building. Because the wife was unable to carry a child, but the couple was eager to have a baby, they decided to hire a woman in California (where surrogacy is legal), to bear a child for them. The American family law attorney who worked with them told me that they wanted to come up with a way to keep legal authorities in Japan from finding out about the surrogacy contract. Furthermore, because surrogacy is frowned upon back home, they did not even want friends and family members to know that an American woman was carrying their child. The solution they came up with was for the intended mother to fake being pregnant. The woman they hired as their surrogate in California played along by sending the couple pictures of her growing belly so that the intended mother could adjust the amount of padding she wore to match. In order to get around having to fake going into labor, the couple spent the last eight weeks of the pregnancy in the United States, claiming that a complication requiring fetal surgery and bed rest required the expertise of American doctors. And then, according to their attorney, "She returned with the baby, and it all worked, but it was like, wow!" Presenting the baby as "naturally" gestated and birthed by the intended mother, the Japanese couple became procreative outlaws in their home country, aided and abetted by their attorney, the surrogate, physicians, and other medical providers in the United States.

This is just one of the stories I heard while researching this book, about the fascinating phenomenon of reproductive tourism to the United States from countries where services like surrogacy, egg donation, and sex selection are illegal, highly regulated, or difficult to access. The attorney who told me the story worked in a family law office in a suburb of San Francisco. When I first walked into her office, the first thing I noticed, aside from a life-sized statue of a Dalmatian dog, were four giant bulletin boards so covered in overlapping photographs of babies there were no blank spaces left. If I had never before set foot in a fertility clinic, an egg donation agency, or a law office that specializes in family-building services, I might have done a double take when confronted with the sight of so many pictures of smiling and crying babies. In fact, I'd been seeing these babies on a regular basis, ever since I started conducting research on the United States fertility industry. Practically every waiting room I'd spent time in—in New York City, in Los Angeles, in San Francisco—it was babies, babies, everywhere, a visual signal to intended parents that this is a place where their dreams for children can come true.

The anecdote about the Japanese couple sounds like it could be the basis of a sitcom farce or a romantic comedy, and the costuming, pretending, and overly complicated maneuverings make the story stand out when I look back on my field notes and interview transcripts. Other aspects of the story, however, sounded all too familiar when compared with other stories I heard during my research, and typify some of the many reasons why foreign nationals come to the United States for assisted fertility services. Traveling thousands of miles for surrogacy, egg donation, sex selection, and other services enables people to circumvent laws and policies, provides them with anonymity and privacy, and gives them access to some of the best medical resources that the world has to offer. Reproduction—including conception, pregnancy, parturition, and childrearing—is a deeply private matter involving deeply private choices. Yet, procreative decision-making is not only a personal issue. Private choices about family building are made in the context of national and global phenomena such as market forces, scientific innovation, state policies, and multilateral agreements.

Procreation has been commodified since at least the days of slavery, with its reproduction of human bodies as property, but the explosion of assisted reproductive technologies (ART) since the 1970s has sped up and spread the commodification process (Davis, 1993; D. Roberts, 1997). These technologies enable reproductive parts and processes to be collected from, transferred to, and performed by multiple entities in commodity chains of baby-making enterprises, in which bodies are pumped with pharmaceuticals, sperm and eggs are harvested, wombs are rented, and embryos are created and selected in the laboratory. Reproduction has long been globalized, too, for example with the migration of women as domestic workers, but the commercialization and fragmentation of procreation produced by reproductive technologies enables the manufacture and handling of those reproductive parts and processes to be outsourced globally. No longer confined to the bedroom or to the body, procreation is a malleable and highly mobile process. The creation of one single child can involve numerous people—not just parents, but also endocrinologists and embryologists, attorneys, egg and sperm vendors, surrogate mothers—who may in fact be scattered across the globe.

Procreation is not only susceptible to commodification and globalization, but it has also long been subject to governance. State actors intervene in shaping their citizens' procreative choices through policies and regulations. Michel Foucault (2007) articulated the concept of "governmentality" in a 1978 lecture, arguing that the family is an instrument through which the state governs population. In *The History of Sexuality*, he introduced the related concept *biopower*, in which norming institutions such as the state, medicine, and education exert disciplinary control over bodies and regulation over populations (Foucault, 1978). Eugenic sterilization in Nazi Germany and the United States, the total ban on abortion in Nicaragua, China's one-child policy, and Romanian pronatalism are just some examples of interventions in the reproductive capacities of a country's citizens and residents that have had serious demographic consequences. The disciplinary arm of the state is not a gender-neutral one, either, and the state's attempts to regulate population have historically occurred through control of the bodies of women (Federici, 2004). Public policies and medical guidelines regarding assisted fertility are both part of this governmental and biopolitical authority.

These dynamics—the commodification, globalization, and regulation of assisted reproduction—are daily expressed and challenged within and through the United States fertility industry. This industry, I argue, is organized to benefit certain classes of American citizens and foreign nationals in their quest to have children through medically assisted conception, buttressed by lax federal regulation and free-market principles. In *Reproductive Tourism in the United States* I present a study of this industry as a particularly American institution and nascent profession that makes it an ideal destination for a phenomenon that has come to be referred to as "reproductive tourism." By focusing on the providers rather than the consumers of assisted fertility services, this book shines a light on how professional ethics and norms, in addition to personal moralities, shape the practice of reproductive tourism. A lack of robust federal oversight, high-technology resources, privatized health care, a pluralist population, and a commitment to professional autonomy combine to make the United States an ideal host for those seeking these sometimes illicit services. Like the Japanese couple mentioned earlier, those who are in possession of enough material resources and political savvy can subvert their countries' norms and laws regarding reproductive technologies, in effect becoming procreative outlaws.

## WHAT IS REPRODUCTIVE TOURISM?

Reproductive tourism is a phenomenon in which people travel significant distances, often across national borders, in order to access such reproductive technologies and services as *in vitro fertilization* (IVF), egg donation, sex selection, surrogacy, and preimplantation genetic diagnosis (PGD). These services enable women and men with infertility issues, single people, and gay and lesbian couples to conceive and bear biologically related children with the assistance of medical technologies and third parties. Some of these services also enable intended parents to reduce the chances of having children with genetic conditions, or to select for certain traits such as sex. Technically, reproductive tourism can also refer more broadly to any kind of cross-border reproduction or reproductive health care, including adoption, contraception, and abortion. However, in its most popular usage by scholars and in the mainstream media, it typically refers to services involving medically assisted conception, and thus it is often framed as a subset of medical tourism, or travel to obtain health care (Martin, 2012).

In 2008, the *New York Times* reported on a strange new phenomenon they called "reproductive outsourcing" (Gentleman, 2008). This remarkable turn of phrase was used to describe the commercial surrogacy market in India, in which citizens of the First World traveled hundreds or thousands of miles to rent the wombs of poor Indian women to carry and bear children for them. Paying another woman to bear a child for you may seem crass or bizarre, but there is historical precedent for this kind of practice. We pay numerous people to perform tasks for us that we do not enjoy, are not capable of, or are inefficient at—yet, is there something specific to reproductive labor, especially, that makes us balk? One source of the squeamishness stems from the history of reproductive labor being tied to the family or private sphere, and the idea that the home should, ideally, be a "place of refuge from market relations" governed by status obligations, not by contract (Glenn, 2010, p. 129; see also Pateman, 1988).

Although the terminology may have been new, the fact of reproductive outsourcing—using a "surrogate" or proxy to perform reproductive labor—is not. The *New York Times* article was explicitly about transnational surrogacy, but the phrase "reproductive outsourcing" may also include all instances wherein reproductive labor is contracted out to be performed by people who are not immediate family members, regardless of whether that labor is voluntary or involuntary, paid or unpaid. Reproductive tourism is just one practice in a chain of practices wherein the seeming interchangeability of laborers and bodies are manifest. By reproductive labor, I refer specifically to those forms of *generative* or physically nurturing labor that are involved with the physical and social reproduction of human beings, such as ova production, gestation and childbirth, lactation, and childcare. Reproductive outsourcing points to the marketization of reproductive labor: physically nurturing labor performed in order to relieve or substitute for the labor of those typically identified as wives and mothers. Reproductive tourism is not even the first instance of transnational outsourcing, if one includes in this expanded definition the migration of nannies and maids (Colen, 1995; Ehrenreich & Hochschild, 2002; Parreñas, 2001; Sassen, 1999).

Slavery in the antebellum United States included at least two instances of reproductive outsourcing: domestic labor and forced procreative labor. Slave owners charged their wives with household management, who in turn discharged the sundry tasks to slaves (Jones, 2009; White, 1999). Domestic labor in the slave household was a cruel example of some of the earliest forms of reproductive outsourcing in the Americas, as the wives of slaveholders directed slave women and children to perform "those duties necessary to maintain the health, comfort, and daily welfare of white families," including fetching wood, lighting fires, making beds, ironing, polishing shoes, preparing meals, dusting, bathing and diapering infants, sewing, and so on (Jones, 2009, p. 21).

As with other forms of reproductive outsourcing, the forced domestic labor performed by slave women contributed to the social reproduction of the slave-owning family and class while it took time, attention, and energy from the slaves' abilities to care for and nurture their own families, thus providing an early example of what Shelee Colen (1995) has termed "stratified reproduction" (see also D. Roberts, 1997). And, as Jones (2009) points out, even the labor the slave woman was able to perform for her own family members in slave quarters still served to benefit the slave owner because it maintained the health and welfare of his property, and the ability for his property to continue to labor for him. All forms of domestic labor—that performed in the slave owner's household as well as that performed in the slave quarters—were part of the social reproduction of the caste system of slavery.

The archetypal instance of the slave as reproductive/domestic laborer is, arguably, the so-called Mammy, who acts as a maternal presence in the slave household. Whereas the slave Mammy was primarily nurturer, and may have formed bonds with the children in her care, her procreative counterpart functioned as a *breeder*. These women, too, formed bonds with their children, but in the structure of slavery, nurturing bonds went against the creed of slavery. Angela Davis (1993) likens the slave woman to a "surrogate mother," because she gestated and gave birth to children that were not, legally, her own (see, also, Collins, 2000). The procreative capacities of slaves were harnessed as a means to create property and future laborers. American slavery was a self-replicating system, almost like some sort of human alchemy: the reproduction of property by property. Both women and men slaves acted as procreative laborers, with such practices as forced "mating," in which slaves were forced to have intercourse with each other, sometimes based on characteristics such as strength or size, much like animals are bred for traits. Slave women also suffered the indignity of rape by their slave masters (D. Roberts, 1997).

Wet nursing is another historical example of reproductive outsourcing. A wet nurse is a woman who breastfeeds a child that is not "hers," typically for wages or as forced labor. Prior to the development of infant formula and knowledge about sterilization that enabled safe bottle-feeding, if a woman died in childbirth or was incapacitated in such a way that she could not breastfeed, obtaining the services of another lactating woman was imperative for the survival of the newborn child. This was not always a market transaction, however, as women throughout time have helped each other in times of need by altruistically sharing their milk with other women's children (Golden, 2001). My own grandmother, for example, used to tell a story of how, during the Nazi occupation of Hungary, she nursed both my father and another child in the ghetto they were confined to, whose mother was so nutritionally deprived she had stopped lactating.

Wet nursing was common in the United States since at least the Colonial era, and was commonly practiced through the nineteenth century (Golden, 2001). In North America, women slaves were sometimes charged with nursing the children of their masters. Even after slavery was abolished, this kind of cross-racial nursing was much more common in the South than in the North (Golden, 2001, p. 72). Outside of plantations, wet nursing was a legitimate, if not highly regarded, occupation. Similar to wet nursing practices in France, what started as a practice in which infants were sent to reside with rural married women became, in the United States, "a temporary occupation for poor urban mothers" who were brought into middle- and upper-class households as live-in servants (Golden, 2001, p. 39; Sussman, 1975).

Families did not only employ wet nurses when the infant's mother was physically incapacitated or had passed away. In many circumstances, wet nursing typifies reproductive outsourcing in a particularly embodied way, much like ovum donation and surrogacy. Children who were "sent out" to reside in their nurses' homes in the countryside made it possible for urban working-class women to retain employment as factory workers or shop girls. In England, France, and the United States, upper class women were sometimes regarded as too "frail" to nurse their own children, as opposed to the robust and hardy lower class women they employed (Baumslag & Michels, 1995; Golden, 2001; A. Roberts, 1976; Sussman, 1975). Wet nursing was sometimes seen as a status marker of the middle and upper classes, but families (particularly mothers) that employed wet nurses have also been regarded as lazy, selfish, or non-nurturing (Golden, 2001; Joshel, 1986).

What is unique about this form of reproductive outsourcing may seem obvious but has enormous implications regarding class and inequality. Namely, it can only be performed by women who are lactating—that is, by women who have recently given birth or who have lactated continuously after having given birth. Every wet nurse is, then, a mother herself. She may, like my grandmother, nurse another woman's child at the same time she continues to nurse her own. In other cases, a wet nurse may have lost a child in its infancy but still have milk to spare. Or, perhaps most commonly, she may reserve her milk solely for the child in her charge. In nineteenth-century England, according to historian Ann Roberts, the fate of wet nurses' own children was grim; although some had already died before their mothers began to sell milk, and some continued to be nursed by their mothers, most were "put out to be nursed by hand," many of them dying from malnutrition (A. Roberts, 1976, p. 286). Infants of wet nurses in the United States, likewise, were often abandoned, sent to orphanages, or died (Golden, 2001, pp. 58–59). As with other forms of reproductive outsourcing, it was not only the reproductive laborer whose body was used to benefit another; at times, her own family also sacrificed, as care, attention, resources—even love—were bestowed upon the children of those who held the pocketbook or the whip.

## Contemporary Instances of Reproductive Outsourcing

Surrogacy and egg donation, like forced breeding and wet nursing, are particularly *embodied* forms of reproductive outsourcing. Contemporary domestic labor, while not directly generative in the same way as these other forms, is still a kind of labor necessary for social reproduction that has been outsourced to paid employees. With the movement of middle- and upper-class women into the workforce and out of the house, domestic duties have been taken up in some households, by nannies, home health aides, housekeepers, and cooks—or outsourced beyond the household entirely in the form of take-out, laundry services, day care, and nursing homes (Hochschild, 2013). This labor also has a transnational element, as much of it is performed by immigrant women, and, as several sociologists and anthropologists have studied, is a form of "stratified reproduction," as labor performed on behalf of another family means less time (or for many, even geographic proximity) to one's own family (Brown, 2011; Colen, 1995; Ehrenreich & Hochschild, 2002; Parreñas, 2001). Domestic workers involved in such organizations as Domestic Workers United have begun to agitate for—and win—rights as workers, but no such grassroots organizing has yet been started on behalf of egg donors and surrogates. Although there are parallels between domestic work and the reproductive work involved in egg donation and surrogacy, these reproductive laborers have not yet been fully proletarianized in the United States as wage laborers (cf. Waldby & Cooper, 2008). As I elaborate in Chapter 5, egg donors and surrogates are placed in an ambiguous position somewhere in between commodities, employees, and entrepreneurs.

Newspaper, magazine, and television media have tended to sensationalize reproductive tourism, with stories about celebrities or so-called baby farms in India. Less attention has been paid to other sought-after services such as egg donation and sex selection, as well as to locations in North America, Eastern and Southern Europe, and the Caribbean that are also popular destinations (Blyth, 2010; Nygren, Adamson, Zegers-Hochschild, & de Mouzon, 2010). Egg donation, sex selection, and other assisted fertility services are arguably just as ethically questionable as surrogacy, but one may speculate that surrogacy has garnered so much media attention because of the starkly embodied nature of it. The actual processes involved with egg donation and sex selection call to mind images of petri dishes and laboratories, whereas surrogacy evokes images of swollen bellies. When there is a cross-racial nature—brown women giving birth to white babies, as is largely the case of surrogacy tourism to India—it is not surprising that reporters and documentarians would find this phenomenon newsworthy.

Knoppers and LeBris (1991) first noted this phenomenon in the early 1990s, and global fertility services have in the past decade become a fast-growing, multibillion-dollar industry (Spar, 2006). Besides individual clinics and providers expanding their market from local clientele to people all over the world, medical tourism entrepreneurs have created specialized agencies to help facilitate communication and services between intended parents, clinics, physicians, attorneys, egg donors, and surrogates across borders. International hubs of reproductive tourism have sprouted throughout the world, enabling people to globe trot in search of affordable, legal, and efficient fertility services, sometimes in a relaxing, vacation-like environment. These agencies are not hard to find, either—all one has to do is Google the phrase "reproductive tourism," and the sheer number of sites with web addresses such as www.reproductive-tourism.com will become immediately apparent.

Like the term "medical tourism," the phrase "reproductive tourism" has been adopted by the mainstream media without being adequately theorized. Definitions of "tourism" are contested within the field of tourism studies, and reproductive tourism, as such, aligns with some and diverges from others. Some define *tourism* as a leisure activity in which people journey for a short period of time to a place that is neither work nor home, and "[consume] goods and services which are in some sense unnecessary" (Urry, 2002, p. 1). This definition is incompatible with the reproductive tourist, who does not travel for expressly leisure purposes, and who consumes goods and services that, from his or her point of view, are in fact necessary for the reproduction of biological offspring. Others argue that people engage in tourism for a number of reasons besides leisure, and that the tourism industry itself does not distinguish much between travel for business or pleasure since all sorts of travelers rely on the same infrastructure and services such as hotels, transportation, and restaurants. One rather loose definition is that "tourism shall be constituted of any kind of travel activity that includes the self-conscious experience of another place" (Chambers, 2000, p. xii). In this definition, a hallmark of modern tourism is the proliferation of reasons for travel; a leisurely vacation is merely one of many rationalizations for riding in an airplane to a distant locale for a weeklong trip. Tourism involves both a spatial and temporal element: it is a temporary interruption of one's daily life to travel to a destination for a bounded set of time, and involves the consumption of goods and services in the course of those travels. As this definition implies, the goal of tourism may be for non-leisure purposes, including reproduction.

The phrase "procreative tourism" was first coined over two decades ago, and over time "procreative" has generally been replaced with "reproductive" (Knoppers & LeBris, 1991). Scholarly disagreement about the nature of tourism has trickled into debates about the very use of the term "reproductive tourism" (Gürtin & Inhorn, 2011). In the course of conducting interviews in the field, one physician began our conversation by telling me how much he hated the phrase "reproductive tourism." (Another physician also expressed offense at my calling his field an "industry"). The physician who hated the title of my research would perhaps agree with those authors who argue that the word "tourism" is derogatory, implying that it is akin to taking a trip to Disney World, all too dismissive of the realities that lead intended parents to travel hundreds or thousands of miles to fulfill their dreams of having children (see, for example, Casper, 2011; Inhorn & Patrizio, 2009; Mainland & Wilson, 2010; Pennings, 2005). Some suggested replacements for "reproductive tourism" include "reproductive exile," "Travel ART," and "cross-border reproductive care" (Ferraretti, Pennings, Gianaroli, Natali, & Magli, 2010; Matorras, 2005; Smith-Cavros, 2010). It is the latter term that seems to have been most widely adopted as an alternative by the fertility industry itself, exemplified by its prevalent use in *Fertility & Sterility,* the journal of the professional organizations the American Society for Reproductive Medicine (ASRM) and the Society for Assisted Reproductive Technology (SART) (see, for example, Blyth, 2010; Mainland & Wilson, 2010; Nygren et al., 2010).

Yet, by neutralizing the term "reproductive tourism" and replacing it with something as benign as "cross-border reproductive care," we lose its linguistic and analytic link to the already established phenomenon of medical tourism (Sengupta, 2011). The use of a neutral phrase such as "cross-border reproductive care" obscures the very heart of the issue that sociologists, anthropologists, and bioethicists who study this phenomenon are grappling with: there are power relations and economic transactions embedded in this practice. Intended parents are not merely traveling to obtain assisted fertility services; they are using their economic capital to purchase the reproductive labor of others, in addition to all of the non-medical goods and services they consume in foreign lands, such as transportation, accommodations, food, entertainment, and souvenirs.

Reproductive tourism is a fascinating case study of globalization in this smaller, interconnected, and interdependent world where people, goods, services, capital, information, and labor flow rapidly across national borders. Unlike other cases of medical tourism, crossing borders for reproductive care frequently involves political, and not merely economic, motives. Forbidden, discouraged, or unable to get their procreative needs met at home, procreative outlaws are reliant upon a global infrastructure of medical providers, attorneys, egg donors, and surrogates, instant communications and information via the World Wide Web, and high-speed transportation and travel services.

## THE STUDY[1]

My research is indebted to what sociologists call the *grounded theory* approach, in which themes and analyses emerge inductively from one's data. The researcher may be drawn to study a particular topic because of his or her preconceived notions, but does not let preliminary hypotheses cloud the data collection or subsequent analysis. As sociologists Anselm Strauss and Juliet M. Corbin write, grounded theory "is inductively derived from the study of the phenomenon it represents. That is, it is discovered, developed, and provisionally verified through systematic data collection and analysis of data pertaining to that phenomenon" (Strauss & Corbin, 1990, p. 23). Grounded theory is typically employed by people who conduct qualitative research (as opposed to statistical or experimental research), and to that end, my studies of the United States fertility industry involved mixed qualitative methods. I conducted in-depth semi-structured interviews with fertility doctors, attorneys, and employees of egg donation and surrogacy agencies, engaged in participant observation of fertility-related events and seminars, and analyzed public policies, websites, and documents from fertility businesses and organizations. This mixed-methods approach allows for a scope that stretches between micro- and macro-level analysis. Ethnographic details and quotations yielded from participant observation and interviews allow for micro-level interpretation of how providers subjectively describe their interactions with clients and make ethical claims regarding their field. This is put into a broader context with analyses of state and global level public policies that structure the actions of providers and the procreative outlaws they serve. Rather than embedding myself in one location (or in one clinic), this research is multi-sited and took me to numerous offices in New York City, Los Angeles, and the San Francisco Bay Area.

## Participant Observation

The first stage of my research, when I knew that I wanted to study reproductive technologies but was not yet sure where to begin, involved attending and conducting unobtrusive participant observation at public events in New York and California that were sponsored by fertility clinics and programs and a non-profit advocacy group. These were publicized as educational events in newspapers, magazines, radio, direct emails, and organizations' websites, and included Open House events, informational seminars, and conferences.

As a participant observer, I registered for and attended the events as a member of the public interested in learning more about the organizations and topics being presented. All of the events were free, except for the conferences, sponsored by a non-profit organization, at which I volunteered in exchange for admission. I took brief notes during the seminars, and typed up longer field notes of my observations afterwards. Because I wanted my presence to be as unobtrusive as possible, for the most part I did not disclose my role as a researcher. For this reason, I have chosen to keep the names of all organizations and seminar presenters that I observed anonymous.

My role as participant observer was twofold. As a participant, my goal was to experience the seminars in the same way as the strangers sitting beside me: Was it a warm, welcoming environment? Did the sessions start on time? Were our questions answered thoughtfully? As an observer, however, my experiences were one step removed, as I took note of how the seminar organizers attempted to appeal to the participants. This entailed taking detailed notes about what kinds of information and materials were distributed to participants (e.g., pens, key chains, brochures, press clippings, egg- or sperm-shaped toys), what the space physically looked and felt like, the content of the presentations, and how presenters engaged with their audience. Although my observations focused on the speakers, I made notes about the composition of the audience in terms of age, race, and gender distribution, and whether people were attending by themselves or with presumed friends and/or partners. I did not record any identifying information about participants or their infertility status if they disclosed it. In addition to participation at these public events, I also wrote extensive field notes and cover sheets after each interview, describing the physical environment of the offices and waiting rooms of each site, providers' appearances, and any presenting questions, concerns, or things to follow up on.

## In-Depth Interviews

The central part of my research involved in-depth, semi-structured interviews. I spoke with twenty people working in the fertility industry whose jobs entail, in part, facilitating or directly providing fertility services for an international clientele. My goal was to investigate how members of the fertility industry subjectively understand their role in the commodification and transnationalization of reproduction. I aimed to interview a broad spectrum of providers (see the Appendix for more information about sampling and recruitment). Of those I interviewed, occupations fell in several general categories, but physicians and egg donor and surrogate "brokers" were the most represented. I also interviewed two attorneys, a licensed clinical social worker, an administrator (director of operations), and a genetic counselor. Half of the providers I interviewed were executives (owners or managing partners) of their organizations. This is a small sample size and is thus not generalizable, but the different occupations of the providers are representative of employees in the fertility industry who have experience working directly with international clients.

Interviews were conducted in person in the fertility industry hubs of New York City, Los Angeles, and the San Francisco Bay Area over a period of three months in 2009. Meeting in person rather than conducting phone interviews enabled me to establish greater rapport with my informants. It also allowed me to approximate as closely as possible the experience a client may have in meeting with providers face to face at their place of business. For this reason, all interviews, with two exceptions, were conducted onsite. One exception was the interview I conducted with Shelby and Rebekah,[2] co-owners of an egg donor and surrogacy agency, whom I had met at a fertility conference in New York City several months earlier. Because they do not have an office but instead both work out of their homes, we met at a coffee shop in a Los Angeles suburb. Theirs was also the only interview in which I interviewed two providers at once. The other exception was Deirdre, the attorney who assisted the Japanese couple described at the beginning of this introduction; although I met her at her office, and was able to observe the giant bulletin boards filled to the brim with photographs of babies, the interview took place at a bustling Chinese restaurant.

## Comparative Policy Analysis

Aside from the ethnographic elements of my research, I also analyzed a number of policies regarding assisted reproductive technologies to identify how regulation impinges on regionally based practice on four different levels: international, national, subnational/regional, and professional. Because of the comparative nature of this project, I contrast policies within the United States with policies of several other nations, including Australia, Germany, Israel, and the United Kingdom. The decentralized and federalist nature of United States government required examination beyond federal policy, and I relied upon data from the National Conference of State Legislatures (NCSL) to identify trends in policies on the subnational level. Because my research focuses on New York State and California, I paid especial attention to these states' policies. Finally, given the laissez-faire orientation of the United States towards assisted fertility (see Chapter 1), much of the practice of the fertility industry is guided not by legislation or government directives but by norms and guidelines of professional organizations (see Chapters 3 and 5). Thus included in the analysis were guidelines disseminated by the American Society for Reproductive Medicine (ASRM) and the Society for Assisted Reproductive Technology (SART).

## WHY STUDY THE UNITED STATES?
## WHY STUDY PROVIDERS?

When I first became interested in the topic of assisted reproductive technologies, I began to conduct participant observation at Open House events at local fertility clinics in New York City. Frequently advertised on the radio or on the clinics' own websites, the events I attended were largely free and open to the public, and usually consisted of a panel of speakers who would make presentations about the services that the clinic offered and then open the floor to questions from participants. Sometimes educational components were included, such as PowerPoint slides featuring animations and video of sperm being directly injected into an ovum. Typically, participants would receive brochures and logo-emblazoned pens, and folders full of information sheets about *in vitro fertilization* (IVF), intrauterine insemination (IUI), egg donation, and other fertility treatments. Sometimes these events allowed participants to tour the facilities, including the high-tech laboratories where embryos are created and stored. When I continued this research in California, the Open House events tended to follow a very similar script.

In addition to Open House events, I also attended two conferences in New York that were organized by a fertility-focused non-profit organization and intended for individuals who were interested in or exploring their options about having children via assisted fertility or adoption. By the time I attended the second conference, I had already begun researching some of the policy issues surrounding reproductive tourism, and was considering framing my research around Americans who had gone abroad, or were considering going abroad, in order to obtain assisted fertility services. At this second conference, I attended a session about reproductive tourism. Unlike most of the other workshops and panels that I attended at this and various seminars, the audience consisted primarily of providers—attorneys, physicians, and social workers—and hardly any intended parents. Rather than an organized speech or panel with professionals behind a dais or a podium, all participants sat in chairs turned towards each other, on the same plane. This physical layout lent itself to an informal conversation among participants, although an attorney was charged with leading discussion.

One person, a middle-aged Indian man in a dark blue suit, revealed to the room that he facilitated a surrogacy program in India. He immediately attracted the attention, and the ire, of many in the room. "But isn't it unethical?" they asked him. "Aren't you exploiting Indian women?" He attempted to defend himself, but the tenor in that room indicated that the majority of people were not persuaded. As a participant observer, I could not help but notice the claims that some of the American providers made about how they treated "their" American surrogates and egg donors, all the while asserting that Indian surrogates could not possibly be treated or paid as well as their counterparts in the United States. Was there not a disconnect, I began to wonder, in how the American providers view their own services, their own relationships with surrogates and egg donors, compared with how they view the same services and relationships in another regional context? Was their outrage at this man based on moral values, or were they angry that he was peeling away some of their own potential business? If Indian surrogates were being exploited by rich foreigners, what did this say about American surrogates and egg donors who labored on behalf of foreign couples? And what if this conversation had happened in Western Europe, where commercial surrogacy and egg donation are largely seen as unethical practices and subsequently banned in several countries? Would the American providers, like the Indian man, also be roundly attacked and forced to defend themselves?

Perhaps I should not have been surprised by the conference attendees' focus on surrogates in India or their blind spots about their role in the reproductive tourism that happens in their own country. Articles in the *New York Times* and other major world newspapers, an episode of Oprah Winfrey, and the recent documentary "Made in India" have focused almost entirely on Americans and Europeans searching for bargains in the surrogacy market in India, despite reports that people also travel to and within Europe,

North America, Southeast Asia, and Latin America in order to obtain fertility services (Nygren et al., 2010). There has been scant attention paid to the United States as a *destination* for intended parents seeking egg donors, surrogates, or access to other forbidden services. As my research reveals, people from all over the world seek out providers in New York and California for egg donation, surrogacy, and sex selection. Some of the most prevalent sending regions, according to providers, include Australia, Japan, China, and Western Europe.

India as a hub for international surrogacy may offer a compelling narrative about exploitation and neocolonialism, but the narrative about the United States as destination is equally compelling: those who are in possession of enough material resources and political savvy can subvert their countries' norms and laws regarding reproductive technologies. If governments enact laws to structure the fertility options of their citizens, yet some individuals, despite these laws, are able to leave their countries' borders to pursue forbidden services elsewhere, what does this say about the reach of biopolitical governance, or of citizenship itself? Unmarried couples and gay men, for example, are excluded from accessing fertility services in many countries, and paying surrogates and egg donors, or using genetic technologies for sex selective purposes, are likewise *verboten* in much of the world. In the United States, however, a laissez-faire orientation towards regulation of reproductive medicine makes assisted fertility services available for anyone with the means to pay for them. The advent of reproductive technologies, which have already contributed to the fragmentation and commodification of procreation, also contribute to the neoliberalization of procreation as a largely unregulated, private, free-market transaction. The United States and other receiving nations capitalize on the unmet international demand for fertility services by allowing hubs of reproductive tourism to flourish within their borders. Although this is an obviously lucrative position for American providers to be in, they speak not in terms of how much money this yields, but in terms of helping international clientele achieve reproductive freedom by so-called American standards.

As a result of the conference discussion, my focus shifted from the United States as a sending nation to the United States as a receiving nation. I went through the reams of material I had collected at fertility seminars and events, and looked at hundreds of websites of fertility clinics and agencies, and discovered that many explicitly advertised and marketed their services internationally. Thus began another stage of my research: in-depth interviews with fertility industry providers who worked with an international clientele. While there already exist ethnographies featuring interviews with intended parents, egg donors, and surrogates, this book focuses on the perspective of the industry insiders: the professionals who facilitate and promote surrogacy, egg donation, *in vitro fertilization*, genetic diagnosis, and sex selection to an international clientele (Almeling, 2011; Becker, 2000; Franklin, 1997; Mamo, 2007; Teman, 2010).

## OVERVIEW OF THIS BOOK

In this book I explore some of the factors that make the United States such a friendly host for the world's reproductive tourists. Chapter 1, "Reproductive Tourism in the Age of Globalization," uses reproductive tourism as a case study of globalization, forming a theoretical underpinning of the book. It examines the tensions between national regulations and the global demand for assisted fertility services that drive the practice of reproductive tourism. In Chapter 2, "The Push and Pull of Reproductive Tourism: The United States as Destination," based on informant interviews and policy analysis, I examine the factors that *push* individuals to search for assisted fertility services outside of their home country, and those that *pull* them to the United States. Chapter 3, "Privatization and Self-Regulation in the United States Fertility Industry," focuses on the factors that make the United States fertility industry unique among its international counterparts, including its lack of federal government funding for research, the largely cash-for-services model of reimbursement, and an overall lack of federal policies regulating the industry. In Chapter 4, "Coming to America: How Providers Manage Work with International Clients," I describe the process and challenges of working with international clients from the perspective of United States providers. Chapter 5, "Ethics, Professional Autonomy and the United States Fertility Industry," focuses on the ethical questions surrounding the work of fertility industry providers, noting how medicalization and the commodification of reproductive body parts makes ambiguous their relationships with donors and surrogates. Chapter 6, "Genetic Imperatives and Selective Technologies in the Global Landscape," explores the imperatives to have biologically/genetically related children, and the resultant ways in which technologies such as egg donation, sex selection, and genetic diagnosis are put to selective ends by domestic and international clients seeking to gain an edge or control over the outcome of their children. The book concludes with "Setting Regional and Global Standards," a discussion of the problems and possibilities of standards to tamp down some of the excesses of reproductive tourism.

The subtitle, "Creating Family in the Mother Country," is an obvious play on words. The *Oxford English Dictionary* defines "mother country" as: (1) "the country of one's birth; one's native land; = MOTHERLAND *n.* 1. Also: the country of one's ancestors or of one's ethnic group"; and (2) "a country in relation to its colonies or dependencies; the country from which the founders of a colony came" ("Mother country," 2014). In the following chapters I complicate the simplistic narrative of imperialism that often shades discussions of reproductive tourism. In this context, the United States is not *that* kind of mother country. Technology, global capital, open borders, and public policies have, however, transformed the United States into a mother country, enabling the creation of family for individuals worldwide.

## NOTES

1. For more details about the methodology, see the Appendix.
2. All names of informants have been changed.

## REFERENCES

Almeling, R. (2011). *Sex cells: The medical market for eggs and sperm*. Berkeley: University of California Press.

Baumslag, N., & Michels, D. L. (1995). *Milk, money, and madness: The culture and politics of breastfeeding*. Westport, CT: Bergin & Garvey.

Becker, G. (2000). *The elusive embryo: How women and men approach new reproductive technologies*. Berkeley: University of California Press.

Blyth, E. (2010). Fertility patients' experiences of cross-border reproductive care. *Fertility and Sterility*, 94(1), e11–e15.

Brown, T. M. (2011). *Raising Brooklyn: Nannies, childcare, and Caribbeans creating community*. New York: NYU Press.

Casper, M. J. (2011, April 13). Reproductive tourism. *The Feminist Wire*. Retrieved from www.thefeministwire.com/2011/04/13/reproductive-tourism/

Chambers, E. (2000). *Native tours: The anthropology of travel and tourism*. Prospect Heights, IL: Waveland Press.

Colen, S. (1995). "Like a mother to them": Stratified reproduction and West Indian childcare workers and employers in New York. In F.D. Ginsburg and R. Rapp (Eds.), *Conceiving the new world order: The global politics of reproduction* (pp. 78–102). Berkeley: University of California Press.

Collins, P. H. (2000). *Black feminist thought: Knowledge, consciousness, and the politics of empowerment*. New York: Routledge.

Davis, A. Y. (1993). Outcast mothers and surrogates: Racism and reproductive rights in the nineties. In L. S. Kauffman (Ed.), *American feminist thought at century's end: A reader* (pp. 355–366). Cambridge: Wiley-Blackwell.

Ehrenreich, B., & Hochschild, A. R. (2002). *Global woman: Nannies, maids, and sex workers in the new economy*. New York: Metropolitan.

Federici, S. (2004). *Caliban and the witch: Women, the body and primitive accumulation*. New York: Autonomedia.

Ferraretti, A. P., Pennings, G., Gianaroli, L., Natali, F., & Magli, M. C. (2010). Cross-border reproductive care: A phenomenon expressing the controversial aspects of reproductive technologies. *Reproductive Biomedicine Online*, 20(2), 261–266.

Foucault, M. (1978). *The history of sexuality: An introduction. Vol. 1*. New York: Vintage.

Foucault, M. (2007). *Security, territory, population: Lectures at the Collège de France, 1977–1978*. New York: Picador.

Franklin, S. (1997). *Embodied progress: A cultural account of assisted conception*. New York: Routledge.

Gentleman, A. (2008, March 10). India nurtures business of surrogate motherhood. *The New York Times*. Retrieved from www.nytimes.com/2008/03/10/world/asia/10surrogate.html

Glenn, E. N. (2010). *Forced to care: Coercion and caregiving in America*. Cambridge, MA: Harvard University Press.

Golden, J. (2001). *A social history of wet nursing in America: From breast to bottle*. Columbus: Ohio State University Press.

Gürtin, Z. B., & Inhorn, M. C. (2011). Introduction: Travelling for conception and the global assisted reproduction market. *Reproductive BioMedicine Online*, 23(5), 535–537. doi:10.1016/j.rbmo.2011.08.001

Hochschild, A. R. (2013). *The outsourced self*. New York: Picador. Retrieved from http://us.macmillan.com/book.aspx?name=theoutsourcedself&author=ArlieHochschild

Inhorn, M. C., & Patrizio, P. (2009). Rethinking reproductive "tourism" as reproductive "exile." *Fertility and Sterility, 92*(3), 904–906.

Jones, J. (2009). *Labor of love, labor of sorrow: Black women, work and the family, from slavery to the present*. New York: Basic Books.

Joshel, S. R. (1986). Nurturing the master's child: Slavery and the Roman child-nurse. *Signs, 12*(1), 3–22.

Knoppers, B. M., & LeBris, S. (1991). Recent advances in medically assisted conception: Legal, ethical and social issues. *American Journal of Law & Medicine, 17*, 329.

Mainland, L., & Wilson, E. (2010). Principles of establishment of the First International Forum on Cross-Border Reproductive Care. *Fertility and Sterility, 94*(1), e1–e3.

Mamo, L. (2007). *Queering reproduction: Achieving pregnancy in the age of technoscience*. Durham: Duke University Press.

Martin, L. J. (2012). Reproductive tourism. In *The Wiley-Blackwell encyclopedia of globalization*. Malden, MA: Wiley-Blackwell. Retrieved from http://onlinelibrary.wiley.com.ezaccess.libraries.psu.edu/doi/10.1002/9780470670590.wbeog495/abstract

Matorras, R. (2005). Reproductive exile versus reproductive tourism. *Human Reproduction, 20*(12), 3571.

Mother country. (2014, September). In *Oxford English dictionary online*. Oxford University Press. Retrieved from www.oed.com

Nygren, K., Adamson, D., Zegers-Hochschild, F., & de Mouzon, J. (2010). Cross-border fertility care—International Committee Monitoring Assisted Reproductive Technologies global survey: 2006 data and estimates. *Fertility and Sterility, 94*(1), e4–e10.

Parreñas, R. S. (2001). *Servants of globalization: Women, migration, and domestic work*). Stanford, CA: Stanford University Press. Retrieved from http://books.google.com/books?hl=en&lr=&id=sbL5UNcvFKEC&oi=fnd&pg=PR9&dq=rhacel+parrenas&ots=whJ3dZZjr1&sig=heuOzoOSZNNee23rseHDWdJbKLQ

Pateman, C. (1988). *The sexual contract*. Stanford, CA: Stanford University Press.

Pennings, G. (2005). Reply: Reproductive exile versus reproductive tourism. *Human Reproduction, 20*(12), 3571–3572.

Roberts, A. (1976). Mothers and babies: The wetnurse and her employer in mid-nineteenth century England. *Women's Studies: An Interdisciplinary Journal, 3*(3), 279–293.

Roberts, D. (1997). *Killing the black body: Race, reproduction, and the meaning of liberty*. New York: Vintage Books.

Sassen, S. (1999). *Globalization and its discontents: Essays on the new mobility of people and money*. New York: New Press.

Sengupta, A. (2011). Medical tourism: Reverse subsidy for the elite. *Signs, 36*(2), 312–318.

Smith-Cavros, E. (2010). Fertility and inequality across borders: Assisted reproductive technology and globalization. *Sociology Compass, 4*(7), 466–475.

Spar, D. (2006). *The baby business: How money, science, and politics drive the commerce of conception*. Boston, MA: Harvard Business School Press.

Strauss, A. L., & Corbin, J. M. (1990). *Basics of qualitative research: Grounded theory procedures and techniques*. Newbury Park: Sage.

Sussman, G. D. (1975). The wet-nursing business in nineteenth-century France. *French Historical Studies, 9*(2), 304–328. doi:10.2307/286130

Teman, E. (2010). *Birthing a mother*. Berkeley: University of California Press.

Urry, J. (2002). *The tourist gaze*. London: Sage.

Waldby, C., & Cooper, M. (2008). The biopolitics of reproduction. *Australian Feminist Studies, 23*(55), 57–73.

White, D. G. (1999). *Ar'n't I a woman?: Female slaves in the plantation south*. New York: W. W. Norton & Company.

# 1 Reproductive Tourism in the Age of Globalization

Reproductive tourism is a growing, global market. In future chapters I provide data from interviews I conducted with United States fertility industry professionals about their experiences working with international clientele. The International Committee Monitoring Assisted Reproductive Technologies (ICMART) recently attempted to collect data from 49 countries about the prevalence of cross-border fertility care. Their data indicate an estimated 5,000 to 7,000 treatment cycles between twenty-three responding countries, but the authors ultimately conclude that non-standardized data collection makes quantification of this practice at present unreliable (Nygren, Adamson, Zegers-Hochschild, & de Mouzon, 2010). Despite the lack of comprehensive numbers about its prevalence, all of my informants indicated that they did not foresee reproductive tourism to the United States—or to other destinations they were familiar with—stemming any time soon.

The websites of some international fertility clinics also hint at this growing market. Fertility Treatment Abroad, for example, is a site that allows users to locate hospitals and clinics by searching by procedure and country of destination (Fertility Treatment Abroad, n.d.). The Pacific Fertility Center in California boasts webpages in both English and Japanese, and advertises that they serve patients from "countries all around the world such as France, Germany, Yugoslavia, England, Vietnam, China, Philippines, and Japan" (Pacific Fertility Center, 2011, para. 1). Connections between reproductive tourism and traditional notions of tourism are made obvious at this clinic's website by hyperlinks to information about San Francisco and local hotel accommodations.

This connection is made even more clearly by the Barbados Fertility Centre, which explicitly markets its services as a holiday getaway. The website boasts photographs of white sand, clear blue sea, and Caucasian couples in bathing suits, with text that reads, "In between your appointments, you have constant access to our team of experts by cellular phone but with the freedom of being on holiday. You can enjoy the soothing sound of the lapping Caribbean Sea, go for a long romantic walk along the white sandy beaches and then enjoy the tantalizing tastes of the Caribbean's cuisine" (Barbados Fertility Centre, n.d., para. 2).

In Spain, the website of the *Centro de Fertilización in Vitro de Asturias* (CEFIVA) is available in Spanish, English, German, French, and Italian. Although it does not boast pictures of sandy beaches and tanned bodies, this clinic uses the "small, peaceful city" in which the clinic is located as a selling point (CEFIVA, n.d., para. 3). One should not overemphasize the conflation of reproductive tourism with leisure activities, however. This clinic also bluntly states, "The present Law governing Assisted Reproduction in Spain allows treatments to be carried out here which are restricted in other countries" (CEFIVA, n.d., para. 1).

Although reproductive tourism may be combined with vacation-like experiences, the focus of the trip is to access fertility services and is thus a very specific type of tourism. People may engage in reproductive tourism in order to access cheaper, more efficient, or a wider range of services, or even to access those services in a relaxing environment; but, as the Spanish clinic's website attests, it is also practiced by those who aim to bypass regulations and laws in their home countries. As I elaborate in Chapter 2, there are several push-and-pull factors operating to drive reproductive tourism from and to various countries. For those driven by political motives, the global fertility marketplace is a space of mediation when tensions bubble up between a nation's laws and regulations and its citizens' particular desires for medically assisted conception. The providers interviewed for this book subjectively discuss their positions in this marketplace as they work with and market their services to an international clientele.

Using reproductive tourism, in which people go abroad for assisted fertility services, as a case in point, this chapter examines the interaction of state policies, global markets, scientific innovation, and other forces of globalization in the transformation of reproductive practices. It has become a truism to state that we are living in an age of globalization, yet scholars and activists have not come to a consensus as to what exactly constitutes globalization, or what distinguishes globalization in the twenty-first century from previous eras of internationalization and transnationalism. When theorists write and speak of globalization, the image that often forms is that of a smaller, interconnected, interdependent world in which people, goods, services, capital, information, and labor flow rapidly across national and regional borders.

Globalization is a transformative force that may produce beneficial and disadvantageous effects simultaneously, offering new opportunities and mobility at the same time it reproduces structural inequalities. This is apparent in the effects of globalization and global capitalism on gender relations and the status of women (Acker, 2004; Eisenstein, 2005). Studies on the transnationalization of reproduction, for example, reveal new patterns of female migration, kinship structures, labor, and childrearing that tend to empower those already privileged by gender, race-ethnicity, class, nationality, and/or immigration status at the expense and exploitation of others (Ehrenreich & Hochschild, 2002; Ginsburg & Rapp, 1995).

One of the questions that globalization raises is the extent to which ease of migration across borders by people, ideas, capital, and consumer products renders those very borders meaningless, or to what degree the sovereignty or law-making capacity of nations has been undermined. This book examines how a global marketplace for assisted fertility services mediates tensions between state control and individual desire, in light of the global variation in policies regarding reproductive technologies. When national and local policies forbid certain procedures (such as sex selection) or prohibit access by particular groups of people (such as unmarried women, lesbians and gay men, or people considered too old to have a child), a fortunate few are able to travel to other jurisdictions to purchase those forbidden procedures or products. One might question whether this behavior undermines the governmental power of the state to regulate its population, at least for those privileged enough to subvert its mandates (Foucault, 2007). In the age of globalization, citizens remain subject to governmentality as it applies to their reproductive decision-making, but some citizens are enabled and transformed into *global* consumers, or biocitizens, able to buy their way out of inconvenient or onerous policies.

Such examples of "flexible citizenship" do not mean that the nation or even national borders are becoming irrelevant (Ong, 1999). Given the range of policies regarding reproductive technologies throughout the world, some nations have capitalized on the unmet international demand for fertility services by allowing hubs of reproductive tourism to flourish within their borders. Tensions between state control and individual desire are mediated by a global marketplace for assisted fertility services. This global marketplace operates in the context of wildly variant national policies regarding reproductive technologies, multilateral agreements and regional confederations that affect trade and the movement of people, and rapidly changing technological developments. Reproductive tourism thus becomes a case study to analyze one central aspect of the globalization debate: to what extent has globalization presaged a declining role of the state? In a world where high-technology fertility clinics now advertise on the World Wide Web for an international clientele, does globalization make national oversight of reproductive technologies and services moot? Does it undermine the regulatory apparatus of the state, that is, its "governmental" power over population?

Consumers of reproductive technologies, like any citizens, are subject to their country's rules and regulations. Government asserts its power over life and death; it affirms and organizes its powers over the social and individual body through discipline of sexuality and regulation of population (Foucault, 1978). One can look to literature regarding population control, abortion, and birth control policies for examples of this governmental function, but one can also look to policies regarding reproductive technologies (Dixon-Mueller, 1993; Petchesky, 1990). These rules and regulations are framed by the interests of the state in managing its demographic needs and reinforcing the ethical, cultural, religious, economic, and political norms and values deemed central in that region.

## GOVERNMENTALITY, BIOCITIZENSHIP, AND THE NEOLIBERAL EXCEPTION

One way to think about how countries regulate fertility services is in terms of Foucault's biopolitical governmentality and the broader context of policies governing reproduction (Foucault, 2007). The state as disciplinarian shapes the population, determining who is "fit" or "unfit" to procreate and raise children—that is, what kind of bodies can or cannot be born and thrive. At the same time, the state creates, limits, reinforces, and defines ethical and moral standards for its populace, or what one can or cannot do with one's body, what counts as a "body" or a "person," and who has ownership or jurisdiction over those bodies and persons (Agamben, 1998; Hashiloni-Dolev, 2007; Rose, 2007). These biopolitical regimes involve not only state actors but also include other institutions with disciplinary functions, including Medicine, Education, and the Family.

Biopolitical regimes play an intimate role in what one can or cannot do with one's body. The state and other norming institutions are involved in overseeing and surveilling end-of-life decisions, organ donation, sex work, and body modification. Policies raise questions, for one, about human biological materials: what citizens may have injected or implanted in their body; what they are allowed to expel or have surgically removed; what they are allowed to buy, sell, rent, or borrow from another person's body. In addition to policies determining what an abstract person may do with his or her body, they also delineate *which types of persons* are allowed to take part in the buying, selling, renting, extracting, and implanting; in what circumstances; and how often. Reproductive practices, including abortion, contraception, sterilization, and assisted fertility, moreover, have *direct* and *immediate* demographic implications.

Regulation of reproductive technologies and services currently varies throughout the world, and this is where the matter of reproductive tourism enters the picture. Reproductive tourism is decidedly *not* only about Westerners traveling to Third World countries to consume cheaper fertility services; reproductive tourism to the United States, where fertility services are quite expensive, is currently thriving. Moreover, those who travel to the United States are not all coming from countries that are wealthier than the United States, or that lack their own fertility industries. A major difference between the United States and these other sending nations is the United States' laissez-faire stance towards assistive technologies and its laws regarding paternity.

If governments enact laws to structure the fertility options of their citizens, and yet some individuals, despite these laws, are able to leave their countries' borders to pursue forbidden services elsewhere, what does this say about the reach of biopolitical governance, or of citizenship itself? All citizens, significantly, are not equally subject to the state's enforcement of rules and regulations. When procreation moves out of the bedroom and into the laboratory, when bodily materials are bought and sold like any other commodity, the hands of the market and the government play powerful roles in both *how* and *what type of* babies are made.

Reproductive tourism may seem to undermine the governmental function of the state if we think of the state as an all-powerful actor enforcing rigorous controls over its population. After all, if citizens can thumb their noses at legislation banning or criminalizing a particular service they then seek out in another country with more lax policies, are they not subverting the governmental reach of the state? Reproductive tourism instead must be seen as a *response* to governmentality, as a practice that is itself *produced* by governmentality: attempts by the state to control the reproductive actions of its citizens through regulation leads to the subversion of those very same regulations. This subversion itself is facilitated by neoliberal free market ideology and practices. Anthropologist Aihwa Ong describes this kind of phenomenon as a "neoliberal exception," in which global capitalist forces undermine regulatory functions (Ong, 2007). Reproductive tourism as a neoliberal exception is, however, a stratified phenomenon that only exists for a privileged subset who are able to subvert the mandates of the state. The less privileged who cannot maneuver around restrictions and prohibitions are still subject to governmental regulations on their reproductive autonomy.

Governmentality does not disappear in the face of reproductive tourism; rather it is interactional, and we see governmental responses *to* reproductive tourism. Just as we can identify different types of governmental regimes, there are also different types of responses. New South Wales, Australia, for example, offers a protectionist response that prohibits even those commercial surrogacy arrangements that occur in other geographic locations. The neoliberal response, on the other hand, capitalizes on the unmet international demand for fertility services by allowing hubs of reproductive tourism to flourish within its borders. This response is exemplified by the United States, India, and some Eastern European nations.

## Biological and Flexible Citizenship Projects

Another useful term to add to the toolkit for understanding reproductive tourism is Rose and Novas's (2005) concept of "biological citizenship" (see also Petryna, 2002; Rose, 2007). The authors refer to a kind of *social identity* that links one's sense of self as a citizen to "beliefs about the biological existence of human beings, as individuals, as families and lineages, as communities, as population and races, and as a species" (Rose & Novas,

2005, p. 440). Biological citizenship can move beyond the self-motivated individual to take on an active, biosocial form, in which people align with others who share similar biological conditions (and/or who act on their behalf as advocates) to advance their position, and may see governments and/or medical authorities as allies or as antagonists (Rabinow, 1996). Acts of biological citizenship may include ACT-UP activists fighting for more federal dollars to go towards HIV/AIDS research, or victims of 9/11 suing the United States to provide for their unique health-care needs.

People with infertility conditions or who are unable to have children on their own for social reasons have started support groups and advocacy organizations, including RESOLVE and the American Fertility Association, and involvement in these organizations is an enactment of both biological citizenship and biosociality. Rose (2007), emphasizing an activist biocitzenry, writes, "Biological citizenship requires those with investments in their biology to *become* political" (Rose, 2007, p. 149). Yet, political acts may not be collective or even conscious. Those who cross national borders in order to obtain fertility services may or may not be involved with any advocacy organizations, but the very act of engaging in transnational reproduction has political overtones, particularly when it occurs as a means to enact one's personal reproductive autonomy in the face of restrictive laws and policies one disagrees with.

In this respect, my interpretation of biological citizenship does not require an activist orientation or even an acknowledgement that this social identity is shared by others. Rather than a politics of social justice, biological citizenship may be motivated by a politics of entitlement. This interpretation of biological citizenship also relates to Ong's "flexible citizenship," which includes "the localizing strategies of subjects who, through a variety of familial and economic practices, seek to evade, deflect, and take advantage of political and economic conditions in different parts of the world" (Ong, 1999, p. 113). Cognizant that different rules apply in different state regimes, a hypermobile, economically privileged segment of the world population seeks to work, invest, be educated, and raise families in the places that are most advantageous for these particular activities. The United States, with its lax regulations, high-technology resources, amenable courts, birthright citizenship, and a class of relatively young and healthy women willing to act as third-party egg donors and surrogates, becomes an ideal Mother Country for those flexible citizens desiring children through assisted fertility.

Those who engage in reproductive tourism do not necessarily forgo one form of national citizenship to take advantage of another but, instead, take their national citizenship for granted as they enact their biological citizenship. This is a different dynamic than cases of so-called anchor babies, in which giving birth to a child in the United States is framed as a first step on the road to securing American citizenship for additional family members. Take for example the recent case in which a French couple has unsuccessfully fought for ten years to get the French government to recognize their twin daughters, born via surrogate in California, as French citizens (Souchard, 2011). By virtue of their birth in the United States, the daughters are American citizens, in the eyes of both American and French law. What is as yet unresolved is whether the couple should be recognized as the natural parents of their daughters and thus transmit to them French citizenship—California law says yes, French law says no. Flexible citizenship and the politics of entitlement plays out in that the French couple felt entitled to subvert French law by traveling to California to obtain a prohibited service, obtain parentage through the California court system, and have their daughters recognized as French citizens despite the illicit nature of their birth in another country.

The collision between biological citizenship and flexible citizenship as exemplified by reproductive tourism may ironically be constructed as a nationalist project, as citizens of one country go to extraordinary ends, involving people, governments, and industries of other nations to produce more citizens for their own home country. Furthermore, as long as the gametes of at least one of the intended parents is being used to produce these transnationally derived children, it is not only *citizenship* that is being transmitted, but genetic continuity. Although Rose (2007) downplays the racialized and eugenic overtones of contemporary manifestations of biological citizenship, the "genetic imperative" is ever present and at play in reproductive tourism and indeed undergirds the entire fertility industry (see Chapter 6 for more on the genetic imperative).

Reproductive tourism is an enactment of what I am here calling *global biocitizenship*. Individuals residing in nations where they cannot obtain the reproductive technologies they desire (because they are too expensive, unavailable, or illegal) are transformed into global biocitizens: they enact a kind of citizenship based on their biological/reproductive desires on a global stage. Reproductive tourism is not the only instance—the same phenomenon is evinced by transnational adoptive parents (Dubinsky, 2010), by people who cross national borders to purchase organs for transplant on the black market or in places where organs are sufficiently commodified (Lock & Kaufert, 1998; Scheper-Hughes & Wacquant, 2002), by those who engage in medical tourism for sex reassignment surgery (Aizura, 2009), and by American seniors traveling to Canada to fulfill their prescriptions (Khosravi, 2003). In all cases, global biocitizens may not imagine themselves being part of a larger social movement. They indeed may be acting purely out of self-interest. Yet, what is true about both organ trafficking and international commercial surrogacy is that global biocitizens cannot act alone: they rely on a global network to facilitate this trade in bodies and body parts, of surgeries and pharmaceuticals, and they travel to places where this facilitating network thrives, either legally or in the shadows.

Global biocitizens do not operate or exist outside the realm of governmentality. Rather, they invoke a kind of free-market subjection, choosing to subject themselves to other regions' modes of governmentality that better suit their biological/reproductive needs and desires than the country in which they are citizens by right of birth or naturalization. We may think of these citizens as "unruly," as they who cannot be contained or constrained—but this unruliness is frequently sanctioned by governments that turn a blind eye to subversion by the socially, politically, and economically advantaged. The less privileged, however, remain subject to governmental controls and often have no choice but to be compliant citizens, without the babies or organs that they, too, desire.

The subjection of global biocitizens to extraterritorial governmentality is exemplified by those individuals who travel to the United States to obtain the services of surrogates. These individuals do not exist in a nether zone absent of law; rather, they turn away from laws in their home countries that forbid contracting with another woman to gestate a baby and towards laws of foreign governments that recognize surrogacy contracts. Thus, we see that providers of fertility services often employ or contract with family law attorneys cognizant of state legislation and court jurisdiction about paternity. Jurists in the United States play a role in this as well, by allowing non-citizens and non-residents to petition American courts for paternity, voiding the legal maternal tie to the surrogate. Yet, as the French case reveals, decisions made in California courtrooms do not necessarily apply in France or elsewhere.

## CULTURAL NORMS AND POLITICAL REGULATIONS

International newspapers are filled with stories of individuals who have been stymied by their efforts to access reproductive technologies in their home countries because of such factors as cost, restrictive regulations, or long waiting lists. The scenario of global biocitizenry may be illustrated by a case discussed in *The Guardian* concerning a British Asian couple (Ramesh, 2006). The couple sought fertility treatment in England for six years before traveling to Gujarat, India, where they found an Asian donor-surrogate at half the price of what it would cost them at home, and who could be implanted with more embryos than is allowed under British policy established by the Human Fertilisation and Embryology Authority. Had the couple used an egg donor-surrogate within the U.K., the surrogate would have had a right to reclaim the child during the first two years of its life, but in India, she has no rights to the child. Although the Indian Council of Medical Research drafted a 2010 Assisted Reproductive Technologies bill implementing oversight and regulation of India's fertility industry, it has yet to be passed by Parliament (Bhalla & Thapliyal, 2013).

The couple was thus able to circumvent both the material and political conditions of their home country: by choosing a surrogate mother in India, they were assured a supply of Asian ova, cheaper services, multiple embryo transfers (to assure a greater chance of pregnancy and live birth), and sole parental rights. Despite the United Kingdom's regulation of reproductive technologies, this couple could bypass their own government's policies. In this case, self-interest trumped national law. In the case of the woman who became this couple's surrogate, she was subjected to practices that would not have been tolerated had she been a British, rather than Indian, citizen: a high-risk multiple embryo transfer, no parental rights, and less compensation. Lack of regulations does not protect reproductive laborers from exploitation, but it does enable some people to have the children of their dreams. Lack of regulations is also good for business and local economies; fertility clinics in such places as India, the United States, or Spain, which have less restrictive policies regarding reproductive technologies than other nations, are able to—and expressly do—market themselves to a niche clientele seeking to bypass what they see as overly restrictive policies and/or overly expensive services.

From "test tube babies" to "designer children," technologies that at first seemed impossible, unthinkable, or untenable are now available at fertility clinics throughout the world. The buying and selling of reproductive parts and labor is a thriving industry (Spar, 2006). The increasing existence and availability of technologies does not suggest, however, that medically-assisted reproduction is universally accepted; cultural lag exists in that these rapidly changing technologies continue to raise many ethical questions, including how nations, professionals, institutions, and individuals should respond to them. In Chapter 5, I elaborate on how these ethics are expressed and put into practice by fertility industry professionals in the United States, and how this relates to ideals of both professional and reproductive autonomy.

Because cultures vary in terms of kinship structures, ethics, attitudes towards science and technology, the autonomy of medical institutions, and tolerance of government regulation, the way that states attempt to intervene and create norms to deal with new technologies and their accompanying ethical dilemmas will ultimately vary (Kabeer, 1996). In addition to policy variation among states is the internal variation of ethics, morals, interests, needs and desires within countries. The ethics inscribed in policies may reflect a position concerning liberties, rights, and autonomy that differs from those held by groups and individual members of the populace (Blyth & Farrand, 2005). This is evident in debates surrounding abortion and stem-cell research, but it is also present in policies regarding assisted reproductive technologies.

When theorizing the ethics of reproductive technologies and the contradictions between state policies and individual desires, one must take care not to equate lack of regulation with more freedom and choice, and regulation with constraint. On the issue of "choice" and procreative liberty, access to reproductive technologies have generally not been touted as a feminist issue of reproductive freedom, nor is there a unified feminist response. Shulamith Firestone (1970), for example, early on envisioned that reproductive technologies could be used as a tool to liberate women from the birth process and the corollary responsibility of childrearing, whereas at the other end of the spectrum Gena Corea (1985) equated reproductive technology with high-tech prostitution and the degradation of women. Feminist scholars writing about the traditional arenas of reproductive rights—abortion, birth control, and sterilization abuse—have noted the limitations of the "choice" frame (Cornell, 1995; Petchesky, 1990; Roberts, 1997; Solinger, 2002), and this frame is similarly problematic for reproductive technologies (Holland, 2007; Rothman, 2000). In the reductive and consumerist "choice" frame, every choice is equally valid and devoid of social, political, and economic context that renders some choices more possible, tenable, desirable, or commendable than others.

Additionally, access to reproductive technology may also get framed as a human-rights issue (Deech, 2003). Like the "choice" frame, a human-rights framework is also tricky. Although "human rights" may be touted as a cultural universal irrespective of national borders, states have different interpretations of what constitutes a right and even, for that matter, what constitutes a "human"—raising questions about *which* humans' rights must be protected (Habermas, 2003). Germany's Embryo Protection Act, for example, accords embryos with the same status as born human beings, and thus some forms of reproductive technology that may result in the destruction of embryos are regarded as violations of human dignity. In the United States, there is no federal standard for what constitutes personhood, but initiatives to define fertilized eggs as persons are regularly debated in the courts and in political campaigns. These definitional distinctions not only have implications for abortion, contraception, and stem cell research but also have widespread consequences for the entire field of reproductive medicine. In the face of countries grappling with these complicated policy and semantic issues looms a growing global marketplace for reproductive technologies, services, and products.

## ETHICS AND RISKS

The *legality* of reproductive tourism depends upon the laws of the country in which one is standing, but some may argue that the *ethics* of the practice are up for universal debate. Some fear that reproductive tourism (and, indeed, all forms of commercial egg donation and surrogacy) exploits the women who sell their reproductive labors, that it may diminish the power and sovereignty of nations to establish their own laws and policies, and that all of the above result in the reinforcement of existing global inequalities. Social scientists, bioethicists, and journalists worry over the living and working conditions of the egg donors and surrogates who provide services to an international clientele, citing possible links, for example, between egg donation and the global sex trade involving

Eastern European women (Waldby, 2008). Others have published alarming reports about commercial surrogacy in India, where it is common for surrogates to reside in dormitories throughout their pregnancies, separated from their own families (Carney, 2010; Chen, 2010; Gentleman, 2008; Hochschild, 2009).

Reproductive tourism has been blamed for the aggressive recruiting tactics of clinics and programs, who attempt to meet the increased demand for egg donors and surrogates despite the large risks that this reproductive labor imposes upon them (Parks, 2010). For example, egg donors and surrogates are injected with hormones that can potentially hyperstimulate their ovaries, a condition that can be life-threatening or lead to infertility (Bodri et al., 2008). For those acting as surrogates, pregnancy and childbirth are, of course, also risky, particularly when carrying twins and other multiples, which is not uncommon for those who become pregnant via IVF. Given the risks involved, one might ask if it is coercive to pay women, particularly those who are poor or who lack education, to endanger themselves for another family's benefit (Donchin, 2010). Is it a kind of bodily imperialism when affluent people rely upon the bodies of poorer women to fulfill their procreative desires?

Or, should reproductive tourism be viewed as a job creation mechanism in places where women lack more optimal employment opportunities? Should we acknowledge reproductive labor as merely another means for women to provide for themselves and their families, and that by paying egg donors and surrogates, we recognize that this is valuable work (Andrews, 1999)? This line of argument may be made on the basis of self-determination, individual liberty, and bodily autonomy, in which a woman is free to contract with others to sell her eggs or carry and give birth to a baby for money because she has rights over her own body (Munyon, 2003). Measures to stem reproductive tourism may thus be framed as acts of paternalism that deny women's agency. Some of these arguments that weigh bodily integrity against bodily autonomy are reminiscent of debates about the global sex trade (Desyllas, 2007) and the international market for human organs (Bilefsky, 2012; Scheper-Hughes & Wacquant, 2002).

A third ethical debate about reproductive tourism focuses not on the rights of the reproductive laborers but on the rights of individuals to become procreative outlaws, subverting the laws of their own countries of citizenship that prevent them from having children in the way that makes most sense to them (Blyth & Farrand, 2005). When laws and regulations discriminate against lesbians, gay men, and unmarried persons, denying them access to fertility treatment, reproductive tourism becomes an act of civil disobedience. As I describe further in this chapter, the lack of any international standards regarding assisted fertility services means that there are immense global disparities in the types of services and technologies that individuals may access. Bioethicist Guido Pennings argues that given this variance in international policies, reproductive tourism can act as a "safety valve," allowing intended parents living in more restrictive nations to travel abroad to fulfill their reproductive needs in a less restrictive nation (2005, p. 127). Yet, one may also argue that this kind of safety valve renders a nation's policies meaningless if its citizens are allowed to subvert them; furthermore, would this not reinforce structural inequalities by enabling a privileged group of citizens to pick and choose which policies apply to them (Martin, 2009)? There is already evidence of regions and countries, including Turkey and New South Wales, striking back against these acts of civil disobedience by imposing criminal and financial penalties on those who have babies via illicit means or who help facilitate the process (Gurtin-Broadbent, 2010; Parliament of New South Wales, 2010).

## INDIVIDUAL INTERESTS, NEEDS, AND DESIRES

Infertility may have been the initial impetus for the research and development of reproductive technologies such as sperm, egg, and embryo donation, surrogacy, and IVF, but they have since been put to other medical and social uses. Once reproductive parts, services, and labor have been commodified for individual consumption, the drive to expand markets leads to new uses, new demands, and an expansion of the very definition of "infertility" itself (Martin, 2010). For some individuals, the demand for reproductive technologies stems from a desire to bear and raise a child who shares a genetic tie, or to undergo the physical experience of pregnancy and childbirth. For others, the desire is to reproduce not just any child, but a particular kind of child with a particular set of traits.

Infertility as such may appear to be primarily a problem on an individual level: when people desire to reproduce, bear, and/or raise children, and cannot do so without medical intervention, infertility can be devastating. Options include remaining childless, adopting and/or fostering children, or calling upon science, medicine, and technology to help them have a biological child. The industry that has developed to address the reproductive needs of the infertile is tremendous: Deborah Spar estimates that in the United States alone, the market for fertility treatment in 2004 yielded almost $3 billion in revenue (Spar, 2006, p. 3).

On an individual level, potential consumers of assisted fertility services have their own interests, needs, and desires to use the technologies that they find appropriate. Yet, these potential consumers are also citizens, subject to their country's rules and regulations. A problem arises when the interest of individual citizens clashes with national interest, when, for example, a lesbian couple is denied access to artificial insemination, or when a couple desiring a son is forbidden from using diagnostic tools to increase their chances. It is at this contradictory juncture of interests, needs, and desires that globalization, and reproductive tourism, specifically, enters. Globalization forces us to push the level of analysis up, beyond the state. Use of reproductive technologies has already been turned into an act of consumption, and globalization widens the market, pushing reproductive decision-making onto the global stage.

## REPRODUCTIVE TECHNOLOGIES AND THE STATE

Government intervention and regulation of reproductive technologies does not necessarily indicate that the state has ultimate control of its members' reproductive decision-making; it does, however, indicate that it continues to maintain an interest in the interplay of demography and technology with culture and ethics. Legislative and ministerial regulations in individual countries or subnational communities may outright ban certain forms of technologies or procedures regarded as morally repugnant, such as genetic screening of embryos, sex selection, or commercial egg donation. Others may attempt to impose limits on who should have access to reproductive technologies—in terms of marital status, age, sexual orientation, and infertility status—whereas other guidelines attempt to regulate the anonymity of gamete donation. At one end of the spectrum are countries such as the United States, which imposes no comprehensive federal regulations concerning reproductive technologies, and at the other end are countries such as Germany, whose parliament has enacted strict guidelines. Most countries fall somewhere in between these two poles.

Assisted fertility services, regulations, and markets vary tremendously from country to country. An infertile couple residing in Canada will have access to an entirely different range of services from one residing in Japan or Slovenia. Even within regional federations such as the European Union, there is not one standard guideline to which all member nations follow but rather a patchwork of disparate regulations. In order to wrap our minds around some of the intense variability, what follows is a brief discussion of the role of the state in assisted fertility services in four nations: Germany, Israel, the United Kingdom, and the United States.

These four specific countries illustrate the range of regulations that are currently in place and are representative of other nations' policies. Although they are not strict "ideal types," they loosely adhere to four modes of biopolitical regulation: conservative (Germany), pronatalist (Israel), liberal (UK), and laissez-faire (USA). Israel and Germany offer excellent counterweights in terms of their international reputations for embracing and rejecting reproductive technologies, respectively (Hashiloni-Dolev & Shkedi, 2007; Hashiloni-Dolev, 2007). Although the United Kingdom and the United States are both regarded as liberal states, their divergence in policies is noteworthy. Regulations, policies, and guidelines are often subject to change. Those discussed below are current as of this writing and are based in part on the International Federation of Fertility Societies (IFFS) 2013 surveillance report (Ory et al., 2013).

Germany has by far one of the strictest policies regarding the uses of assisted fertility services. The basis of Germany's policy lies in the Embryo Protection Act (*Embryonenschutzgesetz*), adopted by the *Bundestag* in 1990, which imposes limitations on (including criminalization of) the uses of reproductive technology, human germ line cells, cloning, and the creation of human–animal hybrids. Scientists and doctors who violate the terms of the Act may be punished by fine or imprisonment for up to three years. Regarding reproductive technology, Germany permits *in vitro fertilization* and artificial insemination but forbids egg donation, embryo donation, and surrogacy; it also limits the number of embryos that may be transferred to a woman's uterus, forbids sex selection with the exception of cases in which severe sex-linked genetic illness is to be prevented, and forbids unmarried or lesbian women access to assisted fertility services (Bundesministerium der Justiz, 1990; Jasanoff, 2005a, 2005b; Robertson, 2004). Preimplantation genetic diagnosis was prohibited until 2011, when the *Bundestag* agreed to allow genetic screening of embryos in cases where parents had a predisposition for a serious genetic disorder (Severin & Kelsey, 2011).

In stark contrast to restrictive Germany, Israel is widely regarded for its pronatalist embrace of reproductive technology and fertility research. In 1987, Israel adopted National Health Regulations regarding IVF (Kahn, 2000, p. 75). IVF, artificial insemination, and egg donation are all permitted, with some limitations. Commercial and altruistic egg donation is forbidden; only surplus eggs from other women who had previously sought medical treatment for infertility may be donated. There are also many guidelines regarding consent and the marital status of all parties involved with gamete donation and embryo transfer (Kahn, 2000). Although the 1987 guidelines initially forbid surrogacy, this restriction was overturned in 1996 when the *Knesset* adopted the Embryo Carrying Agreements Law, which permitted surrogacy agreements subject to the approval of a public committee (Ghent, 1998; Kahn, 1998). Unmarried women may access IVF but are restricted from using donated eggs or a surrogate (Kahn, 2000). As of 2005, Israeli patients may apply to the health ministry for permission to choose the sex of their child through preimplantation genetic diagnosis if they already have four children of the same sex (Siegel-Itzkovich, 2005, p. 1228).

The United Kingdom's policies are guided by the Human Fertilisation and Embryology Authority (HFEA), which was established in 1991 within the Department of Health (Franklin & Roberts, 2006; Morgan, 2004). Recently, the Public Bodies Bill sought to transfer some of the regulatory functions of the HFEA to the Care Quality Commission (CQC) and other government bodies, but it has yet to pass through the legislative process (Human Fertilisation and Embryology Authority, 2011; Lord Taylor of Holbeach, 2011). The Human Fertilisation and Embryology Act of 1990 provides guidance to licensed clinics regarding patient assessment, the welfare of any children resulting from treatment, consent procedures, and donor screening. The Act places age limits on gamete donors and recipients of services, forbids payment to egg donors beyond "reasonable expenses," forbids sex selection except in cases of medical necessity, limits the numbers of embryos that may be transferred during one cycle, and permits prenatal screening and preimplantation genetic diagnosis (Office of Public Sector Information, 1990). Guidelines are continually being updated and reassessed, such as an expansion of availability of preimplantation genetic diagnosis for a wider number of genetic conditions, and a recent prohibition on anonymous gamete donation (Williams, Ehrich, Farsides, & Scott, 2007).

Finally, as I describe in detail in Chapter 3, the United States stands out because of its lack of comprehensive federal regulation of assisted fertility services. Rather than the federal government sanctioning procedures, access to reproductive technologies falls primarily under the jurisdiction of state legislatures and courts. Currently, local policies vary widely in the United States in regard to insurance coverage of infertile patients, parental rights of gamete donors and surrogates, use of surplus gametes and embryos, and the legality of surrogacy agreements (National Conference of State Legislatures, 2007, 2010; Waldman, 2006). With a paucity of federal and state law, regulation of the fertility industry in the United States is largely left to voluntary and non-binding self-policing by professional bodies, such as the American Society for Reproductive Medicine (ASRM) and the Society for Assisted Reproductive Technology (SART).

The United States may be described as laissez-faire, or perhaps more accurately "neoliberal," in its reproductive technology policy, not because no laws exist at all but because of the lack of one central policy or ethical guidepost, and its large reliance on industry self-regulation and market forces.[1] In the United States, procedures that are prohibited in other nations are permitted, such as surrogacy, sex selection, large sums paid to egg donors, and services to unmarried women, lesbians, and women over the age of 45. Because assisted fertility services are largely guided by market, rather than state forces, access to reproductive technology is circumscribed by what the market offers and by patients' health insurance status and/or ability to pay rather than by intervention or interference by the federal government. Even when regulations exist at the local level, those patients privileged enough may engage in within-country reproductive tourism, and travel to another state to procure the desired service or commodity. Considering the United States as a whole, the net effect is ultimately one of non-regulation.

As Table 1.1 illustrates, there appears to be little consistency among Germany, Israel, the United Kingdom, and the United States. Although *in vitro fertilization* is permitted in each of the sample countries, policies vary in terms of who has access to the technology, where the gametes necessary for the procedure can be obtained, and what sort of regulatory oversight the state has, not to mention how the expense of assisted fertility services varies in each country. That services—however limited or restricted—are available in the aforementioned four countries is also

*Table 1.1*  Availability of Reproductive Technologies in Four Countries

|  | Germany[1] | Israel[2] | UK[3] | USA[4] |
|---|---|---|---|---|
| *In vitro fertilization* (IVF) | Yes | Yes | Yes | Yes |
| Embryo donation | No | No | Yes | Yes |
| Surplus egg donation | No | Yes | Yes | Yes |
| Commercial egg donation | No | No | No | Yes |
| Anonymous gamete donation | No | Yes | No | Yes |
| Sperm donation | Yes | Yes | Yes | Yes |
| Surrogacy | No | Yes | Yes | Yes |
| Available to unmarried women | No | Yes (with limitations) | Yes | Yes |
| Available to lesbians | No | Yes (with limitations) | Yes | Yes |
| Age limits | N/A | Yes | Yes | No |
| Non-medical sex selection | No | Yes | No | Yes |
| Pre-implantation genetic diagnosis (PGD) | Yes (with strict limitations) | Yes | Yes | Yes |
| Limits on numbers of embryo transferred | Yes | Yes | Yes | No |
| National insurance coverage | Yes | Yes | Yes | No |
| National oversight | *Bundestag* | Ministry of Health, *Knesset* | HFEA | FDA, CDC |

*Sources*: 1. Bundesministerium der Justiz (1990); 2. Kahn (2000); 3. Office of Public Sector Information (1990); 4. Ory et al. (2013).

significant, as most countries in the developing world cannot offer the same services (Nachtigall, 2006).

The four countries described have each followed a different path to regulation, and it is outside the scope of this chapter to address the cultural and political nuances behind each policy decision, beyond remarking that other countries with similar ideological, moral, and/or historical milieus may be more likely to align with a conservative, pronatalist, liberal, or laissez-faire type (Jasanoff, 2005a). However, because every country is unique in its own right, we may expect to see a continued diversity of regulations, unless globalization proves to be a convergent force. Most importantly, although the state has an interest in the reproduction of its citizens, and the means by which its citizens may need fertility assistance, the citizens' *own* needs and desires may diverge from national mandates. In the age of globalization, the actions of citizens may sometimes supersede the regulatory arm of the state.

## THE DIMINISHED ROLE OF THE STATE?

Government's role in circumscribing, supporting, or ignoring citizens' access to reproductive technologies within the borders of their political communities both contradicts and upholds the tenet that globalization is decreasing the power or reach of the state. On the one hand, states attempt to exert power over reproductive decision-making by enacting and enforcing rules regarding reproductive technologies. On the other hand, despite national regulations, those citizens with the economic, social, and political means to leave the borders of their home countries have the ability to bypass the cultural, ethical, and legal restrictions that the state tries to impose on them. The question arises, then: what is the point of countries enacting guidelines specific to their own cultural and national communities if some individuals can choose to ignore them and seek fertility services in another country?

Reproductive tourism reflects a conflict between individual consumer desire and the state. Globalization serves to mediate this conflict, by offering an "out" to privileged consumers, and it also serves to heighten it, by highlighting the apparent contradictions among states. That is, media, communications, and technology such as the Internet provide a forum for the global consumer to learn about a wide range of services available throughout the world; conflict arises when consumer demand for services does not match the availability and opportunity within one's particular country.

National governments risk increasing reproductive tourism as an unintended consequence when they attempt to change their policies regarding reproductive technologies in a more prohibitive direction. For example, when the United Kingdom's HFEA forbade anonymous gamete donation in 2005, the pool of willing donors, and thus the supply of available ova for *in vitro fertilization*, declined. A number of articles in British newspapers subsequently reported that after this ruling, twice as many British couples are now going abroad to other countries such as Spain or Slovenia to procure eggs, possibly numbering in the thousands (Burne, 2006; Fracassini & Bowditch, 2006).

Another question arises as to the state's ability to monitor and regulate reproductive tourism itself, and whether this infringes on individuals' human rights and reproductive autonomy (Blyth & Farrand, 2005; Deech, 2003). This could involve government intervention, such as denying visas or punishing consumers who accessed forbidden reproductive technologies abroad. Reigning in reproductive tourism also poses a difficulty because of existing treaties and trade relations among nations. This is particularly relevant among member nations of the European Union, which guarantees the free movement of capital, goods, services, and people (Storrow, 2005). Beyond the European Union, the ability of other nations to police the movement of its populace for tourism purposes may be governed by multilateral trade agreements, migration and homeland security policies, and intergovernmental organizations.

The spirit of globalization and multilateralism facilitates reproductive tourism and may in fact undermine the power of the state to regulate the uses of reproductive technologies by its citizenry. This diminished power, however, is stratified, intranationally *and* internationally. That is, reproductive tourism is not an option freely available to all. It necessitates a commitment on the part of a government to the free movement of people, goods, services, and capital, and thus demands a modicum of collusion on the part of the state and a sanctioning of interstate travel and commerce. Absent that commitment and collusion, reproductive tourism cannot take place; those individuals living in authoritarian states, for example, may be more restricted from engaging in reproductive tourism than those in democratic states.

Even within democratic states that allow for the free movement of citizens, the possibility of reproductive tourism remains bifurcated and limited to those who can afford to engage in it. Globalization makes it easier *for a privileged few* to cross borders in search of services or reproductive commodities unavailable or too expensive in their own countries, but it is not the great equalizer. Wealthy, elite, and/or privileged consumers will have an easier time globetrotting in search of reproductive technologies than the poor or less educated. Those who are constrained by material circumstances are the ones most constricted by their government's regulations and ideologies around reproductive technologies. For those without the ability to subvert their country's restrictions, the power of the state remains strong. Local inequalities become reenacted and reinforced on the global stage. The global biocitizen may transcend the state, but that global biocitizen is a member of the tiny elite not representative of the majority of the world. Therefore, on the question of whether reproductive tourism supports the contention that globalization is leading to the diminished role of the state, one can answer that in this case, the effect is limited and not universal.

## BABIES, BODIES, AND BORDERS

Examining reproductive tourism as a case study highlights the "unevenness" of globalization (Held & McGrew, 2002). Although the practice of traveling the world in search of cheap, efficient, and safe assisted fertility services and goods may appear to be a free-for-all in which reproduction and conception have become truly transnationalized, this is not, in fact, the current state of affairs. By discussing reproductive tourism in the context of globalization, what becomes clear is how stratified this practice is. That is, an elite few global biocitizens are able to bypass the laws and culturally inscribed ethics of their own particular country by way of the global marketplace and interstate travel and commerce, yet because of material and political realities, the majority of the world do not have this privilege and freedom.

Reproductive tourism can inform us about the uneven and limited nature of globalization; that is, we are not all equally affected. Globalization may help an elite infertile Japanese couple learn about and patronize a clinic in California that can assist them in locating a suitable surrogate, but for those who cannot afford tens or hundreds of thousands of dollars for treatment on top of travel expenses, infertility and childlessness may continue to be a reality that cannot be overcome. Infertility can be devastating to anyone, but the elite are better equipped to access services in their own countries and, if that is insufficient, to seek them abroad.

A consequence, then, is the reproduction of inequalities on both a local and a global level. This consequence becomes highlighted even more so by those reproductive tourists who seek assisted reproductive technologies for reasons besides infertility treatment. Whether it is to avoid the birth of children with defects or disabilities, or to produce "designer" children, the elite have greater access to these services, too. And, if a nation acts to prevent this genetic stratification of its populace by restricting reproductive technologies, the elite can access them in some other country where those restrictions do not exist. Globalization produces a global citizenry, but this global citizen who transcends borders—political, economic, or cultural—is a tiny minority. Recall the pop star Madonna, an American-born citizen who went to Malawi to adopt a child to bring back with her to England. "Belonging" to no single country, she successfully subverted adoption procedures in three nations (O'Shea, 2007).

Globalization has prefigured the very possibility of reproductive tourism, if only for the elite. Without global standards in place, the practice will probably continue, and inequalities will continue to persist. Technology has given us brand new ways to conceive and bear children that go beyond the limits of the body. What globalization has given us are even more ways to conceive and bear children that go beyond the limits of national and cultural boundaries.

## NOTE

An earlier version of this chapter appears in *Globalizations*, 6(2): 249–263.

1. This argument follows from David Harvey's definition of neoliberalism, which includes the idea that "state interventions in markets (once created) must be kept to a bare minimum because the state cannot possibly possess enough information to second-guess market signals (prices), and because powerful interests will inevitably distort and bias state interventions (particularly in democracies) for their own benefit" (2006, p. 145).

## REFERENCES

Acker, J. (2004). Gender, capitalism and globalization. *Critical Sociology, 30*(1), 17–41.
Agamben, G. (1998). *Homo sacer*. Stanford, CA: Stanford University Press.
Aizura, A. Z. (2009). Where health and beauty meet: Femininity and racialisation in Thai cosmetic surgery clinics. *Asian Studies Review, 33*(3), 303–317.

Andrews, L. B. (1999). Reproductive technology comes of age. *Whittier Law Review*, 21(2), 375–389.

Barbados Fertility Centre. (n.d.). *A holiday with a purpose*. Retrieved from www.barbadosivf.org/holidays.htm

Bhalla, N., & Thapliyal, M. (2013, September 30). India seeks to regulate its booming "rent-a-womb" industry. *Reuters*. Retrieved from www.reuters.com/article/2013/09/30/us-india-surrogates-idUSBRE98T07F20130930

Bilefsky, D. (2012, June 28). Black market for body parts spreads in Europe. *The New York Times*. Retrieved from www.nytimes.com/2012/06/29/world/europe/black-market-for-body-parts-spreads-in-europe.html?_r=2&src=rechp

Blyth, E., & Farrand, A. (2005). Reproductive tourism—a price worth paying for reproductive autonomy? *Critical Social Policy*, 25(1), 91–114.

Bodri, D., Guillén, J.J., Polo, A., Trullenque, M., Esteve, C., & Coll, O. (2008). Complications related to ovarian stimulation and oocyte retrieval in 4052 oocyte donor cycles. *Reproductive BioMedicine Online*, 17(2), 237–243. doi:10.1016/S1472-6483(10)60200-3

Bundesministerium der Justiz. Act for Protection of Embryos (Embryonenschutzgesetz—ESchG), Pub. L. No. Federal Law Gazette, Part 1, No. 69 (1990). Retrieved from www.hinxtongroup.org/docs/Germany2.html

Burne, J. (2006, July 1). Fertile journeys. *Times*. London.

Carney, S. (2010, April). Inside India's rent-a-womb business. *Mother Jones*. Retrieved from http://motherjones.com/politics/2010/02/surrogacy-tourism-india-nayna-patel?page=1

CEFIVA. (n.d.). *International Attention*. Centro de Fecundacion in Vitro Asturias. Retrieved from www.cefiva.com/index.php?option=com_content&view=article&id=57&Itemid=58&lang=en

Chen, M. (2010, June 15). Mailorder wombs: Outsourcing birth to India. *RaceWire*. Retrieved from www.racewire.org/archives/2010/06/mailorder_wombs_surrogacy_across_borders_in_the_global_south.html

Corea, G. (1985). *The mother machine: Reproductive technologies from artificial insemination to artificial wombs*. New York: Harper & Row.

Cornell, D. (1995). *The imaginary domain: Abortion, pornography & sexual harassment*. New York: Routledge.

Deech, R. (2003). Reproductive tourism in Europe: Infertility and human rights. *Global Governance*, 9(4), 425–433.

Desyllas, M.C. (2007). A critique of the global trafficking discourse and U.S. policy. *Journal of Sociology & Social Welfare*, 34(4), 57–79.

Dixon-Mueller, R. (1993). *Population policy & women's rights: Transforming reproductive choice*. Westport, CT: Praeger.

Donchin, A. (2010). Reproductive tourism and the quest for global gender justice. *Bioethics*, 24(7), 323–332.

Dubinsky, K. (2010). *Babies without borders: Adoption and migration across the Americas*. New York: New York University Press.

Ehrenreich, B., & Hochschild, A.R. (2002). *Global woman: Nannies, maids, and sex workers in the new economy*. New York: Metropolitan.

Eisenstein, H. (2005). A dangerous liaison? Feminism and corporate globalization. *Science & Society*, 69(3), 487–518.

Fertility Treatment Abroad. (n.d.). *Fertility treatment abroad—IVF, IUI, surrogacy, ICSI, egg donation*. Retrieved from http://fertility.treatmentabroad.com/

Firestone, S. (1970). *The dialectic of sex: The case for feminist revolution*. New York: Morrow.

Foucault, M. (1978). *The history of sexuality: An introduction. Vol. 1*. New York: Vintage.

Foucault, M. (2007). *Security, territory, population: Lectures at the Collège de France, 1977–1978*. New York: Picador.

Fracassini, C., & Bowditch, G. (2006, January 29). British couples use foreign clinics for fertility treatment. *Times*. London.

Franklin, S., & Roberts, C. (2006). *Born and made: An ethnography of preimplantation genetic diagnosis*. Princeton, NJ: Princeton University Press.

Gentleman, A. (2008, March 4). Foreign couples turn to India for surrogate mothers. *The International Herald Tribune*. Retrieved from www.iht.com/articles/2008/03/04/asia/mother.php

Ghent, J. S. (1998, June 19). Religious issues color reproductive advances in Israel. *JWeekly.com*. Retrieved from www.jweekly.com/article/full/8534/religious-issues-color-reproductive-advances-in-israel/

Ginsburg, F. D., & Rapp, R. (Eds.). (1995). *Conceiving the new world order: The global politics of reproduction*. Berkeley: University of California Press.

Gurtin-Broadbent, Z. (2010, March 22). *Problems with legislating against "reproductive tourism."* *BioNews*. Retrieved from www.bionews.org.uk/page_56954.asp

Habermas, J. (2003). *The future of human nature*. Cambridge: Polity Press.

Harvey, D. (2006). Neo-liberalism as creative destruction. *Geografiska Annaler Series B, 88*(2), 145–158.

Hashiloni-Dolev, Y. (2007). *A life (un)worthy of living: Reproductive genetics in Israel and Germany*. Dordrecht: Springer.

Hashiloni-Dolev, Y., & Shkedi, S. (2007). On new reproductive technologies and family ethics: Pre-implantation genetic diagnosis for sibling donor in Israel and Germany. *Social Science & Medicine, 65*(10), 2081–2092.

Held, D., & McGrew, A. G. (2002). *Globalization anti-globalization: Beyond the great divide*. Cambridge: Polity.

Hochschild, A. R. (2009, October 5). Childbirth at the global crossroads. *The American Prospect*. Retrieved from http://prospect.org/cs/articles?article=childbirth_at_the_global_crossroads#

Holland, S. (2007). Market transactions in reprogenetics: A case for regulation. In L. P. Knowles & G. E. Kaebnik (Eds.), *Reprogenetics: Law, policy, and ethical issues* (pp. 89–104). Baltimore, MD: Johns Hopkins University Press.

Human Fertilisation and Embryology Authority. (2011). *Human Fertilisation & Embryology Authority*. Retrieved from www.hfea.gov.uk/

Jasanoff, S. (2005a). *Designs on nature: Science and democracy in Europe and the United States*. Princeton, NJ: Princeton University Press.

Jasanoff, S. (2005b). In the democracies of DNA: Ontological uncertainty and political order in three states. *New Genetics and Society, 24*(2), 139–156.

Kabeer, N. (1996). *Gender, demographic transition and the economics of family size: Population policy for a human-centered development*. Geneva: United Nations Research Institute for Social Development (UNRISD).

Kahn, S. M. (1998). Putting Jewish wombs to work: Israelis confront new reproductive technologies. *Lilith, 23*, 30.

Kahn, S. M. (2000). *Reproducing Jews: A cultural account of assisted conception in Israel*. Durham, NC: Duke University Press.

Khosravi, F. (2003). Price discrimination in the United States: Why are pharmaceuticals cheaper in Canada and are Americans seizing the opportunities across the border? *Law and Business Review of the Americas, 9*, 427–442.

Lock, M. M., & Kaufert, P. A. (Eds.). (1998). *Pragmatic women and body politics*. New York: Cambridge University Press.

Lord Taylor of Holbeach. Public Bodies Bill, Pub. L. No. HL 2010–11 (2011). Retrieved from http://services.parliament.uk/bills/2010-11/publicbodieshl.html

Martin, L. J. (2009). Reproductive tourism in the age of globalization. *Globalizations, 6*(2), 249–263.

Martin, L. J. (2010). Anticipating infertility: Egg freezing, genetic preservation, and risk. *Gender & Society*, 24(4), 526–545.

Morgan, D. (2004). Ethics, economics and the exotic: The early career of the HFEA. *Health Care Analysis*, 12(1), 7–26.

Munyon, J. H. (2003). Protectionism and freedom of contract: The erosion of female autonomy in surrogacy decisions. *Suffolk University Law Review*, 36(3), 717–744.

Nachtigall, R. D. (2006). International disparities in access to infertility services. *Fertility and Sterility*, 85(4), 871–875.

National Conference of State Legislatures. (2007, July). *Embryo and gamete disposition laws*. Retrieved from www.ncsl.org/IssuesResearch/Health/Embryo andGameteDispositionLaws/tabid/14379/Default.aspx

National Conference of State Legislatures. (2010, September). *Insurance coverage for infertility laws*. Retrieved from www.ncsl.org/default.aspx?tabid=14391

Nygren, K., Adamson, D., Zegers-Hochschild, F., & de Mouzon, J. (2010). Cross-border fertility care—International Committee Monitoring Assisted Reproductive Technologies global survey: 2006 data and estimates. *Fertility and Sterility*, 94(1), e4–e10.

Office of Public Sector Information. (1990). Human Fertilisation and Embryology Act 1990. Text. Retrieved from www.legislation.gov.uk/ukpga/1990/37/contents

Ong, A. (1999). *Flexible citizenship: The cultural logics of transnationality*. Durham, NC: Duke University Press.

Ong, A. (2007). *Neoliberalism as exception: Mutations in citizenship and sovereignty* (2nd printing). Durham, NC: Duke University Press.

Ory, S., Devroey, P., Banker, M., Brinsden, P., Buster, J., Fiadjoe, M. et al. (2013). *IFFS surveillance 2013*. International Federation of Fertility Societies. Retrieved from http://c.ymcdn.com/sites/www.iffs-reproduction.org/resource/resmgr/iffs_surveillance_09-19-13.pdf

O'Shea, G. (2007, October 22). Madonna's adopted lad fast-tracked. *The Sun*. England.

Pacific Fertility Center. (2011, April 17). *Northern California infertility clinic for male & female infertility international care*. Retrieved from www.pacific fertilitycenter.com/global/travel.php

Parks, J. A. (2010). Care ethics and the global practice of commercial surrogacy. *Bioethics*, 24(7), 333–340.

Parliament of New South Wales. Surrogacy Bill 2010, Pub. L. No. Act No. 102 (2010). Retrieved from www.parliament.nsw.gov.au/prod/parlment/nswbills.nsf/0/71C02 4816771A264CA2577C100195683

Pennings, G. (2005). Legal harmonization and reproductive tourism in Europe. *Reproductive Health Matters*, 13(25), 120–128.

Petchesky, R. P. (1990). *Abortion and woman's choice: The state, sexuality, and reproductive freedom*. Boston, MA: Northeastern University Press.

Petryna, A. (2002). *Life exposed: Biological citizens after Chernobyl*. Princeton, NJ: Princeton University Press.

Rabinow, P. (1996). *Essays on the anthropology of reason*. Princeton, NJ: Princeton University Press.

Ramesh, R. (2006, March 20). British couples desperate for children travel to India in search of surrogates. *The Guardian (U.K.)*. Retrieved from www.guardian.co.uk/world/2006/mar/20/health.topstories3

Roberts, D. (1997). *Killing the black body: Race, reproduction, and the meaning of liberty*. New York: Vintage Books.

Robertson, J. A. (2004). Reproductive technology in Germany and the United States: An essay in comparative law and bioethics. *Columbia Journal of Transnational Law*, 43, 189–227.

Rose, N. S. (2007). *The politics of life itself: Biomedicine, power, and subjectivity in the twenty-first century.* Princeton, NJ: Princeton University Press.

Rose, N. S., & Novas, C. (2005). Biological citizenship. In A. Ong & S. J. Collier (Eds.), *Global assemblages: Technology, politics, and ethics as anthropological problems* (pp. 439–463). Malden, MA: Blackwell.

Rothman, B. K. (2000). *Recreating motherhood.* New Brunswick, NJ: Rutgers University Press.

Scheper-Hughes, N., & Wacquant, L.J.D. (2002). *Commodifying bodies.* London: Sage.

Severin, T., & Kelsey, E. (2011, July 7). Germany approves genetic testing of human embryos. *Reuters.* Retrieved from http://in.reuters.com/article/2011/07/07/us-germany-embryo-vote-idINTRE7664HJ20110707

Siegel-Itzkovich, J. (2005). Israel allows sex selection of embryos for non-medical reasons. *BMJ: British Medical Journal, 330*(7502), 1228.

Solinger, R. (2002). *Beggars and choosers: How the politics of choice shapes adoption, abortion, and welfare in the United States.* New York: Hill and Wang.

Souchard, P.-A. (2011, April 6). France rules against children of surrogate mothers. *The Seattle Times.* Retrieved from http://seattletimes.com/html/nationworld/2014694604_apeufrancesurrogatemothers.html

Spar, D. (2006). *The baby business: How money, science, and politics drive the commerce of conception.* Boston, MA: Harvard Business School Press.

Storrow, R. F. (2005). Quests for conception: Fertility tourists, globalization and feminist legal theory. *Hastings Law Journal, 57,* 295.

Waldby, C. (2008). Oocyte markets: Women's reproductive work in embryonic stem cell research. *New Genetics and Society, 27*(1), 19–31.

Waldman, E. (2006). Cultural priorities revealed: The development and regulation of assisted reproduction in the united states and Israel. *Health Matrix, 16,* 65–106.

Williams, C., Ehrich, K., Farsides, B., & Scott, R. (2007). Facilitating choice, framing choice: Staff views on widening the scope of preimplantation genetic diagnosis in the UK. *Social Science & Medicine, 65*(6), 1094–1105.

# 2 The Push and Pull of Reproductive Tourism
## The United States as Destination

New York City, Los Angeles, and San Francisco are three of the largest centers of the global fertility industry, attracting reproductive tourists not only for the quantity and quality of clinics and programs but also for their status as international destinations. As "global cities," they are already popular destinations for business and recreational travel, with infrastructure that includes major airports, hotels, restaurants, museums, and other tourist draws (Sassen, 1999). Providers described the cities where they worked as "international destinations," "destination spots," or "hubs" already known and familiar to people worldwide.

Yet, if one were to pay attention only to media reports about reproductive tourism, in which Westerners travel to Third World nations to contract with surrogates at bargain prices, reproductive tourism to the United States would not make any sense, given that fertility services tend to be *more* expensive in this country, not cheaper. This is because reproductive tourism, as a subset of medical tourism, is not only driven by bargain hunting. It is also driven by public policies that ban or restrict access to particular reproductive technologies, and by a consumerist mentality that transcends national borders. By focusing on the high cost of fertility services alone, researchers and journalists neglect to parse the non-economic factors driving reproductive tourism and, as a consequence, neglect entire regions—such as the United States—where this practice is currently prevalent. Reproductive tourism must be examined through the lens of political economy, but zeroing in on market relations should not come at the expense of political analysis.

Consider the following three scenarios:

A. A middle-class American heterosexual married couple would like to obtain the services of a gestational surrogate because the wife is unable to carry a pregnancy to term. Unfortunately, surrogacy expenses in the United States can cost upwards of $80,000 to $100,000, which is out of their financial reach. The couple travels to Mumbai, India, where the price of surrogacy is as much as 75% cheaper.

B. A gay male couple in France would like to obtain the services of a gestational surrogate and an egg donor in order to have a child. In

France, however, commercial surrogacy and egg donation is not legal. The couple travels to Los Angeles, California, where egg donation and surrogacy are both legal.

C. An Argentine couple has been trying to have a child for several years, but they have not had any success with treatments from local fertility doctors. The couple, after searching on the Internet, finds a clinic in New York City that boasts of a new technique with excellent success rates, and several staff members who are fluent in Spanish.

In each example, "reproductive tourism" happens in quite different contexts—economic, political, and medical. Is it accurate, then, to apply the same set of analyses to such different circumstances?

Those studying reproductive tourism have enumerated numerous explanations for why people cross borders for assisted fertility services. In their overview of existing literature, Inhorn and Gurtin (2011) write:

> Scholars have advanced at least 10 different reasons why individuals engage in CBRC: (i) legal and ethical prohibitions; (ii) denial of access to certain categories of persons (based on age, marital status or sexual orientation); (iii) high costs; (iv) absence of assisted reproduction services in resource-poor countries due to lack of expertise and equipment; (v) long waiting times due to resource shortages; (vi) safety concerns; (vii) low-quality care and/or success rates; (viii) desires for cultural understanding (e.g. language and religion); (ix) proximity to support networks and family members; and (x) concerns around privacy.
>
> (p. 666)

The Ethics Committee of the ASRM (2013) articulate four categories that explain why people travel for reproductive care: access to high-quality care, money, circumvention of law, and privacy. Others focus more on legal issues (Gurtin-Broadbent, 2010; Storrow, 2011; Van Hoof & Pennings, 2011). In this chapter, I reframe the motivating factors in another typology, borrowed from migration scholarship, using the concept of "push" and "pull" factors to explain the directions and motivations behind patterns of reproductive tourism.

In his classic article on migration, Everett S. Lee names four factors that people consider when deciding to migrate from one country to another: "1. Factors associated with the area of origin. 2. Factors associated with the area of destination. 3. Intervening obstacles. 4. Personal factors" (Lee, 1966, p. 50). Negative factors (such as political persecution) associated with one's country of origin may be considered "push" factors, and positive factors (such as social welfare programs for refugees) associated with the destination country may be considered "pull" factors. In aggregate, these factors contribute to larger patterns of migration and demography.

Although not permanent, reproductive tourism is a temporary, micro-migration, and we can use this typology of push and pull factors to better understand why this phenomenon has particular migration patterns—individuals from certain countries traveling to other specific locations. In what countries do reproductive tourists tend to reside? Why do they seek out services in countries where they are not citizens? What is it about the countries or cities where services are popularly sought? How do service providers convince foreigners to travel to their location? Traveling to another country for a short period of time in order to receive assisted fertility services is, obviously, not the same as uprooting oneself for a permanent change of residence, but considering push and pull factors involved in reproductive tourism is useful as an explanatory device.

*Push* factors, as they relate to reproductive tourism, are those factors within a particular country or countries that contribute to making it difficult, onerous, inconvenient, or impossible for citizens to obtain the services and products that they desire. These include expense, legal and procedural barriers, privacy issues, and inadequacy of existing services and products. *Pull* factors are those factors within a particular country that make it a draw for foreign internationals. These include expense (i.e., cheaper), legal climate, quality of services, and reputation. We can now look back at the scenarios posed at the beginning of this chapter in terms of push and pull factors. In Scenario A, the relative expense of surrogacy services acts as both a push and pull factor driving reproductive tourism. In Scenario B, the push and pull factors center around legal and political climates. Scenario C is a bit more complicated: the push factor may be a lack of services, or inadequately trained doctors, but the spark for travel might be more aptly described as what Lee (1966) called "intervening obstacles" or "personal factors." In this scenario, the pull factors are shaped by the information the couple finds on the Internet about a particular clinic: high success rates and an ability to communicate in Spanish. What links all three scenarios is the narrative that the intended parents cannot find what they need in their country of residence and are willing to try to find them by traveling to another country.

In this chapter I use the concept of push and pull factors to explain the pattern of reproductive tourism to the United States, discussing in depth the push factors contributing to reproductive tourism from the eight sending countries most frequently cited by informants, and the pull factors that make the United States an attractive destination. This concept of push and pull factors, however, can also be applied to other geographic patterns of reproductive tourism, such as movements from the United States to India. By discussing push and pull factors, we can answer not only the question of why people seek assisted fertility services outside of their own country, but the equally compelling question of why some countries develop as destinations for reproductive tourism. Doing so helps us to predict from which countries individuals are most likely to originate, and to which countries they are most likely to travel.

Focusing on a single variable, such as the high cost of assisted fertility services, may offer a compelling narrative about stratified reproduction, but it cannot account for why the United States, in particular, has become a hub for reproductive tourism, much less a destination even for those coming from less wealthy nations. Although it is not an explanation for reproductive tourism to the United States, the high costs of assisted fertility services is a significant push factor contributing to intended parents traveling from more expensive to less expensive locations. Given that fertility services in the United States are quite expensive, this factor explains *outbound* rather than *inbound* reproductive tourism. IVF in the United States averages over $12,500 per cycle, at least $10,000 more than what a cycle in the Czech Republic would run (Chambers, Sullivan, Ishihara, Chapman, & Adamson, 2009).[1] Egg donation costs, including fees for donors and brokers and payment to clinics for IVF, can add tens of thousands more dollars, and surrogacy even more so. Seeking out less expensive treatments does not generally factor into why international clients come to the United States, but it certainly operates in the reverse trend of Americans who decide to go abroad. "Made in India," a documentary by Rebecca Haimowitz and Vaishali Sinha (2010), beautifully illustrates this process by shadowing a middle-class Texan couple as they travel to India, contract with a surrogate, and bring their twin babies back home with them, enduring a series of medical and legal complications along the way.

My informants recognize that the high cost of American fertility services drives outbound reproductive tourism, and leads some individuals worldwide to bypass the United States for cheaper locales, reducing their potential global client base. Rebekah, co-owner of a surrogacy agency, spoke of the cost differentials, citing price tags of $4000 per IVF cycle in Europe, versus $20,000 in the United States, and these sums do not even include additional expenses for airfare and accommodations. If demand for their services were based on price tag alone, the United States fertility industry would be the loser on the international market. When potential clients compare the costs between nations, they may balk at how expensive services cost within the United States. When his international patients ask Los Angeles physician Dr. Silverstein why he charges so much, he explains to them that American doctors have much higher costs for malpractice insurance and licenses than their colleagues abroad. Additionally, he explained to me, "They have socialized medicine. You come from London, they think you can break your arm and walk in and just get it set and walk out paying $5. It just doesn't work that way here."

The extreme difference in price means that American fertility providers do not compete on the basis of cost. "Price is always juicy for people," said Deirdre, the San Francisco lawyer who I introduced in the opening of this book. "The majority of people are looking at price, and $20,000 [for IVF in the United States] is significant." She and other providers I spoke with clearly understand the logic that drives reproductive tourism to India and Eastern Europe. Linda, administrator at a fertility clinic in Los Angeles, spoke of a couple that had decided to go to Pakistan "because it's going to hardly cost her anything." When clients decide that it will be cheaper for them to go abroad, the doctors try to dissuade them by citing pull factors—they tout the comparative superiority of their American clinic's technology and success rates compared with clinics in other countries.

My informants were not all as skeptical about the quality of care in other countries. As Los Angeles physician Dr. Randolph put it, "I think as long as, say, the people in India do this very well, it's fine. As long as it's done carefully, sensitively, responsibly, what difference does it make whether you use a gestational carrier in San Francisco or Delhi? I mean, it's just somebody to help carry the baby that's going to allow you to have a child and a family." By framing the "gestational carrier" as some sort of disembodied vessel that can be located anywhere, Dr. Randolph was able to justify the practice of traveling to another country to purchase a cheaper vessel.

I do not mean to discount the power of such bottom-line decision-making. For those who feel financially constrained, India or Eastern Europe provide a less expensive alternative to New York or California. Although high expenses explain one of the patterns of reproductive tourism—from wealthy nations to less wealthy nations—it cannot account for reproductive tourism to these three United States cities. Yet, because business is booming in the global fertility markets of New York City, Los Angeles, and San Francisco, a cluster of other push and pull factors that go beyond the financial must be playing a role in decisions made by clients coming from abroad. In the next section, I outline some of the non-economic push factors that contribute to individuals seeking assisted fertility services outside of their countries' borders.

## NON-ECONOMIC PUSH FACTORS FROM SENDING COUNTRIES

### Inadequacy of Facilities

Reproductive tourists come to the United States from all over the world. When asked what countries their international clients hail from, many providers replied something along the lines of, "They come from all over," or "Everywhere." When pressed for more details, some replied in broad terms, classifying their clients as European, Asian, Middle Eastern, or Latin American. Throughout my interviews, informants named the following long list of sending countries: Afghanistan, Argentina, Armenia, Australia, Belgium, Brazil, Canada, Chile, China, Dubai, Egypt, France, Germany, Greece, Hong Kong, India, Israel, Italy, Japan, Korea, Kuwait, Mexico, Mongolia, New Zealand, Norway, Peru, Russia, Singapore, Slovenia, Spain, Switzerland, Taiwan, Thailand, the United Kingdom, and Vietnam. Although "Africa" was cited as a region from which a provider has seen clients, Egypt was the only nation in Africa specifically named.

By naming particular countries or states, the providers did not imply that they regularly see clients from all of the above with the same frequency.

Some countries, such as Afghanistan and Mongolia, appeared to be named as one-off examples by providers to prove how "exotic" or widespread their client base is. Of the countries that were singled out by name, several were repeated throughout many interviews. As one can see by the list of 35 countries that my informants explicitly named, many of them are highly industrialized, democratic nations, eighteen of which are members of the Organisation for Economic Co-Operation and Development (OECD). Although large numbers of international clients are traveling from Australia, Japan, and England, reproductive tourism is clearly practiced by citizens from a range of countries, not merely from wealthy, industrialized nations. Moreover, the narrative promoted in the mainstream media and even in scholarly journals, that reproductive tourism is akin to neo-imperialism, in which wealthy Westerners travel to poorer regions to exploit the bodies of brown women, is also incomplete. The United States, one of the wealthiest, most developed countries in the world, is a receiving nation of reproductive tourism from both the developed and the developing world.

The eight most frequently cited countries were the United Kingdom (mentioned by 13 providers), Japan (12), Australia (11), China (10), France (8), Italy (7), Canada (6), and Mexico (6). Given that these countries were most frequently named as sending countries, it is useful to take note of the state of assisted fertility services in each one. That is, do they lack their own robust industries? Is a lack of trained physicians and fertility centers a push factor boosting reproductive tourism to other countries? The International Federation of Fertility Societies (IFFS) estimates that there are 3,706 to 3,895 fertility centers worldwide (Ory et al., 2013, p. 11). The second column in Table 2.1 shows the number of fertility centers in each country as reported in their international survey of clinics, with the United States' numbers supplied for comparison.

*Table 2.1*  Absolute and Per Capita Number of Fertility Centers in Nine Countries

| Country | Number of Fertility Centers (2013)[1] | Number of Centers per 1,000,000 People (based on 2014 population estimates)[2] |
| --- | --- | --- |
| Australia | 63* | 2.8 |
| Canada | 26–27* | .75–.78 |
| China | >200 | >.15 |
| France | 100 | 1.5 |
| Italy | 350 | 5.67 |
| Japan | 591 | 4.65 |
| Mexico | ~30 | ~.25 |
| United Kingdom | 71–117 | 1.11–1.84 |
| United States | 430 | 1.35 |

*Sources*: 1. Ory et al. (2013); 2. Population estimates from Central Intelligence Agency (2014).

*2010 estimate (Jones et al., 2010).

In the third column of Table 2.1 is the per capita ratio of fertility centers in each country per one million residents, calculated based on population estimates from the CIA World Factbook (2014).[2] While the United States in absolute terms has one of the largest fertility industries in the world, boasting up to 430 fertility centers (second only to Japan's 591 centers), Australia, Italy,[3] and Japan have more fertility centers per capita. France and the United Kingdom have a comparable number of clinics per capita with the United States. For this group of sending countries, lack of an adequate number of fertility clinics may only be a significant push factor for intended parents in Mexico and Canada, having fewer fertility clinics than the United States on both an absolute and per capita basis. The other 27 sending countries cited by informants vary widely in terms of reported numbers of fertility centers, from three in Slovenia to 500–600 in India, and possibly zero in countries that did not respond to the IFFS survey, such as Afghanistan, Armenia, and Mongolia. Residing in a country that does not have any or enough fertility clinics may be a factor for some intended parents who travel to the United States for assisted fertility services, but a further explanation is necessary. The countries of origin of many intended parents who are traveling to the United States from abroad have fertility industries that are just as big as, if not bigger than, that of the United States.

## Restrictive Laws and Policies

According to my informants, it is not typically a lack of an adequate number of fertility clinics in their home countries that drives most reproductive tourism to the United States, but laws and regulations. The political motive for reproductive tourism remains both underreported and underanalyzed, leaving entire fertility markets such as the United States out of the conversation. A burgeoning fertility industry exists throughout the world, largely in high- and middle-income nations, with great variation in the number of clinics and agencies, scientific and technological resources, and types of services offered. A variety of clinics and services are matched by a global variety of policies and laws regulating assisted reproduction. From highly regulated countries like Germany, to the United Kingdom's middle ground, to an almost complete absence of regulation in the United States, there is clearly no universal standard when it comes to reproductive technologies.

Types of regulation vary from country to country, as well. United States regulations largely focus on laboratory protocol and consumer-oriented legislation mandating reporting of success rates. Although state-level legislation exists permitting or proscribing particular procedures, there is no national-level promotion or ban, unlike in many other nations. Surrogacy, egg donation, and sex selection, for example, are all procedures that are highly regulated if not outright banned in a plurality of countries. In the previous chapter, I compared policies regarding reproductive technologies in

*Table 2.2*   Existence of National Laws and Policies Regulating Assisted Reproductive Technologies

| Country | Relationship Status | Embryo Transfer | Gamete Donation | PGD | Surrogacy | Sex Selection |
|---|---|---|---|---|---|---|
| Australia | | X | X | | X | X |
| Canada | | | X | | | |
| China | X | X | X | X | X | X |
| France | | X | X | X | X | X |
| Italy | X | | X | | X | X |
| Japan | X | X | X | X | X | X |
| Mexico | | | X | | | |
| U.K. | | X | X | | X | X |
| U.S. | | | | | | |

*Source*: Ory et al. (2013).

the United States, the United Kingdom, Israel, and Germany. In this section, I discuss in more detail how policies act as push factors.

Again using the eight most frequently cited sending countries as an example, Table 2.2 presents data from the 2013 IFFS report about a number of regulations that vary regionally.

To sum up Table 2.2, China, Italy, and Japan require that people seeking assisted reproductive technology (ART) be in married or stable relationships. Australia, China, France, Japan, and the United Kingdom place limits on the number of embryos that may be transferred during IVF. China, Italy, and Japan forbid egg donation. Italy forbids sperm donation, and Japan only allows sperm donation when used with artificial insemination (i.e., not with IVF). Australia, China, and the United Kingdom do not allow anonymous gamete donation. Italy forbids all use of preimplantation genetic diagnosis (PGD); France and Japan forbid the use of PGD to screen embryos for chromosomal abnormalities. France, Italy, and Japan do not allow gestational surrogacy. Federally, the United States, by contrast, has no relationship requirements, no limits on embryo transfer, allows egg and sperm donation, PGD, and gestational surrogacy. As described in Chapter 3, the United States is not entirely laissez-faire: regulations are determined by state law, and professional organizations maintain practice guidelines for their members.

There are at least four distinct policy issues that contribute to *pushing* intended parents out of their countries of origin in search of assisted fertility services: prohibition and criminalization of services, exclusion of populations from access to services, inaccessibility of services due to regulations, and issues of privacy and anonymity.

## Policy Issue 1: Desired Services Are Prohibited or Criminalized by Law or Policy

The most obvious push factor are those policies, statutes, laws, and guidelines that outright forbid a particular assisted fertility service or treatment, such as gamete donation, surrogacy, PGD, or sex selection. This is distinct from policies that shape *how* these services may be offered, such as those that regulate who may have access to them (policy issue 3) or payment to third-party donors and surrogates (policy issues 2 and 4), because those regulations presume that the services, even if in a highly restricted form, are allowed to be transacted within the borders of the country. For example, the IFFS reports that sperm donation is not allowed for ART purposes in Italy and Australia (Ory et al., 2013, p. 58). These two countries, in addition to Norway and Switzerland, also forbid egg donation (Ory et al., 2013, p. 60). Additionally, embryo donation is not allowed in 22% of countries responding to the IFFS survey (Ory et al., 2013, p. 61). Such blanket policies prohibiting gamete and/or embryo donation means that intended parents who desire these particular services in order to have a biological child *must* seek those services in another country.

Sex selection is another example of a service that is widely banned but sought out by intended parents worldwide. In the IFFS survey, out of forty-six countries, only Belgium, the Czech Republic, Greece, Hong Kong, Israel, Libya, Russia, Saudi Arabia, and the United States permit sex selection via PGD or sperm sorting (Ory et al., 2013, p. 140). In some cases, sex selection is prohibited for social reasons, such as gender balancing or personal preference, but permitted for medical reasons. For example, Australia's National Health and Medical Research Council instituted a ban on sex selection except in cases of serious genetic conditions in 2004; the ban is, however, more of a guideline than a legally binding protocol throughout the country (Feikert, 2009). The states of Victoria, Western Australia, and South Australia have instituted their own stricter prohibitions on sex selection (Feikert, 2009).

Prohibitions against and impediments to obtaining sex selection in Australia (among other countries) lead to inquiries by individuals desiring the procedure.[4] While I was interviewing New York physician Dr. Bradley, he happened to receive an email from someone in Australia. The doctor turned his computer monitor around to show me his email inbox, pointed at the screen, and said, "This was what I'm talking about. Referred from New South Wales, Australia, stating he wants gender selection. [*Reading from screen*] 'The legislation in Australia doesn't allow such treatments and thought of taking it a step further.' . . . That's their reason for contacting me! Not because I'm some super doctor."[5] Despite attempts in Australia to restrict sex selection, those with the desire and the wherewithal still seek those restricted services outside their country's borders. The United States offers one of the best options for those seeking this service, despite the geographic distance.[6]

Finally, surrogacy (via insemination or IVF) is prohibited in at least seventeen countries, according to the BioPolicyWiki (2014b): Austria, China, Finland, France, Germany, Italy, Latvia, Norway, Poland, Singapore, Slovenia, Sweden, Switzerland, Taiwan, Tunisia, Turkey, and Vietnam. The IFFS, reporting on IVF surrogacy alone, reports slightly different numbers, with 24 out of 62 responding countries not "allowing" the procedure, but not necessarily banning, prohibiting, or criminalizing it (Ory et al., 2013, pp. 110–117). Blanket prohibitions on PGD also exist in Austria, Germany, Lithuania, and Switzerland (BioPolicyWiki, 2014c).

## Policy Issue 2: Desired Services Are Regulated to Such an Extent that They Are De Facto Unavailable or Difficult to Access, and/or Such Regulation Affects the Quality of Services

Far more common than outright bans and prohibitions of services are regulations and restrictions that impose limits on how services may be offered within a country or region. For comparison's sake, consider some state-level restrictions on abortion within the United States, such as waiting times, the requirement for doctors to have hospital privileges, or facility standards for clinics that make abortions in certain localities difficult if not impossible to obtain, despite the *de jure* legality of abortion nationally. A similar situation exists globally in the context of assisted fertility. For example, there are very complicated policies and statutes regarding gamete and embryo donation that do not ban donation per se, but place restrictions such as how much a third-party donor may be compensated for his or her gametes, the number of cycles an egg donor may undergo, and, as will be discussed as policy issue 4, requiring or prohibiting anonymity of third-party donors (Ory et al., 2013, pp. 58–72). Such restrictions on gamete donation act as push factors in a different way than outright bans: in these cases, restrictions on donation shapes the gamete "market" by, in some cases, reducing both the number and quality of sperm and egg "donors."

Commercial gamete donation is prohibited in many of the countries that have fertility industries.[7] By relying only on "altruistic" donors, countries attempt to impede (or at least regulate) the development of egg and sperm markets. Yet, demand for sperm and eggs outstrips supply, particularly when rules against donor compensation consequently results in a limited pool to draw from. Egg donation, in particular, is a process that involves weeks of hormone injections, minor surgery, and medical risks such as ovarian hyperstimulation. Rather than rely on a pool of young women induced to donate their eggs by paying them thousands of dollars (as is common in the United States), donors in countries such as Australia or the United Kingdom are limited to other recipients of assisted fertility services who have excess gametes to donate, friends and family members of the intended parents, or altruistic young women who wish to donate their eggs out of the goodness of their hearts. This not only limits the *number* of gametes available for donation, but it also limits the viability and *quality* of the gametes, including in terms of variation in physical characteristics and ethnic markers. This last point about the quality of gamete markets will be further elaborated in Chapter 6's discussion of egg donation as a selective technology.

Using Australia as an example again, this country does not allow women to overtly sell their eggs. Article 6.5 of the Regulations states: "Do not trade in human gametes. Gamete donation must be altruistic. Commercial trading in human gametes and/or the use of direct or indirect inducements, must not be undertaken" (Australian Government, 2007, p. 27). As discussed previously, bans on compensating women for their eggs lead to gamete shortages and/or a reduction in gamete diversity and quality because fewer people will be willing to donate gametes without financial remuneration. Thus, even though transferring eggs from one woman to another is not illegal in Australia, the ban on *commercial* egg donation acts as a push factor for reproductive tourism from Australia. These bans ultimately benefit American providers, as implied by Dr. Leveque, who recalled that "the Australians emerged" as patients at his clinic after Australia enacted restrictions governing egg donation. "And we now have a reputation because we produce so many babies, . . . that if people want to do egg donation, they come here to do it. It's an easy trip. There are direct flights from Australia."

Like bans on commercial gamete donation, prohibitions on commercial forms of surrogacy (in which women are paid large sums to carry a child for another individual or couple) are far more common than outright prohibitions on surrogacy. Countries with bans on commercial surrogacy include Australia, Canada, Denmark, Greece, Israel, the Netherlands, New Zealand, and the United Kingdom (BioPolicyWiki, 2014b). Canada's 2004 Assisted Human Reproduction Act, for example, states the following under the "Prohibited Activities" section:

> No person shall pay consideration to a female person to be a surrogate mother, offer to pay such consideration or advertise that it will be paid. . . . No person shall accept consideration for arranging for the services of a surrogate mother, offer to make such an arrangement for consideration or advertise the arranging of such services. . . . No person shall pay consideration to another person to arrange for the services of a surrogate mother, offer to pay such consideration or advertise the payment of it.
>
> (Canada Legislative Services Branch, 2012, para. 5)

As with prohibitions on commercial gamete donation, prohibitions on commercial surrogacy vastly limits the pool of willing and able women available to act as surrogates. This leaves the United States, once again, along with India and a handful of other countries, as some of the only global marketplaces where women are legally enabled to enter into a commercial surrogacy contract.[8] Tammy, a social worker who provides psychological assessments for a Los Angeles–based surrogacy agency, called it "a shame" that a country like Australia has "every element that is important to do surrogacy"—that is, according to her estimation, technology and people willing to be surrogates—but many of its policies against commercial surrogacy make those elements irrelevant. She saw a *mismatch* between what individuals want and what their countries of origin have decided is ethically normative. In order to exercise their desire for children through commercial surrogacy, Tammy found it only rational for them to come to the United States to do so, but that rationale is not based on economics. It is based on desire and political circumstance.

## Policy Issue 3: Desired Services Are Restricted to Certain Populations, Excluding People on the Basis of Age, Infertility Diagnosis, Relationship Status, and/or Sexual Orientation

Another type of regulation that pushes intended parents to seek services outside of their home countries addresses what classes of people, based on biomedical and/or social factors, have access to assisted fertility treatments. People prevented from accessing assisted reproductive technology services include lesbians and gay men, single people, unmarried couples, and older people. Italy provides one of the clearest examples of this practice, limiting access to assisted reproductive technologies to "stable heterosexual couples who live together, are of reproductive age, are over the age of 18, have documented infertility, and have been first provided the opportunity for adoption" (Riggan, 2010). The IFFS reports that forty-five out of sixty-two countries responded that marriage was necessary for access to ART, "of which 13 countries have been reported to have requirements that state this as an absolute prerequisite; these countries are mainly Islamic and Southeast Asian" (Ory et al., 2013, p. 31). Additionally, thirty-three countries responded that intended couples must be in a "stable relationship" (if not legally married), twenty-six allow single people access to ART, and only fourteen permit treatment for lesbian women (Ory et al., 2013, p. 31).

## Policy Issue 4: Desired Services Are Regulated to Such an Extent that They Impinge on Intended Parents' and/or Third Parties' Privacy or Anonymity

Anonymous gamete donation is prohibited in many countries, meaning that information about sperm and egg donors are kept in a registry, and offspring conceived from third-party sperm or eggs have the right to access information (identifying or not), about their parentage (Ory et al., 2013, pp. 74–79). In Australia, for example, the National Health and Medical

Research Council prohibits anonymous gamete donation (Australian Government, 2007). Because the country acknowledges the right of children to information about their genetic parentage, gamete donors must consent to having their identifying information released to any future genetic offspring. Such prohibitions on anonymous gamete donation have two particular implications for reproductive tourism. The first is that, similar to policy issue 2, such regulation may in effect lead to a decline in men and women willing to donate or sell their gametes if they cannot remain anonymous. Resulting gamete shortages and waiting lists become a push factor for intended parents anxious to have a child. The second implication is that families may wish to keep gamete donation anonymous because they do not want to disclose to their offspring the nature of their conception. Dr. Leveque expressed to me that he believes that these laws that require donors to identify themselves create "huge problems," because children conceived through gamete donation are "going to find out about it through the state." If they get their services in a country without these laws against anonymous donation, they can keep their medical records and the circumstances of their child's conception private. "And that's the way it should be," said Dr. Leveque, "because conception is a private matter between adults, and I don't think the state has a role in that, except for perhaps safety issues."

Individuals throughout the world face a mismatch between personal desire and government policy, and this mismatch drives reproductive tourism. Whereas the logic of bargain-hunting assumes that services are similar, abundant, and widespread such that a consumer only needs to locate the cheapest place to get his or her reproductive needs met, additional push factors relating to policy point to the global variation in regulation and access. Not only do people need to be financially savvy in their search for assisted fertility services, they must also be savvy enough to navigate the laws in both their home countries and those they intend to travel to. The other side of push factors is, obviously, pull factors. That is, faced with the inability to get desired services in their own country, people may seek those same services elsewhere.

## PULL FACTORS: THE COMPETITIVE ADVANTAGE OF THE UNITED STATES

When price is not the most relevant issue, the United States is positioned remarkably well to act as a destination for reproductive tourism. Such pull factors include a friendly regulatory climate, technical superiority, reputation, and other external factors. Aside from bargain-hunting or evading government restrictions, savvy and discerning individuals may also be driven by a logic of global consumption, taking into consideration such factors as reputation, success rates, personal recommendations, and a host of perks and benefits that a particular clinic, physician, or other provider offers them.

With such a delicate and high-stake transaction as assisted fertility services, consumers can choose to work with those providers who they believe are most likely to offer them the highest quality service and the greatest likelihood of success.

Pull factors may act independently of push factors. Even if individuals do not feel "pushed" out of their home countries because of onerous laws and regulations, they may still feel compelled to search the entire global market for what they view are the highest quality and least risky services. In the age of globalization, consumers may consider a range of goods and services regardless of location and international borders. Given the advertising and information sharing made possible by the Internet and other communications media, consumers can research goods and services in locales hundreds if not thousands of miles away from them, as Dr. Bradley's query from Australia about sex selection indicated. Moreover, commerce, shipping, and high-speed travel options enable consumption on a global scale. This type of transnational consumption is not limited to imports; overseas travel itself is an act of transnational consumption, in which the consumer travels to the point of origin of the good or service.

## Lax Regulatory Climate

As briefly described in the previous chapter, the overall regulatory climate of the United States as it pertains to assisted reproductive technology is generally laissez-faire. The policy issues that act as push factors for reproductive tourism do not generally apply in the United States (at least on a national level; state-level regulations do exist, as described in Chapter 3). Sex selection, gamete donation, and surrogacy services may all be obtained legally within the United States, and there are no bans on compensation for third parties or requirements for medical justifications for any of these services. Although individual clinics and providers, using their own discretion, may choose what types of people to work with, United States law does not forbid lesbians, gay men, single people, or people of advanced maternal or paternal age from consuming fertility services. There is no government prescribed registry for gamete donors or any restrictions on anonymous donation.

## Egg Donor Quality

Another factor cited by providers is tied specifically to egg donation, and speaks to the racialized "genetic imperative" I analyze in Chapter 6. For patients who want a gestational surrogate and will provide their own fertilized egg (i.e., their own genetic material), India is a low-cost option. If they want or need to use an egg donor, however, the impression made by several of my informants is that the United States has better quality in terms of "the selection of donors we have available for people."[9] While it is unclear whether or not individuals actually decide to come to the United States because of the variety and quality of egg donors, this is, at least, one way in which providers have made sense of their industry. It is a means for them to assess how their field differs—or is superior to—industries in other nations. As I describe in Chapter 6, it is unthinkable to most American providers *not* to match egg donors with intended mothers.

The United States is not the only country with egg markets; there is also a booming egg market in Central and Eastern European countries, including Romania and the Czech Republic.[10] Yet, as I detail in Chapter 6, the very pluralism of the United States is a competitive advantage: the United States boasts young women of almost every conceivable hue, race/ethnicity, and religion. Not only is there a high likelihood of finding a young, white egg donor—particularly one who has the education and cultural capital that intended parents often desire—but there are also specific niches of Asian or Jewish egg donors, for example, that may be more easily fulfilled in such a large, pluralist nation.

## Reputation of United States Health Care

If reproductive tourists were most concerned with the ability to legally access assisted fertility services, they would be far better off obtaining them in other countries, where they are much cheaper, such as India for surrogacy, or Romania for egg donation. Yet, hundreds, if not thousands of people choose to come to the United States for fertility services. Providers cited the quality, superiority, and safety of American health care as an explanation, especially when compared to services in these and other countries. Intended parents from abroad may not have experienced firsthand the quality of American medical services, but the reputation of the United States as a wealthy world power may translate into an implicit trust in the safety and above-board nature of assisted fertility services, both medically and legally. Dr. Randolph explained that his international patients "need to be well taken care of. And they need to know what system they're getting into. And how good that system is." It is a matter of faith for them that these needs can be met in the United States. At the same time, he conceded that this may be a false hope. Where quality and ethics are concerned, the country one chooses may not be as important as the individual clinic, and that "Where you're going to end up is very important, relative to how good of a clinic are they, how ethical are they, how much money are you going to end up spending, that kind of thing."

Even if an individual or couple decided to pursue fertility treatment in a particular country, their search has only just begun: they still need to find a particular clinic or doctor within that country who they feel comfortable working with. If we conceive of fertility and pregnancy as matters of gambling and risk, people seeking treatment may believe that they have the best odds of finding suitable doctors and clinics in a country such as the United States, with its advanced medicine and technology. Several informants speculated that American success with assisted fertility is borne from decades of accumulated experience. For those who are "really desperate" in their quest to conceive, proven success rates are often more important than any other factor, including cost. Success rates of individual clinics in the United States are not difficult to obtain for anyone in the world with an Internet connection and facility in the English language: annual reports are posted online by the United States Centers for Disease Control and Prevention, and many clinics list their statistics on their own websites (CDC, 2014). These publically available statistics may also serve as assurance to intended parents in other countries, offering more proof of the legitimacy of American providers.

Some informants conjectured that intended parents have concerns about the conditions for surrogacy and childbirth in other countries, either out of sympathy for the women who will carry their babies or for the outcome of the babies themselves. India again emerges as the foil for comparisons of reproductive tourism. Anne, program coordinator of a surrogacy agency, argued that in the United States, "everything is done properly medically," but she herself would not trust that India can offer the same care in a field that is laden with so many potential risks. She stated,

> We have a lot of things that go wrong, medically. That's why these [American] doctors are the best in the world when they're looking at a high density ultrasound, and they can see that, "Oh, gee, there looks like a bubble on that baby's brain. Let's track that." This is part of our work. I doubt that's going on there [in India]. And, if a baby, . . . needs a high-level NICU [neonatal intensive care unit], I doubt that's being provided. So, I think the overall medical care is highly questionable.

Her assessment, however, was not based on any firsthand experience or knowledge about surrogacy in India; instead, she relied upon her own assumptions and speculation about American versus Indian health care.

## Legal Clarity

Similar to the medical reputation of the United States being a competitive advantage is the perception that the United States offers clarity and/or ease in establishing legal parentage, once again ameliorating concerns about risk. This advantage was mostly cited by providers who broker in surrogacy, where issues of parentage are most contested. If a woman is contracted to gestate and give birth to a child for someone else in exchange for a sum of money or out of the goodness of her heart, is she or is she not the legal mother of that child? Ironically, the answer to this question is *not* so cut and dried, even in the United States. Yet, providers cite "clarity" of this legal issue as an advantage of acquiring the services of a surrogate in the United States, with India once again as the foil.

Providers found the laws in the United States—as complex as they may be—ultimately clearer and more favorable than in other nations. This could be explained, however, by their built-in familiarity with United States law and ignorance of policies elsewhere. For example, Anne assumed, incorrectly, that India, like the United States, has birthright citizenship, and stated, as a drawback, that a child born in India to an Indian surrogate "is a citizen of India when it's born."[11] She went on to say, speaking of Americans and others traveling to India for surrogates, "I don't know what they're all doing about getting the legal documents done, or the name put on the birth certificate that has their names legally. And these are things I know when couples call they go, 'Oh, you're kidding! I never thought of *that*.' They just don't understand the complexity of what it takes to get a name on the birth certificate here." While she acknowledged that securing parentage on birth certificates is a complex legal process, even in the United States, she speculated that it is even more so in other places. Intended parents who have far less experience and knowledge than Anne, who has been working in this field for decades, may similarly make assumptions about the legal situation in the United States compared with other nations.

Liam, CEO of a surrogacy agency, also saw surrogacy tourism to other countries as "risky." Speaking of surrogacy in India or Russia, he stated, "If everything goes smoothly and you get out of the country, you're good. But, if the surrogate suddenly decided she was going to challenge it, you don't have any law that says she's not the mother." This is a risk, he said, that many are not willing to take. "I think, for some clients economically they don't have any choice but to take that risk. And that's understandable. But for clients who can afford to come to the United States, that would be their preference."

Although Anne and Liam spoke of United States law being much less complex, the two family law attorneys I interviewed made the process seem quite complicated. When I sat down with Michael in his posh office in Los Angeles, I made him stop several times to explain to me the complex legal process involved with transnational surrogacy, which varies from state to state. In order to establish parentage in cases of surrogacy, special documents may be required, such as powers of attorney, advanced health-care directives, and "guardianship documents that help protect the rights of the intended parents to make decisions for the child," even when that child is still *in utero*. In many states, attorneys also have to go through a court process, which "involves preparing court documents, filing them in court, going before a hearing, representing the parties in front of the court, and then getting a court order saying they are the legal parents, or whatever that state will allow."[12] The process can be even more complicated when third-party donors are involved, such as with surrogacy involving gay male couples. In those cases, some states automatically allow both men to be on the court order as legal parents, but in others, only the genetic parent is initially recognized, and the other parent must do a second-parent adoption. Even with all of this complexity, it still seemed manageable to Michael, especially for heterosexual married couples using their own genetic materials: "In a lot of states it's a pretty easy process. In all the states the process is *doable*, but in some states it's just simple, and you don't have to go court; the attorney can go for you." Furthermore, if the surrogacy occurs in California or a handful of other states, the process is well established and the laws about parentage are clear.

Clarity of laws in the United States does not necessarily guarantee a smooth legal process, however. Deirdre, the San Francisco family law attorney, told me about a number of cases that made her reconsider whether it was worth the hassle of working with international clients. One couple that had contracted with a surrogate went through a divorce during the pregnancy, and decided they no longer wanted the child. Because they were in another country, she "couldn't get [her] hands on them," causing both Deirdre and the eight-month-pregnant surrogate to, reasonably, panic until the situation was resolved.

In another case, a couple went against her advice to bring their twin babies back to France with a United States passport and apply for French citizenship a few years later. Instead, they contacted the French consulate on their own. Because surrogacy is not legal in France, and the government "had indicated they would not give citizenship that was born of a surrogate without a full-on adoption . . . the consulate decided they were going to make an example of this couple." After France threatened to take the children away and put them in foster care, Deirdre had to involve the Department of State, since the children were American citizens:

> So, we worked it out on a crappy compromise with the French govern-ment, that they would not take the children, but the family had to go through adoption, and abandonment, because they said 'No, this birth mother has no rights to sign on anything. You can't *do* it. You're run-ning afoul of international stuff.' So we finally worked it out, and the children were being placed with them—it was very screwy—in foster care, but with the same people, and they were going to have to do an adoption under French law. It all worked, but it was all very convoluted and should not have had to happen.[13]

Although the aforementioned case is an example of an international couple going to great lengths to ensure the citizenship of their children in their home country, it also illustrates what for others may be construed as another advantage that the United States has to offer: birthright citizenship. That is, providers in California who broker between intended parents and surrogate mothers cited the fact that if the child is born on United States soil—regardless of the circumstances of its birth or the status of any of the parties involved—that child is an American citizen. Granted, almost anyone who comes to the United States to acquire the services of a surrogate is already quite privileged. Surrogacy can cost upward of $100,000, requires time necessary to travel, and some savvy in navigating contracts and legal issues. According to some of my interview subjects, American citizenship is not a life-or-death issue but would be an added benefit—more so than, say, if a child had birthright citizenship from one of the other countries where commercial surrogacy is legal. These dual-citizen children may be the pint-sized versions of Aihwa Ong's "flexible citizens," brandishing multiple pass-ports throughout their lifetimes as it suits their convenience (Ong, 1999).

## America as a Luxury Brand

Globalization has made the world a "tiny place," as Dr. Bradley described it:

> I mean, everybody lives the same, everybody's got aspirations. A comfortable home. Food. So they're trying to have children. . . . I'm dealing with a patient from Norway. She could be an American. She happens to be a physician. She's seeing me. If she didn't have an accent when she's talking to me, I could be talking to any American. Same humor, same interests, same questions. Everything exactly the same.

The "everybody" that Dr. Bradley spoke of, however, is clearly limited to the global elite, living lives that are, from his perspective, virtually indistinguishable. Globalization scholars may refer to this effect as a "leveling" or "flattening" of culture, in which people throughout the world begin to resemble each other in their dreams, habits, and even the way they build families. Liam, the CEO of a gay-focused fertility agency, also sounded like a champion of globalization when he said "I think that because the world really is more one now, it's not as different. You know, I travel all over the world myself, and I don't feel, unless I'm going to a Third World country, it's pretty much the same everywhere." In this statement, Liam, unlike Dr. Bradley, at least acknowledged differences between highly developed and developing countries.

The "smallness" of the (global elite) world means that intended parents may be more willing to travel across geographic borders to get their needs met. The globalization of the market only emphasizes the need for providers to distinguish themselves. Providers of fertility services compete not only on the basis of price but also on type and quality of service. Some see their services as so superior that they are beyond competition. As Dr. Gorman told me,

> There are [clinics] that . . . cannot offer the quality that is being offered here, because the patients who come to us are in higher quality places in the first place, and they can't even get it there. You know? So it doesn't make sense to go to India for those. So this [India] does not represent competition for us.

Even more succinct is an analogy he made using Wal-Mart and Bergdorf Goodman:

> If you do things because you want to save money, it's one thing. If you do things because you're trying to get better quality, or because you're . . . trying to get something that you cannot get elsewhere, it's something else. It's not that different than in any other sphere of the economy. If you go to Wal-Mart, you do not expect to find the same items as you find in Bergdorf Goodman, for example. Yeah? Same thing here. And there are certain things that I think everybody can buy at Wal-Mart and be perfectly happy, and there are others, which you either don't buy at Wal-Mart, or you won't find at Wal-Mart.

In the logic of global consumption, the United States is a luxury brand.


## BASTION OF FREEDOM?

The way that providers described their international clients, it sometimes appeared that coming to the United States was their last resort. From the perspective of the individual desiring a child by means of gamete donation, surrogacy, or IVF, traveling to another country and paying a higher premium may seem like the only option. Many providers, sympathetic to their clients' needs (and their credit cards), described the situation by invoking the language of *necessity* or lack of options:

> *Linda (fertility clinic director of operations)*: It's illegal to do egg donation in other countries. You know, not all other countries, but some. So they have no choice if they want to have a baby but they're old, or they need an egg donor.
> *Tammy (social worker)*: It's pretty much a necessity. Most countries don't allow this. And, so, in order to, for this to be possible, they have to come to another country. And a lot of them choose California because . . . we're some of the most established agencies. So, they don't really have a choice, unfortunately.

Providers were able to frame the United States fertility industry as a safe refuge or a beacon for intended parents worldwide who happen to reside in or be citizens of countries with much more restrictive policies that prevent them from fulfilling their dreams of a biological child.

> *Liam (CEO of a surrogacy agency)*: [Surrogacy is] pretty much illegal in their own country. Pretty much, surrogacy's not legal in any country around the world. And, their options if they didn't do it in the U.S.,

would be to do it in India or perhaps Russia, and in those countries they don't have the same protection.

*Jen (genetic counselor)*: I think we are kind of free to do more than most countries are, and that's a lot of times why people from other countries come here, is because they can't get those services where they're from, whether it's that they have, you know, socialized medicine, or that there's religious issues related to reproductive medicine. But I think because we're open in both of those respects that people come here to get their services.

In these statements made by providers, lax regulation becomes a cognate for "freedom" and "choice" in the neoliberal language of the free market. American providers operate in the social, political, and moral context of liberal United States values, which holds that individuals should have the right to sell and purchase products and services without government interference. As I elaborate in Chapter 3, this liberal context is especially salient when it comes to medical services.

## THE PUSH AND PULL OF REPRODUCTIVE TOURISM, REVISITED

Providers offer more than high-quality services and advanced technologies. They offer intangibles: a mystique of luxury, an aura of privilege and entitlement. Reproductive tourism is both a result and a determinant of "stratified reproduction" (Colen, 1995). For those seeking fertility services, different classes of fertility markets have emerged, both within and between countries. To reiterate a point, the logic of the bottom line is *not* the sole determinant for reproductive tourism, particularly for the elite. This is not to say that *value* does not matter. Paying hundreds of thousands of dollars for a surrogate to carry your child may strike some as an extremely good value, worth every penny.

Although money is not a major component of travel to the United States for fertility treatment, this motive is still paramount in any discussion of reproductive tourism. Given the high costs associated with assisted reproductive technologies, many individuals seek out cheaper locations to fulfill their demand for services. Rather than travel to New York City, Los Angeles, and San Francisco, those motivated by financial reasons would be more likely to travel to India, the Caribbean, or Eastern Europe.

My informants cited policy issues as a more compelling push factor for reproductive tourism. As American providers of assisted fertility services, they work in a country that is free of many of the regulatory hurdles and prohibitions found in nations such as Australia, Japan, the United Kingdom, and Italy. Those residing in countries where there are bans or severe restrictions on egg donation, surrogacy, and sex selection seek these services elsewhere, and find that the regulatory environment in the United States is much more open to these practices.

Yet, given that assisted fertility services are quite expensive, politics alone does not adequately explain why reproductive tourists do not automatically go to those countries that boast both a friendly regulatory environment *and* bargain prices. The United States draws in those reproductive tourists, particularly those from affluent backgrounds, who view the fertility marketplace in global terms. They are savvy consumers, choosing particular clinics and doctors based not on bargain prices but on other tangible and intangible factors, such as reputation, success rates, and quality of care. Furthermore, they choose the United States in particular not only for its lax regulations but for its high technology resources, clarity of laws regarding parentage, and status as a global destination. Despite the fact that assisted fertility services in the United States are some of the most expensive in the world, it has emerged as a major destination for international reproductive tourists seeking egg donors, surrogates, and sex selection services from well-established and reputable providers.

## NOTES

1. A website for a clinic in the Czech Republic cites US$2,259 per IVF cycle (Fite & Fite, n.d.).
2. The discrepancy in dates between the two sets of data means that the per capita ratio cannot be taken at face value; however, the numbers provide a generalized snapshot of the size of each country's fertility industry.
3. Until 2004, the regulation of assisted fertility services in Italy was similar to that found in the United States, with virtually no national restrictions on its use, enabling a fertility industry to develop absent government oversight. This changed in 2004 with the passage of Law 40/2004 by the Italian Parliament, which dramatically shifted the orientation of Italy from a laissez-faire stance to a conservative one, in which previously available services were now prohibited (Boggio, 2005).
4. Dr. Silverstein estimates that about 80% of his international clientele come to his clinic for sex selection.
5. I should note that the computer monitor was not close enough for me to read (nor did Dr. Bradley expect me to actually read the contents of his email inbox), thus confidentiality of this inquiring potential patient was not violated.
6. Traveling to relatively nearby New Zealand is not an option, as sex selection is banned there, with penalties of up to NZ$100,000 for violation (Clarke, 2009).
7. These countries include Australia, Belgium, Canada, China, Czech Republic, Denmark, Estonia, Finland, France, Greece, Hungary, Israel, the Netherlands, New Zealand, Singapore, Slovenia, South Korea, the United Kingdom, and Vietnam (BioPolicyWiki, 2014a).
8. New South Wales, attempting to prevent surrogacy tourism, recently enacted a law that will criminalize commercial surrogacy even when it takes place outside the country's jurisdiction (Noone, 2010).
9. Interview transcript, Dr. Leveque.

10. According to Daisy Deomampo, who is studying reproductive tourism in India, a new practice is emerging in that country in which intended parents bring their own donors with them from out of the country, or import frozen embryos (personal correspondence).
11. India eliminated birthright citizenship in 1987.
12. Interview transcript, Michael.
13. Although it is unclear if this is the same case that Deirdre described, since she obviously must keep the names and details of her clients confidential, France recently denied citizenship to twin girls that had been born to a surrogate in California, after a ten-year battle by the parents to have them legally recog nized (Souchard, 2011).

## REFERENCES

Australian Government. (2007). *Ethical guidelines on the use of assisted reproductive technology in clinical practice and research.* Canberra, Australian Capital Territory: National Health and Medical Research Council. Retrieved from www.anu.edu.au/ro/ORI/Human/ART-Ethical-Guidelines-Research.pdf

BioPolicyWiki. (2014a, April 28). *Eggs for assisted reproduction.* Retrieved from www.biopolicywiki.org/index.php?title=Eggs_for_assisted_reproduction

BioPolicyWiki. (2014b, April 28). *Surrogacy—BioPolicyWiki.* Retrieved from www.biopolicywiki.org/index.php?title=Surrogacy

BioPolicyWiki. (2014c, April 29). *Preimplantation genetic diagnosis.* Retrieved from www.biopolicywiki.org/index.php?title=Property:Preimplantation_genetic_diagnosis

Boggio, A. (2005). Italy enacts new law on medically assisted reproduction. *Human Reproduction, 20*(5), 1153–1157.

Canada Legislative Services Branch. (2012, September 30). *Consolidated federal laws of Canada, Assisted Human Reproduction Act.* Retrieved from http://laws-lois.justice.gc.ca/eng/acts/A-13.4/page-2.html?texthighlight=surrogacy#s-6

CDC. (2014). *ART Reports and Resources.* Retrieved from www.cdc.gov/art/ARTReports.htm

Central Intelligence Agency. (2014). *The world factbook.* Retrieved from https://www.cia.gov/library/publications/the-world-factbook/

Chambers, G. M., Sullivan, E. A., Ishihara, O., Chapman, M. G., & Adamson, G. D. (2009). The economic impact of assisted reproductive technology: A review of selected developed countries. *Fertility and Sterility, 91*(6), 2281–2294.

Clarke, S. F. (2009, June). *Sex selection & abortion: New Zealand. Law Library of Congress.* Retrieved from www.loc.gov/law/help/sex-selection/newzealand.php

Colen, S. (1995). "Like a mother to them": Stratified reproduction and West Indian childcare workers and employers in New York. In F.D. Ginsburg and R. Rapp (Eds.), *Conceiving the new world order: The global politics of reproduction* (pp. 78–102). Berkeley: University of California Press.

Ethics Committee of the ASRM. (2013). Cross-border reproductive care: A committee opinion. *Fertility and Sterility, 100*(3), 645–650. doi:10.1016/j.fertnstert.2013.02.051

Feikert, C. (2009, June). *Sex Selection & Abortion: Australia—Law Library of Congress. Law Library of Congress.* Retrieved from www.loc.gov/law/help/sex-selection/australia.php

Fite, C., & Fite, M. (n.d.). *IVF Vacation/cost of IVF/IVF in Europe/affordable ivf alternative.* Retrieved from http://ivfvacation.com/

Gurtin-Broadbent, Z. (2010, March 22). *Problems with legislating against "reproductive tourism." BioNews.* Retrieved from www.bionews.org.uk/page_56954.asp

Haimowitz, R., Sinha, V. (Directors), Fledgling Fund, & Chicken & Egg Pictures (Production). (2010). *Made in India* [Motion picture]: United States: Made in India, LLC.

Inhorn, M. C., & Gürtin, Z. (2011). Cross-border reproductive care: A future research agenda. *Reproductive BioMedicine Online, 23*(5), 665–676.

Jones, H. W., Jr., Cooke, I., Kempers, R., Brinsden, P., & Saunders, D. (2010). *IFFS surveillance 2010: Fertility and sterility.* Retrieved from www.iffs-reproduction.org/documents/IFFS_Surveillance_2010.pdf

Lee, E. S. (1966). A theory of migration. *Demography, 3*(1), 47–57. doi:10.2307/2060063

Noone, R. (2010, November 22). Childless couples face jail as part of international baby ban. *Daily Telegraph*. Australia. Retrieved from www.dailytelegraph.com.au/news/national/childless-couples-face-jail-as-part-of-international-baby-ban/story-e6freuzr-1225958115275

Ong, A. (1999). *Flexible citizenship: The cultural logics of transnationality.* Durham, NC: Duke University Press.

Ory, S., Devroey, P., Banker, M., Brinsden, P., Buster, J., Fiadjoe, M. et al. (2013). *IFFS surveillance 2013.* International Federation of Fertility Societies. Retrieved from http://c.ymcdn.com/sites/www.iffs-reproduction.org/resource/resmgr/iffs_surveillance_09-19-13.pdf

Riggan, K. (2010, October 1). *G12 country regulations of assisted reproductive technologies.* Retrieved from http://cbhd.org/content/g12-country-regulations-assisted-reproductive-technologies

Sassen, S. (1999). *Globalization and its discontents: Essays on the new mobility of people and money.* New York: New Press.

Souchard, P.-A. (2011, April 6). France rules against children of surrogate mothers. *The Seattle Times*. Retrieved from http://seattletimes.com/html/nationworld/2014694604_apeufrancesurrogatemothers.html

Storrow, R. F. (2011). Assisted reproduction on treacherous terrain: The legal hazards of cross-border reproductive travel. *Reproductive BioMedicine Online (Reproductive Healthcare Limited), 23*(5), 538–545. doi:10.1016/j.rbmo.2011.07.008

Van Hoof, W., & Pennings, G. (2011). Extraterritoriality for cross-border reproductive care: Should states act against citizens travelling abroad for illegal infertility treatment? *Reproductive BioMedicine Online (Reproductive Healthcare Limited), 23*(5), 546–554. doi:10.1016/j.rbmo.2011.07.015

# 3 Privatization and Self-Regulation in the United States Fertility Industry

As described in Chapter 1, sovereign nations construct their own rules and protocols regarding the political economy of assisted fertility that may orient them with various "fertility regimes" or governing styles. The United States' orientation to a laissez-faire fertility regime (at least regarding assisted fertility, in great contrast to the ongoing "culture wars" over contraception, abortion, and sex education), makes the United States fertility industry a somewhat peculiar American institution. Individual aspects of the United States fertility industry are not in themselves exceptional. However, the fertility industry has developed in a particular way that makes it stand out from fertility industries in most other capitalist democracies.

Structures and practices of the American fertility industry have been largely shaped by the following three factors: (1) funding streams for research in infertility treatment and reproductive medicine; (2) payment for fertility services; and (3) the relative absence of national regulation of assisted reproduction. Compared to other nations, the United States government has a striking lack of both financial and regulatory input. The net effect of private (rather than government) monies financing both research and clinical practice is a fundamentally less regulated industry. As I articulate below, this is a field that is almost entirely *privatized* and *market-driven*, not only in its research funding and compensation for services, but in its regulation. It is this nexus of privatization that offers a competitive advantage to clinics and providers in the United States reaching out to consumers in a global marketplace.

## RESEARCH FUNDING

Although scientists in the United States, along with the United Kingdom and Australia, were early pioneers of reproductive technologies, in particular *in vitro fertilization* (IVF), American scientists lacked the government support that their British and Australian counterparts received. In 1974, only a few months after the Supreme Court passed the landmark 1973 *Roe v. Wade* decision, the United States Congress instituted a "temporary" moratorium

on the federal funding of fetal research (Boonstra, 2001). Although reproductive medical researchers faced questions and condemnation in each of
the three countries, government responses ultimately swung in different
directions (Spar, 2006). The United Kingdom legitimated IVF as a valid
treatment for infertility and established a regulatory body called the Human
Fertilisation and Embryology Authority (HFEA) in 1990. Australia, likewise, validated IVF with regulatory bodies established in different states. In
the United States, the National Commission for the Protection of Human
Subjects of Biomedical and Behavioral Research in 1975 recommended that
the temporary ban on funding for fetal research be ended in order to support research in IVF; however, both anti-abortion fervor and political inertia
kept the ban in place (Boonstra, 2001; Henig, 2004; Spar, 2006, pp. 26–28).
This "de facto moratorium" on federal funding for IVF research (Boonstra,
2001, p. 3) persisted for decades, and is now in arguably murky territory
with President Obama's 2009 executive order lifting the ban on federal funding for stem-cell research that relies in part on discarded embryos resulting
from IVF procedures.

That private, rather than public, monies largely financed IVF research in
the United States is significant for a number of reasons. In her history of IVF,
journalist Robin Marantz Henig (2004) argues that bans on government
monies for fetal and embryonic research (the underpinnings of IVF, stem-
cell research, and a host of other applications) turned the field into a "cow-
boy science driven by supply and demand" (p. 12). That is, because the U.S.
government did not fund research, an opportunity was missed to *direct* the
research, provide quality-control measures, and ultimately regulate practices
that later grew out of this research. There were financial consequences as
well. The doctors who Spar describes as "victims of the ambiguous ban on
federal funding," ultimately became victors (2006, p. 28). "Quietly," Spar
writes, "doctors began to see the field of reproduction not only as a cutting
edge of medicine but also as a distinctly profitable endeavor—expanding,
unregulated, and catering to a population that seemed ever eager to pay"
(2006, p. 29).

At least two of my informants appeared to agree with Henig's thesis
about the path-dependent role that initial (and subsequent) lack of government financed research had on the direction of the field and existing practice
today. Dr. Leveque, a Bay Area physician in practice since the late 1980s,
told me, "There's really no established funding for doing research in this
field. It's all privately funded, all of it. And so programs like mine will start a
clinical protocol, and establish it, without that big research network behind
it." This has implications for the development and promotion of particular
technologies, and clinical practice more generally:

> [As] technologies have matured in the laboratory, we've been able to
> bring those out into clinical practice very quickly. The problems that
> emerge along . . . that pathway are that we have clinical needs that

require use of technologies that are not clearly established. You know, you don't have an elaborate ten-year safety record, and proof of efficacy and all that kind of stuff. Sometimes we have to adopt technologies before they're proven, is what it comes down to.

(Dr. Leveque)

This history of the field was echoed by Dr. Gorman, a New York doctor who first began practicing in Chicago in the early 1980s, when IVF was in its infancy. Lack of government research grants created an atmosphere ripe for technological innovation. Moreover, because this was such a new field with low success rates, patients also had low expectations, which pushed doctors to be daring and creative. According to Dr. Gorman, "Since there's so little to lose, and so much to gain, that experimentation, even if it is not well controlled, is warranted. And it was this trial and error that drove the field very quickly." Unlike their counterparts in the United Kingdom and Australia, who got government support for research coupled with government oversight, reproductive scientists and clinicians in the United States were researching and developing new protocols in privately funded clinics and medical schools, largely without government interference.

The United States may have backed away from funding early research in reproductive medicine, but this is not necessarily reflective of American attitudes towards using public monies for science and medical research. Rather, research that involves reproductive materials is a particular *type* of science that government has been loath to finance, with all of its implications about "playing God," tinkering with life, and dredging up long-entrenched cultural schisms surrounding abortion politics. Dr. Leveque referred to reproduction as a "political hot potato," elaborating that "people don't want to think about it, on a public basis. The President doesn't want to talk about reproduction. Congress doesn't want to think about reproduction."

Ironically, as Melinda Cooper (2008) points out, federal money began to pour into the life sciences in the 1980s, making it "the most heavily funded area of basic science research in the United States, apart from defense" (p. 27). Whereas fetal and embryonic research remained in the private sphere, other scientific research (including in the biological sciences) developed in the context of alliances between public and private entities, leading to the creation of the biotech and pharmaceutical industries (Cooper, 2008). Thus, although Henig, Spar, and practitioners in the field conclude that lack of government funding was ultimately a boon to the highly lucrative fertility industry, Cooper's research implies that had the moratorium on fetal research been lifted, the fertility industry may have still wound up a mostly privatized capitalist enterprise (see also Waldby & Mitchell, 2006). What is unclear is the extent to which federal funding would have shaped the direction of research.

That the United States has not financed embryonic research does not mean that the government did not take any interest in the field. Ethical and political motivations ultimately led to *de jure* and *de facto* bans on govern-ment financing of research involving human reproductive materials. Under the second Bush administration, bans on funding for stem-cell research had clear echoes of the bans faced by reproductive scientists in earlier decades. But bans on federal funding do not necessarily quell research in a given field. In the case of IVF and other assisted reproductive technologies, bans on funding merely shifted the research beyond the purview of government. By not financing research, the government voided its influence over the direction of research and clinical practice. The absence of government fund-ing and oversight, and the subsequent domination by industry and market forces, signaled the privatization of reproductive medicine.

## REIMBURSEMENT FOR ASSISTED FERTILITY SERVICES

A second factor in which the United States fertility industry differs from countries with comparably robust fertility programs is in payment or reim-bursement for assisted fertility services. According to a comparative study of several nations with prominent fertility industries, the national govern-ments in the United Kingdom, Scandinavian countries (Denmark, Sweden, Norway, Finland, and Iceland), Japan, and Australia all reimburse for some fertility treatments (Chambers, Sullivan, Ishihara, Chapman, & Adamson, 2009, p. 2286). In Canada, the province of Ontario reimburses for fertility treatments, but this is not the case in the rest of the federation (Chambers et al., 2009, p. 2286). Of the sixty nations surveyed by the IFFS (Interna-tional Federation of Fertility Societies), 52% reported coverage of assisted reproductive technology treatment by a national health plan (twenty-three nations with partial coverage, and eight with complete coverage; Ory et al., 2013). As the authors of the survey point out, high-income countries are more likely to offer national health plans that cover treatment than middle- and low-income countries "with the main exception of the United States" (Ory et al., 2013, p. 22). In addition to the United States, the other coun-tries that only offer coverage through private insurance plans are Argentina, Libya, the Philippines, and Saudi Arabia (Ory et al., 2013).

The United States federal and state governments do not directly reim-burse for assisted fertility services or medications, although people with government-issued health insurance may have some services and medica-tions covered under their particular programs.[1] Payment for assisted fertility services (to medical providers, clinics, gamete donors, surrogates, pharma-ceutical companies, and so on) is privatized and may be provided by health insurance and managed-care corporations, paid out of pocket by individu-als utilizing services, or a combination of the two. This is, of course, not unique to the field of reproductive medicine, but is an aspect of health-care provision and payment in the United States more generally (Hacker, 2002; Quadagno, 2004). The financing of the American fertility industry is in part a legacy of one of the primary examples of American exceptionalism: our lack of a national health-care system (Hacker, 2002; Quadagno, 2004). The enactment of the Affordable Care Act has also somewhat changed the landscape of fertility treatment coverage, and advocates hope to see coverage mandated as an "essential health benefit" in future revisions of the law. As of this writing, coverage for infertility treatment is not mandated, with the exception of states that had already included coverage in their benchmark plans (Resolve, 2014).

Only fourteen states currently have legislation mandating that insurance companies cover or offer some infertility treatment (see Table 3.1, Column 1), leaving millions of Americans residing in states where insurance coverage for fertility services is not mandated. Even in those states that require that insurance companies cover treatment, the services may only cover diagnosis and inexpensive procedures, or may outright exclude IVF, which is one of the most costly reproductive technologies. Of the fourteen mandated states, only eight specify coverage for IVF (see Table 3.1, Column 2). Six will continue to mandate IVF coverage as an essential health-benefit benchmark, but Arkansas and Maryland will not include infertility treatment as a benchmark benefit (Table 3.1, Column 3; RESOLVE, 2014). Most individuals in the United States, even those with health-care insurance, must pay out of pocket for fertility treatment.

There are several consequences of the private compensation model in the United States, namely high prices for assisted fertility services, stratification

*Table 3.1* Insurance Mandates

| States with insurance mandate | Mandate included coverage for IVF prior to ACA | IVF mandate continues under ACA |
| --- | --- | --- |
| Arkansas | X | |
| California | | |
| Connecticut | X | X |
| Hawaii | X | X |
| Illinois | X | X |
| Maryland | X | |
| Massachusetts | X | X |
| Montana | | |
| New Jersey | X | X |
| New York | | |
| Ohio | | |
| Rhode Island | X | X |
| Texas | | |
| West Virginia | | |

*Sources*: National Conference of State Legislatures (2012); RESOLVE (2014).

of users of fertility services and mismatch of supply and demand, and implications for regulation. The prices for assisted fertility services and technologies in the United States may be higher since service providers are largely dealing with individual consumers and private insurance companies rather than one central agency that can negotiate prices. This is similar to arguments made about lowering the costs of prescription drugs by government negotiating directly with pharmaceutical corporations (Frakt, Pizer, & Hendricks, 2008). Given these very high costs, most individuals in the United States who would like to access assisted fertility services cannot actually afford them. Some may travel to countries where services are cheap enough that they can pay out of pocket. Besides lacking negotiating power over the costs of services, technologies, and medications, the government also lacks power as a regulatory arm. By not paying for either research *or* the use of services, the government essentially loses the power of the purse. Fertility treatment and assisted reproduction are left in private hands.

## Relative Cost of Assisted Fertility Services

In regard to insurance coverage for fertility treatment affecting its relative cost, my informants pointed to legislation in other localities (states, countries, and/or global regions) that they believed resulted in consumers having to pay less for services there. For example, Robin, the director of a Los Angeles-based egg donation program, named Massachusetts (a state that mandates IVF coverage) as a model for California to follow. She stated:

> Right now, most people in California don't get [IVF] paid for at all. Zero. . . . So I believe that the more that we can get that paid for, the better. And, that will make it accessible to a broader range of people. Right now the costs of the medical piece are so high that—and a lot of that is pharmaceuticals—the cost is so high it just automatically excludes a whole lot of people.

Mandated insurance coverage of IVF in California would not necessarily bring down the *price* of IVF treatment, but having some or all of it covered by health insurance would at least reduce the out-of-pocket expenses for some consumers. Depending on how legislation were written, mandated coverage could expand the number of people who will have access to treatment—and thus expand the market for fertility services in California and other states. Consumers benefit by having greater access, but fertility services providers also benefit by gaining more clients.

Researchers have found several consequences related to mandated insurance coverage. A 2008 study found a greater increase in use of assisted reproductive technologies in states that have adopted mandated insurance coverage for infertility treatment (Henne & Bundorf, 2008). Additionally, mandated states had lower rates of high-risk multiple pregnancies and births, particularly in those states that have what the authors describe as "comprehensive" insurance coverage (Henne & Bundorf, 2008). Using more updated data, another study found that providers in states without mandated insurance coverage for IVF are more likely to transfer multiple embryos than those in mandated states, resulting in higher pregnancy, live-birth, and multiple pregnancy rates (Martin, Bromer, Sakkas, & Patrizio, 2011).

In addition to state-to-state comparisons, providers I spoke with compared the United States as a whole with other nations that have more "socialized medicine" (a term that came up frequently in my interviews), arguing that costs are cheaper in countries with more financial support. According to Dr. Leveque, because European countries with comprehensive health-care coverage have lower costs for treatment, this results in more overall treatment cycles happening in Europe than in the United States. Furthermore, he and others I spoke with provided anecdotal evidence for claims about the relationship between insurance coverage and multiple pregnancies. Michael (attorney) argued that when patients have to pay for IVF cycles out of pocket (which can run at least $12,000 per cycle), there is a greater incentive on the part of the patient to push for more medically risky procedures, such as multiple embryo transfers:

> You're like, you know, "I'll be damned if I'm going to risk it and then wait and save some embryos for later. Let's do three. Let's transfer three and we'll hope that we'll get one, or two." So there's this sort of motivation because of the insurance and the cost, to go for it.

Indeed, in a 2009 study of six countries/regions, researchers noted that the United States was the only country without any federal or state funding of assisted reproductive technologies and also had the highest multiple birth rate (Chambers et al., 2009). It also had the highest cost ($12,513) for an IVF cycle, compared to $8,500 in Canada, $5645 in Australia, $5,549 in Scandinavia, and the lowest costs in Japan at $3,956 per cycle (Chambers et al., 2009, p. 2288).[2]

## Stratification of Users of Reproductive Technologies

In her remarkable essay about West Indian nannies, Shellee Colen introduced the phrase "stratified reproduction" to delineate how social location (based on race, socioeconomic status, nationality, and immigration status) stratify women's reproductive options, circumstances, and livelihoods (Colen, 1995). Although Colen wrote primarily about caretaking and childrearing, Ginsburg and Rapp (1995) have extended the term to other aspects of reproduction, including conception, pregnancy, and childbirth. Use of reproductive technologies is also highly stratified, and the privatization of the industry makes it even more so. Because most Americans do not currently have access to insurance that covers all aspects of fertility treatment (even those in mandated states such as Massachusetts and New York), use of reproductive technologies is highly stratified, limited to those who can afford to pay out of pocket for treatment.[3]

Anecdotally, most of my informants acknowledged that their clients—both domestic and international—were a relatively privileged group. When asked to estimate the income range of their typical clients, from high-income (above $100,000 per year), to middle-income (between $30,000 and $100,000 per year), to low-income (under $30,000 per year), a few hedged that they knew nothing about their clients' finances. For example, Michael, the Los Angeles attorney, gave a very vague, lawyerly answer, circling around the fact that the majority of his clients are probably well off:

> We never really ask them what their income levels are. I could make an assumption, that because they have the finances to afford the process, they're probably not low-income. They may not even be middle-income . . . [They] can find the resources, whether it's through home equity lines of credit, or whatever else. They may have family helping them out. So I'd say at least middle-income and higher-income, generally speaking.

Tammy, a Bay Area social worker gave a similarly evasive answer about her clients' income, preferring to call them middle- and upper-middle-class rather than wealthy. She also provided a broader, more nuanced demographic description of her typical clients:

> They have earning power. They tend to be professionals. They tend to have enough earning potential where they can eventually pull themselves out of debt. They have supportive families, or they borrow from their home, or their family members.

Others were wary of describing a "typical" client, and replied that their clients' incomes were highly variable. Most providers I spoke with, however, were quite blunt in noting that their clients are high earners. In fact, many recognized that one would *require* a high income in order to access their services. For example, Liz, coordinator of an egg donation program in New York City, estimated that the majority of her patients are high income, particularly because at her clinic, patients tend to go through several cycles of IVF using their own ova before turning to egg donation. Costs quickly add up, draining financial resources. By the time they see her for egg donor services, they "have already spent fifty, sixty, seventy thousand doing IVF." Ironically, she says, "By the time they finish all of their IVF and come to donor egg, I don't think they're as wealthy as when they started off, you know?" According to a recent qualitative study, the median cost of IVF using donated eggs was approximately $14,000 more than IVF alone (Katz et al., 2011).

Robin was even more straightforward about her clients' high incomes. "Yes, absolutely," she says. "They can't afford it otherwise." Shelby and Rebekah, co-owners of a surrogacy agency in Los Angeles, went back and forth with each other about how wealthy one needs to be to acquire various services, with surrogacy being the most costly of all expenses:

*Shelby*: It's not cheap, and it's not getting cheaper. So, it would be great if, you know, everybody could afford it, but it's just not the case. . . . Infertility affects everybody. Unfortunately, only—

*Rebekah*: Only a slice can get services.

*Shelby*: . . . Egg donation, a bigger bracket. IVF, an even bigger bracket. But surrogacy is just . . . We get these calls all the time. You know, 'Can I do it for $30,000?' It's like, no, unless you have a sister willing to do it.

*Rebekah*: And frozen embryos. The pregnancy itself costs.

*Shelby*: Yeah! Forget us! Even if you do it on your own . . . you should have a contract, you should do psych, you need the medications, you need the IVF, you need the monitoring for your sister or friend.

*Rebekah*: With an agency, you have to figure for non-international clients, it's $80 to $100,000. . . .

Regional stratification also exists, as clinics are not evenly dispersed in all states. Of the 456 fertility clinics reporting statistics to the Centers for Disease Control and Prevention, two (Wyoming and Maine) have zero fertility clinics, whereas California, Illinois, Florida, New Jersey, New York, and Texas each have over twenty (see Table 3.2; CDC, ASRM, & SART, 2010). The fertility industry is also concentrated *within* those states, with the largest numbers of clinics concentrated in Southern California, Chicago, greater New York City, the San Francisco Bay Area, Houston, and Dallas/ Fort Worth (in Florida, clinics are spread throughout the state). Egg donor and surrogacy programs are also concentrated in a handful of states. On the published list of ASRM-approved egg donor agencies, 31 out of 79 agencies are located in California (American Society for Reproductive Medicine [ASRM], 2011). Depending on what state or part of the country one is located in, one will have more or less access to fertility clinics and services. People in fertility clinic deserts will have to travel long distances to access treatment.

Dr. Randolph, a Bay Area physician, told me that the industry has concentrated in these areas as a direct result of the high cost of fertility treatment. Because these expensive procedures tend not to be covered by insurance, clinics and agencies have opened in cities that have large populations and high numbers of people with expendable incomes. Of the five states with the highest concentration of fertility clinics, only Illinois and

*Table 3.2*   Concentration and Number of Fertility Clinics in the United States (including D.C. and Puerto Rico)

| Zero clinics | 1–5 clinics | 5–10 clinics | 11–20 clinics | 21–30 clinics | Over 30 clinics |
|---|---|---|---|---|---|
| Maine | Alaska (1) | Alabama (6) | Arizona (10) | Illinois (25) | Calif. (69) |
| Wyoming | Arkansas (1) | Colorado (8) | Michigan (12) | Florida (28) | New York (38) |
| | Delaware (2) | Conn. (9) | N. Carolina(11) | New Jersey (21) | Texas (41) |
| | District of Col. (4) | Georgia (8) | Ohio (11) | | |
| | Idaho (1) | Hawaii (5) | Penn. (18) | | |
| | Iowa (2) | Indiana (10) | Virginia (13) | | |
| | Kansas (4) | Kentucky (5) | Washington (10) | | |
| | Louisiana (4) | Maryland (7) | | | |
| | Mississippi (3) | Mass. (9) | | | |
| | Montana (1) | Minnesota (5) | | | |
| | Nebraska (2) | Missouri (8) | | | |
| | Nevada (3) | Tenn. (8) | | | |
| | New Hamp. (1) | Wisconsin (7) | | | |
| | New Mexico (1) | | | | |
| | North Dakota (1) | | | | |
| | Oklahoma (3) | | | | |
| | Oregon (4) | | | | |
| | Puerto Rico (3) | | | | |
| | Rhode Island (1) | | | | |
| | S. Carolina (3) | | | | |
| | South Dakota (1) | | | | |
| | Utah (4) | | | | |
| | Vermont (1) | | | | |
| | West Virginia (3) | | | | |

*Source:* Centers for Disease Control and Prevention (CDC, 2014).

New Jersey mandate that insurers cover IVF. California and New York mandate some coverage for infertility diagnosis and treatment, but exclude IVF. Texas mandates that insurers offer IVF and other treatments, but does not mandate coverage. Florida currently has no legislation regarding mandated insurance coverage for infertility diagnosis and treatment (National Conference of State Legislatures, 2012).

Consumers of assisted reproductive technologies are also stratified by race, ethnicity, and sexual orientation. Although higher percentages of Hispanic and African American women report infertility than do white women, they are less likely to access treatment (Jain, 2006; Missmer, Seifer, & Jain, 2011). Asian American, Black, and Hispanic women also have worse outcomes than White women who use fertility treatment, including decreased odds of achieving pregnancy and live birth (Fujimoto et al., 2010). Lesbians and gay men also face barriers to treatment. Some fertility clinics still actively or implicitly exclude lesbians and/or unmarried women from receiving services (Johnson, 2009; see also Mamo, 2007).

High costs and lack of insurance coverage also mean that all those who request or desire assisted fertility services cannot access it (Chambers et al., 2009). Dr. Liu, Bay Area physician, put it in stark terms: "The only reason [patients] can't do it is because they can't pay for it. That's pretty sad." Other providers described scenarios in which insurance companies claim on paper that they cover fertility services, but in reality they have caps that restrict both the quality and quantity of treatments. Sometimes insurance companies will cover diagnosis of infertility but will not cover its treatment.

## Implications of Privatization on Regulation

Providers have a unique perspective on how the financing of assisted fertility services impacts the nature of regulation of their industry. Dr. Gorman stated that, ideally, physicians—with some input from their patients—should have the greatest voice in determining just how regulated the fertility industry should be. Input from "the payers," as he put it, almost comes as an afterthought. "I think the payer's entitled to have an opinion," he said, "Whoever that payer is. But I think in the final analysis, it should be the physician who has the greatest input." Yet, Dr. Gorman recognized that this is only an ideal, and that globally, the collective payer—whether that is an insurance company or a government body—exerts power over the organization and practice of reproductive medicine. To back up this claim, he compared the private insurance-driven system in the United States with the more socialized systems in Europe:

> I think our European colleagues are coming from a different administrative governing philosophy than we do. Many of these countries come from socialized medical systems, or work in socialized medical systems

where the government is the principal payer for services. And that, of course, changes the dynamics of who decides what should be done and shouldn't be done.

Since the United States government is not the payer, lawmakers have less reason—or right—to make rules about infertility treatment and assisted fertility services. Access filters down to what insurance companies are willing to pay for, and beyond that, what individual consumers can afford to pay for on their own.

Dr. Liu appeared to concur with this idea of Dr. Gorman's. Liu described the fertility industry in California as largely a "cash business." Since most of his patients pay out of pocket, "There's no reason for anybody to regulate it." Later, when I asked him to compare the American fertility industry with that of other nations, his words echoed Dr. Gorman's comparison of European socialism with American individualism: "We have much less regulation compared to everywhere else. Because everywhere else, there is government payment involved, and along with that comes government regulation." Although many of my informants lamented the fact that the current system was so stratified that the majority of people who want assisted fertility services cannot afford them or do not have insurance that will cover treatment, this system does work in their favor. As a largely "cash business," providers avoid both government regulation and the bureaucracy of insurance companies. This harkens back to the "golden age of doctoring," in which physicians were largely self-employed businessmen who operated on a fee-for-service basis, beyond the control of both government and managed care (McKinlay & Marceau, 2009).

Yet, even though Dr. Liu and others spoke of the lack of regulation as a consequence of the cash business nature of the fertility industry, they were also quick to describe how the insurance industry, rather than the government, sometimes fills in the role of determining the nature of services that physicians are able to offer. One physician provided the example of an insurance company that mandated that before covering any IVF cycles, couples must try a particular number of insemination cycles (a much less expensive treatment), even if the physician determines that IVF is a more appropriate treatment. This is not only a waste of money, but it is a waste of time. Because time is of the essence in infertility treatment (the older we are, the harder it becomes to conceive), mandating cycles of ineffective treatment can waste precious months that could be spent trying IVF.

I conducted my interviews in the midst of the health-care reform debate, and details of the Affordable Care Act had yet to be decided by the United States Congress. In light of this sense of foreboding change, I asked my informants to put on their fortune-telling lenses and speculate about how health-care reform would affect infertility treatment. One Los Angeles physician did not see health-care reform as a positive development for his field. He used New Jersey, which is a mandated state, as an example of a negative outcome of insurance coverage:

New Jersey covers infertility. Huge, huge numbers, okay? The poor doctors are working for next to nothing. And so what it's done is disheartened everyone. I've got an embryologist working for me from New Jersey who says, "Listen, it's a *mill*."

From his perspective, mandated insurance coverage has decreased the quality of care in New Jersey. If national health-care reform mandated insurance coverage, he did not see the situation improving any.

I think that they'll probably put some things in there about infertility being covered, and it'll immediately be followed by limitations on that coverage. It'll be the same as everywhere else. . . . Like here, the Screen Actors guild . . . [covers] infertility, [but with] a thousand dollar maximum. Well, you know, that's like not even the first visit. Yeah, it's covered, but it's not covered. I could see that coming in a national plan.

Besides mandated coverage for IVF and other fertility treatment, providers also offered conflicting answers regarding their views on movement towards universal coverage or single-payer-style systems. In New York, Dr. Gorman worried about long waits under "socialized medicine," arguing that it can reduce quality of care. He gave the example of a 39-year-old woman who has to wait a year for an IVF cycle, and becomes 25% less likely of achieving a pregnancy because she is one year older. "No other area in medicine," said Dr. Gorman, "projects the difference as clearly as IVF."

Robin had a nuanced response, seeing positives and negatives. Although she would be happy that "more people will have access, then more people will have babies," she does not want to see a system that prevents people from using their own money to purchase health care. Nor would she want to see a government program like Medicare that does not adequately compensate physicians. That scenario would be "disastrous," causing the few good fertility doctors that are out there to leave the field.

Others were not as pessimistic. Linda, for example, operations director of a Los Angeles clinic, thought health-care reform could level the playing field between "ethical" doctors who "don't charge an arm and a leg" and wealthy doctors. Several providers also made "wish lists" for things they would like to see covered by insurance where gaps currently exist, including coverage for pregnancy, surrogacy, egg donation, and newborn babies born to international clients.

## EXCEPTIONALISM IN PUBLIC POLICY

Financing is not the only—or even the primary—difference between the United States and other fertility industries. Even more than the issue of who pays for infertility research and treatment, what most makes the United States stand out is its lax public policy. It is not exceptional in its lack of federal or national policy, but it is the *combination* of high-quality services and lax public policy that largely act as pull factors of reproductive tourism to New York City, Los Angeles, and San Francisco.

When I attended a fertility and adoption conference in New York City in 2006, I watched a debate between a prominent reproductive endocrinologist and a bioethicist about the ethics of paying young women for their eggs for IVF or stem-cell research. Aside from the lively debate about consent and coercion, one of the most interesting comments I took note of was made by the physician, who stated something to the effect of, "People think that the fertility industry is not regulated. That is untrue. We are one of *the* most regulated fields of medicine."[4] My ears perked up at this statement because the idea that reproductive medicine in the United States is highly regulated was in great contrast to descriptions of this country as the "wild West" of infertility (e.g., Hecht, 2001). It was my impression that the United States is one of the *least* regulated countries in the matter of assisted fertility services.

Yet, the physician was not comparing reproductive medicine in the United States to reproductive medicine in other countries. Rather, he was comparing the regulation of reproductive medicine to the regulation of other medical fields. This is an important distinction. Before addressing how the providers I interviewed saw their field from both angles—as compared to other countries, as well as in comparison with other medical fields—it is first necessary to outline the existing public policies in the United States.

## Federal Policies

Contrary to the notion that the United States is absent any national regulation regarding assisted fertility and third-party reproduction, there are at least three federal policies applicable to reproductive medicine. Chronologically, these three policies include the Clinical Laboratory Improvement Amendments (CLIA), established by Congress in 1988; the 1992 Fertility Clinic Success Rate and Certification Act; and the 2005 FDA guidelines entitled Eligibility Determination for Donors of Human Cells, Tissues, and Cellular and Tissue-Based Products.

CLIA is administered by the FDA and the Centers for Medicare and Medicaid Services (CMS), and sets national standards for laboratories that test human specimens, affecting fertility clinics with on-site laboratories, and providers who outsource testing and lab work, such as egg donor and surrogacy programs (FDA, 2009). Although it sounds relatively benign, some of the providers I spoke with portrayed the FDA and other regulators as fearsome tools of surveillance. According to Linda, an administrator at a Los Angeles fertility clinic,

> The FDA doesn't tell anybody when they're going to come. But it's really hard, because since 2005, they've been training inspectors, and

you just never know when they're going to walk through your doors, when they're going to come out.

Moreover, some providers perceived a blurred line between "suggested" and "mandated" standards. According to Linda,

Some of the laboratory testing, what they do is they . . . aren't telling you [that] you have to do it, but they're recommending you *should* do it, so you better do it. Because if you get inspected and you're not doing it, even if they didn't tell you [that] you have to do it, you're still going to get cited.

However burdensome CLIA is, it is not *unique* to reproductive medicine, but affects all sorts of medical fields.

The 1992 Fertility Clinic Success Rate and Certification Act, however, is specific to this field. It was issued by the Department of Health and Human Services (HHS) and the Centers for Disease Control and Prevention (CDC), and developed in consultation with professional organizations including the American Society for Reproductive Medicine (ASRM), the Society for Assisted Reproductive Technology (SART), the College of American Pathologists (CAP), and the American Association of Bioanalysts, as well as the infertility advocacy group RESOLVE (Department of Health and Human Services, 1999, p. 39375). According to its description in the *Federal Register*, it "was intended to provide the public with comparable information concerning the effectiveness of infertility services and to assure the quality of such services by providing for the certification of embryo laboratories" (Department of Health and Human Services, 1999, p. 39374). In addition to establishing standards for laboratories that handle embryos, this Act requires collection of data from fertility clinics regarding pregnancy rates, to be compiled and published by the CDC in annual reports. Consumers can then view these statistics (by individual clinic or in aggregate) on the CDC website in order to help them choose a clinic to work with.

There have been some unintended consequences of this Act, including a possible rise in high-risk multiple pregnancies by clinics wishing to improve their now publicly available pregnancy success rates. Some providers also complained that regulations mandating statistics reporting and laboratory standards are onerous. According to Dr. Leveque, his clinic was already reporting statistics prior to this Act. "And honestly," he said to me, "they just made the process a lot more complicated without making it any better when they passed this law."

The national policy that informants were most upset by was issued in 2005, when the FDA and the United States HHS issued guidelines regarding tissue donation. The "Eligibility Determination for Donors of Human Cells, Tissues, and Cellular and Tissue-Based Products" is aimed at industry members as a means to assist them in determining the eligibility of prospective donors of cells and tissues, including sperm, eggs, and embryos, to prevent the transmission of communicable diseases. The guidelines require that establishments dealing in the donation of human tissues and cells test, screen, and determine donor eligibility, keep and maintain records of test results and interpretations, quarantine cellular materials while they are being tested, and use the FDA's extensive list of risk factors and conditions, as well as clinical and physical evidence (FDA, 2007).

Significantly, the guidelines exclude entire classes of people from donating cells and tissues because they are deemed to be "at risk" for communicable diseases because of their medical history, social position, and/or behavior. This long list of excluded classes includes men who have had sex with other men, intravenous drug users, sex workers, people who have been imprisoned, and people who have been exposed to a wide variety of diseases, including HIV, hepatitis, and syphilis. Also excluded are people who lived abroad in Europe during specific time periods (such as during the Mad Cow Disease scare), or who were born or lived in certain African countries (FDA, 2007).

This quite extensive list of donors who should be considered ineligible presented a constant source of irritation and frustration to providers. Although they understood the risks of disease transmission involved in tissue transfer, many argued that these risks apply more to blood transfusions and organ donation, and not to reproductive medicine. Had the FDA consulted with practitioners of reproductive medicine, I was repeatedly told, those practitioners would have explained that the same risks do not apply universally to all sorts of tissue transfer. For example, Robin complained that the FDA regulations make "no sense" when it comes to egg donation. When I asked her to elaborate, she told me the following:

> We are not able to accept any donors that have been to Europe, or England, during the Mad Cow time. . . . Basically, any bright college student who's around 25 and did a semester abroad is pretty much screwed. And so that really reduces . . . our egg donor pool, and I think it's unfortunate, because I'm told there isn't a single instance anywhere of eggs being infected by Mad Cow. There is no medical science behind it.

Linda, similarly, was frustrated by the ways in which overly rigid FDA regulations exclude donors:

> Some of the laboratory testing that's required for third-party cycles . . . don't make sense for certain ethnic groups. Meaning, they are going to come out positive. But it's not going to, in the doctor's knowledge . . . jeopardize the pregnancy, harm a fetus, nothing like that. But, as far as the FDA goes, the way they're reading it is, it could. So, you might end up with positive results, and have to disqualify a perfectly good donor candidate . . . for no medical, real reason.

Liam, CEO of a surrogacy agency that works primarily with gay men, also argued that some of the FDA eligibility guidelines "weren't medically sound as they applied to sperm donation and egg donation. And so, it actually created an impact that is excluding certain donors that before, could have donated, but now are not allowed to," including gay men and people who had lived abroad. Like Robin, he saw that a policy developed "to protect the health and well-being of society" was being applied too broadly.

Interestingly, the egg donor coordinator of a program at a large fertility clinic in New York City explained to me that despite these FDA guidelines, there are ways to get around them.

> *Liz:*       I like [the guidelines]. It brings a sense of reassurance.
> *Lauren:*  How so?
> *Liz:*       Just, you really feel like you're doing the right thing. You know? Not cutting corners. Not compromising.
> *Lauren:*  Do you ever feel that it gets in the way of doing things that you would like to do? Or how you'd like the program to grow?
> *Liz:*       No, I don't think it gets in the way. I mean, I know that there have been patients that have felt that. An example is, if the patient presents with . . . a known donor, and she's a carrier of an infectious disease, they want to proceed anyways. We can do it, and we did do it, and we have to get exceptions from regulations, from the DOH [Department of Health] to do it. FDA—doesn't matter. . . . Doesn't matter if it's a known donation situation, and one is a carrier of another, as long as the physician is informed, that's all you need to do with the FDA.

Although guidelines were created as national standards, Liz's experience with the FDA led her to see them as somewhat flexible. Many of the other providers, however, made the opposite conclusion. This may speak to the relative institutional power of various programs. Liz works at a large, established, university-affiliated fertility clinic where her colleagues may have less difficulty maneuvering and finessing bureaucratic rules than would smaller, less established programs.

## U.S. Supreme Court Decisions

Besides federal regulations and congressional legislation, the other area of policy that affects the fertility industry on a national level is Supreme Court decisions. There are no specific decisions that explicitly deal with assisted fertility, surrogacy, or genetic testing, but there are at least four decisions that have implications for this field: *Skinner v. Oklahoma, Griswold v. Connecticut, Eisenstadt v. Baird,* and *Roe v. Wade.* Scholars of reproductive rights point to all four as landmark decisions that impinge upon issues of reproductive autonomy and bodily integrity, establishing rights to procreate, to contraception, and to terminate pregnancy, respectively.

In the 1942 case of *Skinner* v. *Oklahoma*, the Supreme Court struck down that state's punitive compulsory sterilization laws, establishing the "right to have offspring" as a Constitutional and indeed human right (316 U.S. 535). *Griswold* v. *Connecticut*, decided in 1965, reversed prohibitions against contraception for married people (381 U.S. 479). Five years later, the Supreme Court decision in *Eisenstadt* v. *Baird* extended the right to contraception to unmarried people, arguing that to do otherwise would discriminate against the unmarried (405 U.S. 438). *Roe* v. *Wade*, most famously, established the right to abortion in 1973. Just as in *Griswold*, the Supreme Court decided that the right to privacy includes the termination of pregnancy (410 U.S. 113).

Although none of these Supreme Court decisions deal explicitly with assisted fertility or third-party reproduction, they have implications for the field, notably the codification of the right to privacy in the arena of sex, pregnancy, and childbirth. This right to privacy can be interpreted as a right between adult couples, as well as between physicians and their patients, both of which are of paramount importance in reproductive decision-making, including whether or not use of reproductive technologies is of merit. Should a legislative body in the United States attempt to more actively regulate the uses of reproductive technologies or assisted fertility services, on par with the sort of regulations in nations such as the United Kingdom or Germany, it may conflict with some of these Court decisions.

## State Policies and Case Law

On a national level, the United States does not play a large role governing the fertility industry or citizens' access to assisted fertility services, but if one drills down to the state level, one can find a handful of laws, regulations, and case law that pertain to reproductive technologies and assisted fertility services. Georgia, Louisiana, and Oklahoma, for example, prohibit the sale of oocytes, whereas Indiana, Florida, and Virginia explicitly permit women to be compensated for their eggs (Cone, 2012, p. 206). An additional fourteen states (Arkansas, California, Colorado, Idaho, Maryland, Massachusetts, Michigan, Minnesota, Missouri, North Dakota, Pennsylvania, South Dakota, and Virginia) prohibit the sale of oocytes for research purposes but do not prohibit their sale to intended parents for procreative purposes (Cone, 2012, p. 207). As discussed previously, one of the areas in which states play a role is in infertility insurance laws, albeit implementation of the Affordable Care Act shows that these laws may be in flux. The other areas governed by state legislation and case law are the disposition of gametes and embryos, and the legality of surrogacy.

As of 2007, sixteen states have laws regarding the disposition of procreative materials: California, Colorado, Connecticut, Florida, Louisiana,

Maryland, Massachusetts, New Jersey, New York, North Dakota, Ohio, Oklahoma, Texas, Virginia, Washington, and Wyoming. These laws cover such issues as informed consent, parentage, embryo donation for adoption or research, destruction of embryos, disposition of sperm, eggs, and embryos in case of divorce or death, inheritance rights of offspring, personhood, and prevention of incest (National Conference of State Legislatures, 2007). California, for example, has several Codes and Statutes regarding the use of human reproductive materials. They require informed or written consent by a number of parties in different circumstances: by sperm, egg, and embryo donors for use of their reproductive materials in assisted reproductive technology; by infertility patients for disposition of surplus embryos after fertility treatment; and by egg donors for use of their ova in research. California law also prohibits buying and selling eggs for research purposes, entitles children to death benefits if they were conceived and born after the death of a parent (as long as informed consent had been obtained prior to death), and extends the right to petition the court for parentage to those who conceive using assisted reproductive technologies (National Conference of State Legislatures, 2007). New York Code is much less extensive. It prohibits creating embryos using donor eggs and donor sperm except for use by a patient for her own fertility treatment; forbids creation of embryos using gametes of close blood relatives; and requires informed written consent by sperm, egg, and embryo donors (National Conference of State Legislatures, 2007). New York explicitly permits the sale of eggs for research purposes (Cone, 2012).

Another area of policy in which there is no uniformity or harmony in the United States is the legality of surrogacy arrangements. In an analysis of the legal status of surrogacy, attorneys Diane S. Hinson and Maureen McBrien attempt to assess how surrogacy law is actually practiced, rather than relying on how case law is written, by both studying legal statutes and speaking with providers of assisted fertility services throughout the country. They write, "ART attorneys who practice in a specific state know that the actual practice in that state is often 180 degrees different from what the statute might suggest. . . . Our thesis was that we would find 'some' variation from at least some of the states' written statutes, but the degree of variation surprised even us" (Hinson & McBrien, 2011, p. 32). They group the fifty states plus the District of Columbia into eight general categories:

- "Red Light: Statute makes surrogacy contracts criminal and surrogacy not practiced (DC)."
- "Proceed at Your Own Risk: Statute prohibits enforcement of GS [gestational surrogacy] contracts, but surrogacy continues in practice (AZ, IN, MI, NY, NE)."
- "Yellow Light: Even though no statutory prohibition exists, courts will not grant parentage orders. GS continues in practice, but parents must adopt child after birth (LA)."

- "Squeeze into the Statutory Box: Statute permits GS, but only if various restrictions are met (FL, NH, NV, TX, UT, VA, WA)."
- "Green Light: Statute permits surrogacy and provides regulatory structure to bypass courts (IL)."
- "Statute Permits Surrogacy, but Without Much Detail (AR, CT, IA, ND, NM, TN, WV)."
- "Published Case Supports Surrogacy, but No Statute (CA, OH, MA, MD, NJ, PA, SC)."
- "Vacuum—No Statute/No Published Case." [CO, GA, KS, KY, ME, MT, OR, RI, SD, AK, MN, MS, NC, WI, DE, HI, ED, MO, OK, VT, WY, AL] (Hinson & McBrien, 2011, p. 35)

As indicated in the last column of Table 3.3, some states have statutes that explicitly permit surrogacy and find valid the legality of contracts between surrogates and intended parents. Others have statutes that explicitly prohibit surrogacy and void all such contracts. Some have a blend, permitting some types of surrogacy and prohibiting others, or permit surrogacy but forbid compensation to the surrogate by the intended parents. Most states, however, have *no* statutes permitting or prohibiting gestational agreements, relying on previous case law or on a case-by-case basis if an issue arise (Hinson & McBrien, 2011; Human Rights Campaign, 2011).

Like their opposite positions regarding the sale of eggs for research purposes, California and New York have polar approaches to surrogacy—only in this case their positions have reversed, with California being the permissive state and New York the prohibitive. As sociologist Susan Markens writes in her comparison of the two states,

> New York's policy was constructed to discourage surrogate parenting; California's proposed policy was designed to regulate the practice in order to allow it to continue with as few problems as possible. More specifically, New York expanded its laws on adoption and the prohibition of baby selling to cover surrogate parenting arrangements, whereas California's approach to surrogacy was an explicit attempt to accommodate this new reproductive practice by circumventing existing adoption law.
> (Markens, 2007, p. 4)

The contrasting surrogacy policies have shaped the two states' fertility industry in divergent ways. California has the most favorable legal climate for surrogacy, which, according to Robin, accounts for why so many IVF doctors moved to the state, followed by egg donor and surrogacy agencies. New York, despite the less favorable legal climate for surrogacy—and the most stringent health regulations, according to my informants—is still the third most popular state for the fertility industry. (Texas, the state with the second highest number of clinics, is more ambiguous when it comes to the legality of surrogacy contracts.)

This favorable climate for surrogacy makes California attractive to those who live in regions (other states or internationally) where commercial

*Table 3.3*   States with Laws Regarding Assisted Reproductive Technologies

| State | Laws re: insurance[1] | Laws re: gamete & embryo disposition[2] | Laws permitting surrogacy[3] | Laws prohibiting surrogacy |
|---|---|---|---|---|
| Arizona | | | | X |
| Arkansas | X | | X | |
| California | X | X | X | |
| Colorado | | X | | |
| Connecticut | X | X | | |
| D.C. | | | | X |
| Florida | | X | X | |
| Hawaii | X | | | |
| Illinois | X | | X | |
| Indiana | | | X | X |
| Louisiana | | X | | X (prohibits compensated AI surrogacy [AIS]) |
| Maryland | X | X | | |
| Massachusetts | X | X | | |
| Michigan | | | X | X |
| Nebraska | | | X | X (prohibits compensation) |
| Nevada | | | X | |
| New Hamp. | | | X | |
| New Jersey | X | X | X (permits uncompensated IVF surrogacy [IVFS] only) | X (prohibits compensation and AIS) |
| New Mexico | | | X (permits uncompensated only) | |
| New York | X | X | X | X |
| North Dakota | | X | X (permits IVFS) | X (prohibits AIS) |
| Ohio | X | | | |
| Rhode Island | X | | | |
| Texas | X | X | X | |
| Utah | | | X | |
| Virginia | | X | X (permits uncompensated only) | |
| Washington | | X | X (permits uncompensated only) | X (prohibits compensation) |
| West Virginia | X | | | |
| Wyoming | | X | | |

*Sources*: 1. National Conference of State Legislatures (2012). 2. National Conference of State Legislatures (2007). 3. Human Rights Campaign (2011).

surrogacy is not legal. In a nutshell, to quote Liam, in California, "there's no chance, or the chance would be so drastically slim, where a judge would ever award custody of your baby to the surrogate." Michael, the family law attorney, called the state "very surrogacy-friendly," explaining that "We have case law in California that's been decided by the Supreme Court indicating that intended parents going through assisted reproduction are the legal parents, providing they get a court order of parentage." This is *not* the case in New York, where surrogacy contracts are not recognized by the state.

Even among the states where surrogacy is legal, some providers recognize different *cultures* of surrogacy. Tammy, for example, noticed a difference between a program she worked for in Kansas versus the one she now works for in California. In Kansas, the whole process was kept anonymous, and the surrogate and intended parents never met each other, not even at the birth. In contrast, she found that

> California really opened up and started to demystify and address the fear that people had of this being a real relationship, and being a relationship between parties that can work, with management and guidance. People can get together and start as strangers, and really do something important and special together. And I would say that that's been where CA has been a pioneer in surrogacy.

Although surrogacy is not legally recognized in the state of New York, providers do find ways around this. Dr. Silverstein, who has clinics in both New York and California, provides information about surrogacy at his New York clinics, but then clients fly out to Los Angeles for the actual surrogacy process. Even more conveniently, Dr. Maynard's clinic has a "sister clinic" in New Jersey, where non-commercial surrogacy is legal. Dr. Gorman stated that his clinic does not "participate" in surrogacy, but, he explained, "it's just an open donation process, and from one couple to another woman, . . . and then, they have surrogacy agreements amongst themselves and through surrogacy agencies outside of the state." Liz's clinic in New York City will provide gestational services, but only for cases where the surrogates are sisters or first cousins of the intended parents.

Liz: The New York law is very tricky, and it's not anything that physicians usually want to take a chance with. Because the contracts are not recognized in New York State between the carrier and the biological parent, so the rights of the birth mother would prevail.

Lauren: And if it's a family member, then there's no need for a contract? Is that how it works?

Liz: Well, I mean, usually we also recommend that there's a contract, but if it's a family member, it's generally non-compensated, so it's the compensation thing, combined with the contract that we like to stay removed from.

As Liz and other providers told me, when in doubt, they consult with attorneys who are expert in family and reproductive law.

## Industry Self-Regulation

In addition to the various levels of government regulation of reproductive technologies and assisted fertility services, the fertility industry is also self-regulated by the guidelines issued by its professional organizations. Two of the primary professional organizations, the American Society for Reproductive Medicine (ASRM) and its affiliate the Society for Assisted Reproductive Technology (SART), jointly dispense practice guidelines, positions, and opinions for their members on such topics as gamete and embryo donation, embryo transfer, laboratory standards, preimplantation genetic diagnosis, and egg freezing (Society for Assisted Reproductive Technology, 2011). The Ethics Committee publishes documents offering ethical considerations of various technologies and practice scenarios, including the disposition of abandoned embryos, embryo and oocyte donation to women of advanced age, and sex selection (Society for Assisted Reproductive Technology, 2014).

Informants claimed membership in these and several other professional organizations, as well as two non-profit consumer advocacy groups, indicated in Table 3.4. As a member of professional organizations, providers gain access to marketing resources (such as being listed in Internet databases available to the public), practice guidelines, policy updates, and professional status. The director of operations at a Los Angeles clinic told me that by

*Table 3.4*  Organizations in which Providers Claim Membership

**Professional Organizations**

American Academy of Adoption Attorneys (AAAA)

American Academy of Assisted Reproductive Technology Attorneys (AAARTA)

American Bar Association (ABA)

American Congress of Obstetricians and Gynecologists (ACOG)

American Medical Association (AMA)

American Society for Reproductive Medicine (ASRM)

Egg Donor Surrogate Parenting Association (EDSPA)

National Society for Genetic Counselors

Society of Reproductive Surgeons

Society for Assisted Reproductive Technology (SART)

Society of Reproductive Endocrinology and Infertility (SREI)

**Consumer Advocacy Groups**

American Fertility Association (AFA)

RESOLVE

being certified by professional organizations, her clinic looks "impressive" to other clinics—from her point of view, professional membership is a signal to others that one possesses a good set of morals. Membership and accreditation is a source for peer review and esteem.

Unlike government regulation, industry self-regulation is largely non-binding. The goal of guidelines and best practices is to provide guidance to professionals as they navigate some tricky procedures involving human life. Because these organizations do not have the force of law behind them, however, industry professionals are not legally required to follow the guidelines or opinions of their organizations. If a provider does not follow a state or federal policy, he or she faces the possible risk of criminal penalty, fine, or loss of license. It is less clear what the consequences are of not following the professional guidelines, however. When asked if they knew of any repercussions of going against ASRM/SART guidelines, providers gave a series of contradictory responses. A New York physician stated that if you are not in good standing and do not "conform to a certain kind of conduct," the organization "could kick you out. Reprimand you." Yet a physician working in San Francisco said the precise opposite, that "SART doesn't really have the power to sort of kick someone out. So when it comes to enforcement, yeah, you get a nasty letter from SART, and you can just tear it up (*laughs*). You can grow a thicker skin, that's all you need to do."

Although several providers explained to me that in order to be a member of these professional organizations one must comply with the guidelines, there did not seem to be any greater repercussion beyond the stick of being, perhaps, a "pariah of the profession" (Dr. Liu). Overwhelmingly, the language that providers used indicated that absent the power of *law*, professional organizations do not exert much control over individual practitioners:

| | |
|---|---|
| *Michael*: | There's no meat and bones behind [the guidelines]. |
| *Dr. Gorman*: | You don't go to jail if you didn't follow guidelines. |
| *Dr. Maynard*: | I mean, there's no law that makes you follow the guidelines. |

Despite their cynicism about the role that their professional organizations play in self-regulating behavior and practice, many providers still expressed positive messages about the guidance and associated benefits they gained through membership. Sometimes this came across as a kind of double-speak, or maybe just lack of reflexivity. Dr. Leveque, for example, claimed that professional organizations "do not have the power to shut somebody down," but still saw them as forces for self-regulation: "I think it works in that while mistakes can be made within our system, they get resolved. They get out, the group that has the problem is identified, and within the system we work to improve that group." From Dr. Leveque's perspective, the system is "functional" and works through negative sanctions reinforced by other clinics and providers. If word gets out that there is a group that is not following the standards of their profession, it may not be "shut down" through any formal or legal mechanisms, but others in the field will choose not to work or collaborate with them.

This kind of extralegal professional normalization also applies beyond the medical and legal fields. While physicians and attorneys (and also the clinical social worker and genetic counselor I interviewed) are licensed and regulated by the state and their professional organizations, they do not make up the entire workforce of the fertility industry. If we take into account all of those who own and work at egg donor and surrogacy agencies, we can see that there are huge swaths of this industry working entirely free from professional *or* government regulation. If agencies want to be listed on the ASRM website, they must comply with ASRM guidelines, but there is no *obligation*, legally or professionally, to do so. Some clinics and doctors require that egg donor and surrogacy agencies sign documents attesting that they will comply with ASRM guidelines—but again, agencies are not obligated to work with those clinics or doctors.

Nor is there currently any licensing of egg donor or surrogacy agencies in the United States, although several providers argued in favor of the creation of such licensing programs. Robin, for example, imagined that licensing could serve as "a sort of Good Housekeeping seal of approval." She believed it would help protect vulnerable intended parents from being exploited, and help them assess the quality of programs. Other providers pointed to recent scandals in which surrogacy agencies absconded with millions of dollars given to them by intended parents for donor and surrogate services that were meant to be transferred to surrogates and egg donors (see also Saletan, 2009; Yoshino, 2009). Dr. Silverstein blamed the lack of professionalism and government oversight for these rogue agencies:

> In order to be a surrogate agent, all you need to do is buy a business license for $10, put it up on the wall, and you're a surrogate agent. No professional training, no educational requirements, nothing.

He has written to the California legislature about this problem, saying "Listen, there's twenty more like this," but has yet to get a response.

Deirdre spoke of how her legal license kept her accountable to her clients and the surrogates they contract with, but was ambivalent about licensing egg donor and surrogacy agencies:

> I tend to be more the anti-government licensing thing—I don't like a lot of bureaucracy, because they tend to put in regulations that are not enforceable or they don't know what they're doing. But it would be nice to have some oversight. But, we also have the economics. The government doesn't have the money to oversee all this stuff, so what good is regulation if the regulation is violated and you can't get anyone to prosecute it?

Shelby and Rebekah were also ambivalent:

*Rebekah*:   There are pros and cons. I'd like to see some kind of self-regulatory board. Not government licensing. You know, if there had been licensing when I started my company, I'm sure I wouldn't have fit into the requirements, you know? Now, we are probably, I don't want to say *the* most reputable, but *among* the most reputable agencies out there. There are other good ones, is what I'm saying.

*Shelby*:   And so we would probably be able to get licensing.

*Rebekah*:   Yeah.

*Shelby*:   But, the start-up wouldn't.

Yet even licensing may not stem abuse. More recently, a licensed family law attorney in Southern California pleaded guilty to operating an international baby-selling ring (Associated Press, 2012).

Providers continually made arguments for self-regulation from within the industry, but they did not always make this argument without apprehension or trepidation. Tammy, the social worker, summed up the situation as a "kind of double edge" when it comes to insuring safety for all parties involved: the industry is capable of causing harm to people, but if it is "over regulated" by lawmakers, the industry may be too confined, which could also harm intended parents. This is precisely the argument that Dr. Leveque made when he told me that when governments in other countries imposed standards, "the care has disappeared."

Again, this fear of government regulation was not only expressed by physicians. One surrogacy broker expressed that she "would never trust" elected officials to make policy about assisted reproduction, and another said that government involvement is her "biggest fear." Deirdre said that she "[does] not particularly like government regulation." She is working with other attorneys to establish a national standard of care created by practitioners in the field because she "did not want the government to come in and regulate, regulate, regulate."

There is an inherent contradiction here. Many of the providers I interviewed argued that the fertility industry should self-regulate, without arduous interference from government regulation; yet, at the same time, they expressed ambivalence about the effectiveness or even existence of enforcement mechanisms. As I indicated earlier, providers expressed wariness about lawmakers and bureaucrats making policy in areas in which they lack the specific expertise (particularly medical expertise) that they believe is necessary to help intended parents have children—or, in other words, that would interfere with the way they conduct business. This attitude may not be unique to Americans, yet skepticism about government and belief in the triumph of market forces aligns with neoliberal or free-market ideologies, a trait that is inherent in American politics.

I sat down with twenty fertility-industry professionals in three cities to talk about their work as United States providers in an emerging global market. Their descriptions of the United States fertility industry began to form a collective portrait. Providers spoke of a technologically robust landscape, with medical breakthroughs, new techniques, and better success rates. They saw this field growing exponentially larger—locally, nationally, and internationally. More clinics and agencies were popping up, leading to increased competition, but the demand for assisted fertility services was also constantly on the rise. Those who had been working in the field since the 1980s witnessed changes in public attitudes regarding assisted reproductive technologies, seeing them more accepted, commonplace, and open, rather than something to fear or hide.

The providers also spoke of shifts in laws and regulation, of having to be on top of policy changes in several different arenas and regions. They expressed feelings of being burdened by paperwork and bureaucracy, of being overregulated by policies that came down to them from the state, the federal government, and their professional organizations. Although they had concerns about the industry, and were cynical about how easy it is to ignore professional norms, many were fearful of government interference, and desired keeping regulation of the field within the industry itself. Ironically, the regulatory playing field in the United States, when compared to other nations, is quite laissez-faire. On some level, the providers understand this, as they repeatedly told me that their international clients come to the United States because of overly strict regulation in their own countries. While they may not be currently clamoring for *less* regulation, most providers were happy with the regulatory status quo: keeping the fertility industry privatized, and the government out of their business.

## NOTES

1. Women veterans, for example, may receive limited infertility diagnosis and treatment, but not IVF (U.S. Department of Veterans Affairs, 2014).
2. A recent qualitative study finds that of the cohort of 398 women pursuing fertility treatment who they surveyed, median costs for IVF treatment was $24,373 (Katz et al., 2011).
3. An estimated 85% of IVF consumers in the United States pay for fertility treatment out of pocket (Katz et al. 2011).
4. Field notes.

## REFERENCES

American Society for Reproductive Medicine (ASRM). (2011). Egg donor agencies. *American Society for Reproductive Medicine*. Retrieved from http://asrm.org/detail.aspx?id=856

Associated Press. (2012, February 25). Surrogacy lawyer Theresa Erickson pleads guilty. *San Francisco Chronicle*. Retrieved from www.sfgate.com/cgi-bin/article. cgi?f=/c/a/2012/02/24/MNDO1NC40O.DTL

Boonstra, H. (2001). Human embryo and fetal research: Medical support and political controversy. *The Guttmacher Report on Public Policy*, 4(1), 3–4, 14.

Centers for Disease Control and Prevention. (2014). *2012 preliminary ART fertility clinic success rates report*. Atlanta, GA: CDC. Retrieved from www.cdc.gov/art/ARTReports.htm

CDC, ASRM, & SART. (2010). *2008 assisted reproductive technology success rates: National summary and fertility clinic reports*. Atlanta: U.S. Department of Health and Human Services. Retrieved from www.cdc.gov/art/ART2008/index.htm

Chambers, G. M., Sullivan, E. A., Ishihara, O., Chapman, M. G., & Adamson, G. D. (2009). The economic impact of assisted reproductive technology: A review of selected developed countries. *Fertility and Sterility*, 91(6), 2281–2294.

Colen, S. (1995). "Like a mother to them": Stratified reproduction and West Indian childcare workers and employers in New York. In F.D. Ginsburg and R. Rapp (Eds.), *Conceiving the new world order: The global politics of reproduction* (pp. 78–102). Berkeley: University of California Press.

Cone, K. L. (2012). Family law—Egg donation and stem cell research—Eggs for sale: The scrambled state of legislation in the human egg market. *UALR Law Review*, 35, 189–226.

Cooper, M. (2008). *Life as surplus: Biotechnology and capitalism in the neoliberal era*. Seattle: University of Washington Press.

Department of Health and Human Services. (1999). Implementation of the Fertility Clinic Success Rate and Certification Act of 1992. *Federal Register*, 64(139), 39374–39392.

FDA. (2007, August). *Guidance for industry: Eligibility determination for donors of human cells, tissues, and cellular and tissue-based products*. Retrieved from www.fda.gov/biologicsbloodvaccines/guidancecomplianceregulatoryinformation/guidances/tissue/ucm073964.htm

FDA. (2009). *Clinical Laboratory Improvement Amendments (CLIA)*. Retrieved from www.fda.gov/MedicalDevices/DeviceRegulationandGuidance/IVDRegulatory Assistance/ucm124105.htm

Frakt, A. B., Pizer, S. D., & Hendricks, A. M. (2008). Controlling prescription drug costs: Regulation and the role of interest groups in Medicare and the Veterans Health Administration. *Journal of Health Politics, Policy and Law*, 33(6), 1079–1106.

Fujimoto, V. Y., Luke, B., Brown, M. B., Jain, T., Armstrong, A., Grainger, D. A., & Hornstein, M. D. (2010). Racial and ethnic disparities in assisted reproductive technology outcomes in the United States. *Fertility and Sterility*, 93(2), 382–390. doi:10.1016/j.fertnstert.2008.10.061

Ginsburg, F. D., & Rapp, R. (Eds.). (1995). *Conceiving the new world order: The global politics of reproduction*. Berkeley: University of California Press.

Hacker, J. S. (2002). *The divided welfare state: The battle over public and private social benefits in the United States*. New York: Cambridge University Press.

Hecht, A. N. (2001). Wild wild west: Inadequate regulation of assisted reproductive technology. *Houston Journal of Health Law & Policy*, 1, 227–261.

Henig, R. M. (2004). *Pandora's baby: How the first test tube babies sparked the reproductive revolution*. Boston, MA: Houghton Mifflin Harcourt.

Henne, M. B., & Bundorf, M. K. (2008). Insurance mandates and trends in infertility treatments. *Fertility and Sterility*, 89(1), 66–73. doi:10.1016/j.fertnstert. 2007.01.167

Hinson, D. S., & McBrien, M. (2011). Surrogacy across America. *Family Advocate*, 34(2), 32–36.

Human Rights Campaign. (2011). *Surrogacy laws: State by state.* Retrieved from www.hrc.org/issues/parenting/surrogacy/surrogacy_laws.asp

Jain, T. (2006). Socioeconomic and racial disparities among infertility patients seeking care. *Fertility and Sterility, 85*(4), 876–881.

Johnson, K. M. (2009). The (single) *woman question: Ideological barriers to accessing fertility treatment.* Presented at the Annual Meeting, Society for the Study of Social Problems, San Francisco, August 7–9.

Katz, P., Showstack, J., Smith, J. F., Nachtigall, R. D., Millstein, S. G., Wing, H. et al. (2011). Costs of infertility treatment: Results from an 18-month prospective cohort study. *Fertility and Sterility, 95*(3), 915–921.

Mamo, L. (2007). *Queering reproduction: Achieving pregnancy in the age of technoscience.* Durham, NC: Duke University Press.

Markens, S. (2007). *Surrogate motherhood and the politics of reproduction.* Berkeley: University of California Press.

Martin, J. R., Bromer, J. G., Sakkas, D., & Patrizio, P. (2011). Insurance coverage and in vitro fertilization outcomes: A US perspective. *Fertility and Sterility, 95*(93), 964–969.

McKinlay, J. B., & Marceau, L. D. (2009). The end of the golden age of doctoring. In P. Conrad (Ed.), *The sociology of health and illness: Critical perspectives* (pp. 213–239). New York: Worth.

Missmer, S. A., Seifer, D. B., & Jain, T. (2011). Cultural factors contributing to health care disparities among patients with infertility in Midwestern United States. *Fertility and Sterility, 95*(6), 1943–1949.

National Conference of State Legislatures. (2007, July). *Embryo and gamete disposition laws.* Retrieved from www.ncsl.org/IssuesResearch/Health/EmbryoandGamete DispositionLaws/tabid/14379/Default.aspx

National Conference of State Legislatures. (2012, March). *Insurance coverage for infertility laws.* Retrieved from www.ncsl.org/research/health/insurance-coverage-for-infertility-laws.aspx

Ory, S., Devroey, P., Banker, M., Brinsden, P., Buster, J., Fiadjoe, M. et al. (2013). *IFFS surveillance 2013.* International Federation of Fertility Societies. Retrieved from http://c.ymcdn.com/sites/www.iffs-reproduction.org/resource/resmgr/iffs_surveillance_09-19-13.pdf

Quadagno, J. (2004). Why the United States has no national health insurance: Stakeholder mobilization against the welfare state, 1945–1996. *Journal of Health and Social Behavior, 45,* 25–44.

RESOLVE. (2014, February 17). *The Affordable Care Act and Infertility RESOLVE: The National Infertility Association.* Retrieved from www.resolve.org/get-involved/the-affordable-care-act-and-infertility.html

Saletan, W. (2009, March 24). If you stop paying a surrogate mother, what happens to the fetus? *Slate.* Retrieved from www.slate.com/id/2214498/

Society for Assisted Reproductive Technology. (2011). *ASRM guidelines for practice.* Retrieved from http://sart.org/Guidelines/

Society for Assisted Reproductive Technology. (2014). *Ethics committee reports and statements.* Retrieved from http://sart.org/EthicsReports/

Spar, D. (2006). *The baby business: How money, science, and politics drive the commerce of conception.* Boston, MA: Harvard Business School Press.

U.S. Department of Veterans Affairs. (2014). *Medical benefits package.* Retrieved from www.va.gov/healthbenefits/resources/publications/hbco/hbco_medical_benefits_package.asp

Waldby, C., & Mitchell, R. (2006). *Tissue economies: Blood, organs, and cell lines in late capitalism.* Durham, NC: Duke University Press.

Yoshino, K. (2009, March 21). Money woes reported at firms involved in surrogate births. *Los Angeles Times.* Retrieved from http://articles.latimes.com/2009/mar/21/local/me-surrogate-agency21

# 4 Coming to America
## How Providers Manage Work with International Clients

A central question that arises with reproductive tourism to the United States is *how does it work?* This seemingly simple question can be broken down into several smaller questions. Some of these questions deal with how clients and providers find each other: *How do you reach out to potential clients from abroad? How do your international clients find you?* Others are even more pragmatic: *How do you communicate with your clients who live far away, in other time zones? What are the specific challenges of working with international clients? Do you offer any special services for your out-of-town clients?* In the first three chapters I have outlined the regulatory landscape of assisted fertility services and reproductive technologies on the international and local level, dealing largely with the *what* and the *why* of reproductive tourism. In this chapter, I deal with the *how*, grounded specifically in the context of the United States fertility industry.

### FINDING EACH OTHER

Chapter 2 described the pull factors that draw international clients to the United States. In this section, I focus on how providers assess the ways their international clients find and select them, and relatedly, how they market their services on a global level. This process can be intensely personal—through word of mouth referrals—or facilitated by Internet searches, carefully calibrated websites, and Google metrics. In this respect, finding an assisted fertility provider is not unlike the kind of research that many of us undergo in order to select a consumer good or service like a new car or a contractor: we rely on information from a number of sources, including recommendations by friends and colleagues, customer reviews on sites such as Yelp or Amazon, reports from reputable consumer agencies and media outlets, and haphazard Google searches. Consumers in this day and age are able to research and select from a wide variety of goods and services regardless of geographic location, and this is also true for those seeking assisted reproductive technologies. An infertile heterosexual couple in France, for example, may not limit their search for a reproductive endocrinologist to their own country or even to Europe, but may expand their search to encompass the *global* fertility market, basing their selection on any number of criteria. The best clinic to suit their needs may be twenty-five miles away, or they just might be 2,500 miles away.

Some providers deliberately market their services internationally by way of press releases to garner interviews and media attention, and by advertising in markets where soliciting fertility services is not prohibited. Providers also may travel to particular countries to generate referrals. People from Liam's surrogacy agency, for example, go to England, Australia, Spain, and Italy to consult with potential clients and "just get to know that country better, and talk to other folks there." Interestingly, he expressed that it has not been effective to go to a country where he doesn't tend to have many clients in order to generate new clients because "we can't create the market." As he elaborated,

> You know, it's not like going in and introducing a new product like a Coke versus a Pepsi. The market really is created by people's desire to have a child, and their openness about their sexuality, or if they're a straight couple, their openness about whether they're willing to use an egg donor, things like that. So, the market really evolves on its own, and then they start searching people out, who can either give them information, or a friend who's done it. So, yeah, generally it's more effective for us to go somewhere where we already have a good base of clients, and it's kind of already evolving. And then we get more people that we talk with.

As indicated by Liam's comment, word of mouth is a particularly powerful marketing tool. Personal recommendations from friends who have had success with a specific provider count for a lot, as Dr. Bradley described: "We live in a global world. . . . At the end, they're going to go where they think the doctor's great. They'll do what they have to do. . . . I've had many patients come because I enjoy a good reputation. I got their friend pregnant, so their friend sent them to me." Patient referrals were cited by most of the providers. Dr. Maynard told me, "A lot of the non-American patients that we see are referred through other patients who have been in the same situation. You know, they'll tell them 'Oh, go see [physician at her clinic]. Go visit.' So, word of mouth has a lot to do with it."

Similar to snowball sampling, in which participants are drawn from the networks of prior research subjects, so too do client referrals "snowball." Clinic administrator Linda, for example, explained that "We have a whole lot of Chinese patients, and the way that happened was . . . one couple came, many years ago, and conceived, and ever since then they've told all their friends. So we've had quite a few couples just from that one pregnancy, which is pretty nice. I mean, that's your best referral, right?" Liam's description of how international clients made their way to his donor/surrogacy agency was remarkably similar:

> What tends to happen, which is interesting, is you have kind of . . . we call them "circles of influence." So, you'll have one or two people in a country go through the process, that tend to be the first. They then kind of create this wave of people who come after them. And so, that's what tends to happen in a country, and it just depends on how small a country is, and how big that wave is. Like, Norway is a huge country for us. I think because it's a small country, it's very affluent, you know, it happened that way. We had a few clients and now it's just constant.

In this globally integrated fertility industry, physicians and agencies also make referrals, both within and without the United States, and these may be spontaneously generated or carefully cultivated. Dr. Leveque, for example, explained that his Australian and Chinese patients tend to be sent to him by their local doctors. When asked how Australian and Chinese doctors know about his clinic, he replied, "The American Society of Reproductive Medicine's professional group met here [in San Francisco] last year, in October. And we hosted a number of the docs from other countries here. We gave them tours, did a dinner, a luncheon, and a lot of different celebrations and welcoming things. And that was very well attended. It was just a matter of them knowing us. And we get referrals from those people." Liz, egg donation coordinator, also mentioned that the physicians at her clinic "have a presence globally, with all the research, and the physicians are constantly going to speak at different conferences." In addition to networking at meetings, professional referrals arise from clinicians' international reputations garnered by research published in medical journals, offices held in professional organizations, and media coverage.

Referrals are frequently made between donor/surrogate agencies, clinics, and family law attorneys, highlighting a symbiotic relationship. Providers at agencies and clinics described keeping lists of other professionals to which they refer patients. Thus, an intended parent from abroad seeking assisted fertility services involving gamete donation or surrogacy may first select an American clinic that then refers them to a third-party agency, or may first select a third-party agency that then refers them to a clinic or physician. This scenario is more common for services in California, where brokers for third-party donors and surrogates typically act independently of clinics. In New York, fertility clinics are more likely to have in-house donor programs (and no in-house surrogacy services, given its prohibited status in the state). Many of the various international professional meetings that physicians and clinic workers mentioned are also attended by the egg donor and surrogacy agencies and other assorted programs that make up the fertility industry, which again provides opportunities for networking. Referrals to family law attorneys specializing in assisted reproductive technology also tend to come from both the agencies and clinics that intended parents are already working with.

Intended parents may also seek out information about providers on their own, rather than relying upon referrals and recommendations from friends and professionals. Although many providers claimed not to aggressively market their services abroad, their web presence functions at least as a passive form of marketing. According to my informants, their domestic and international clients tend to find them via the Internet. Global fertility markets are dependent upon technology for the spread of information, enabling intended parents to virtually shop for global fertility services through Internet searches and the viewing of websites of clinics and programs. Robin, owner of an egg donation agency, described the process as "someone's looking for, you know, infertility support, or egg donor agencies, or surrogacy. . . . So if they type in those keywords, they find us." Several others spoke in terms of precise keyword search terms and Google rankings. Liz, a fertility clinic egg donation coordinator, mentioned how some sophisticated consumers will even "look up the statistics online. If they know a lot about what they're doing, then they'll look up pregnancy rates, and statistics, and they'll go to the SART [Society for Assisted Reproductive Technology] website. . . . And there's chat rooms, and there's LISTSERVs, and all sorts of things like that."

Beyond passive marketing, many clinics deliberately use their web presence to market their services to potential clients. All of my informants' organizations have a website, and this is not uncommon for fertility-industry programs. If we examine the publically accessible database of providers maintained by ASRM (American Society for Reproductive Medicine) and SART, we find that 762 out of 3,376 providers include a URL address in their listed contact information (ASRM, 2013). Not included in this particular database are potentially hundreds of other programs, including independent gamete and surrogate agencies, that individuals may happen upon with an Internet search, on a message board, or other online sources.

Promoting one's services with a website is particularly important for programs that wish to reach a global audience, and some clinics and programs tailor their Internet presence to this market by translating their sites into multiple languages, or by having special pages specifically targeting people who may be coming from out of state or abroad. Michael, a family law attorney, answered that his organization does not target or market itself to an international clientele "in a proactive way." But, he continued, "We mention on our website that we do provide services to international clients. We've thought about having a homepage of our website translated into multiple, different languages, and encouraging them to contact us for more information. But no, we haven't made any specific marketing efforts." As he and other providers made clear, this kind of passive marketing is especially important in countries where physicians and lawyers are prohibited from advertising and soliciting in television or print media.

In order to maintain the confidentiality of my informants, I will not divulge specific information found on their program's websites. Instead, to point out some more general marketing trends among United States fertility clinics, I performed a content analysis of the 438 programs with unique URLs included in the ASRM/SART database.[1] Of these 438 programs, 104 were identified as having content relating to services for "international," "global," or "out of country" patients. While these clinics and programs are spread all over the United States, they are most densely concentrated in the states of California (34), Florida (13), New York (10), and Texas (10). Clinics' websites signaled openness to working with international clients through such means as blatant statements about serving clients from all over the world, special tabs or hyperlinks on the homepage (frequently labeled "international" or "out of town"), or even pictures of a globe or an airplane. If a potential client from another country finds the homepage of such a fertility program, he or she can easily click on the tab or hyperlink to find information that is specifically designed and written with foreign clients in mind.

As an example of an overt statement, the homepage of California's American Reproductive Center (ARC) states, "ARC offers national and international patients the most sophisticated fertility treatments available today. These services are available to patients in southern California as well as patients from other states and even other countries. We have extensive experience treating patients from around the world" (American Reproductive Centers, 2014, para. 1). Someone looking at the website of IVF Florida would find the statement "We recognize that patients will travel great distances to receive the care that best fulfills their needs. At IVF FLORIDA, we treat patients from all across the region, the nation, as well as the world" (IVF Florida Reproductive Associates, 2014, para. 1). The Reproductive Medicine Institute of Illinois claims, "The physicians and staff at Reproductive Medicine Institute are committed to providing quality care and attention to patients throughout the world, regardless of language, ethnicity or location" (Reproductive Medicine Institute, 2011, para. 5). Were someone from abroad Googling in order to find a clinic in the United States, they may be inclined to contact those programs that seem comfortable and already familiar with working with people coming from another country.

The propensity of clinic websites to identify some of their clients' home countries also works to evoke a sense of familiarity and comfort. Among the 104 websites analyzed, thirty-seven list the countries or regions from where they have received clients. For example, the Institute for Human Reproduction in Illinois states "Our Egg Donation Process has an international following, with couples from Europe, the Middle East, China and other Asian countries, as well as South America, routinely passing through our Chicago offices" (Institute for Human Reproduction, n.d., para. 12). Eighty-four specific countries in total were named as sending countries on these websites, in addition to Africa, Asia, Europe, Central and South America, the Middle East, and the Caribbean. In this website analysis, the most frequently named countries were Australia, Canada, China, France, Germany, India, Japan, Mexico, Spain, and the United Kingdom. Note the overlap between this list of most frequently named countries and those cited by my informants in Chapter 2.

Additionally, many programs market specific aspects of their organization on their websites. They emphasize several reasons for international patients to choose a particular program, including quality of medical care, with explicit references to years of experience, reputation, and success rates; reasonable prices or even discounts for international patients; availability of services illegal in other countries, such as sex selection or gestational surrogacy; quality of donors and/or surrogates; availability of particular services; convenience of location; and the program's location as a tourist destination.

This final point about being a tourist destination was also mentioned in many of my conversations with providers about their locations in the global cities of New York, San Francisco, and Los Angeles. As three of the largest centers of the fertility industry in the United States (and, indeed, the world), the sheer quantity and quality of clinics and programs act as a draw. Additionally, these cities have status as international destinations. To accommodate his international patients, Dr. Bradley and his staff provide them with lists of restaurants and Broadway shows. "They like to come to New York," he said. "They just happen to be getting some good treatment here." Jen, a genetic counselor, summed up the draw of New York City: "I mean, I just think New York is New York. Just being a huge place for technology and medicine. We have so many huge medical centers with great reputations. I think it's just a place that people come for lots of things, not just medicine." While New York may have Broadway, California, in turn, has its beaches. Dr. Leveque described how international patients' knowledge about California translates into an expectation for high quality medical care:

> It's interesting, if you talk to somebody from Europe, from Eastern Europe, about the United States, and California. They all know California. They know the beach, and they know Sacramento, because they've been taught the state capitals. So they'll come to a major city, Los Angeles, San Francisco, Sacramento, and expect that it's a center of excellence.

Consumers may decide among these and other United States cities for a number of reasons, including their accessibility by plane and surface transportation and the distinct attractions each city has to offer. Shelby and Rebekah, the co-owners of a Los Angeles surrogacy agency, both pointed to the weather as a major appeal of California compared to New York. And, in fact, our interview took place outside a café in the beautiful July sunshine of Southern California. Thinking of the oppressive heat and humidity I knew was waiting for me back in New York, I could not help but understand their logic.

## WORKING WITH INTERNATIONAL CLIENTS

Locating clinics and agencies to work with across national borders is only the first step in a long process. Just as technology has enabled the spread of information about the types of fertility services that are available throughout the world, and about the reputations and success rates of individual clinics and providers, so too does technology facilitate communications among the various parties involved.

### Breaking Down Borders: Technology and Globalization

The Internet has transformed the ways that physicians, clients, surrogates, lawyers, and other interested parties communicate transnationally. Email, for example, has become an essential tool of service provision, and many providers indicated how they often preferred this method of communication over telephones and fax machines. Email gives providers time to answer questions at their leisure or after they conduct research, rather than having to respond immediately to a client on the other end of the phone. For transnational communications, it is even more important. Email circumvents the problems that arise from bad phone connections, reduces or even eliminates expensive phone bills for international calls, and makes the difficulties of communication across different time zones moot. Rebekah, surrogacy agency co-owner, explained that her clients frequently have "a very small window of opportunity" when they can make phone calls, and for those who live far away, "their hours are off from our hours." When clients and clinics rely on the phone to communicate, she and her business partner frequently act as intermediaries, conveying messages between the two when the hours to communicate do not overlap.

These communication problems get ameliorated when clients and providers shift to using email. As Dr. Leveque described it,

> Our communication [with international patients] is a bit different, given that we're often eight to twelve hours off from these other countries. We communicate by email, and that works great. They can email me at 8 o'clock in the morning their time, and I get it when we arrive in the office here. There might be a twelve-hour delay, but it works out great for the kinds of treatments that we do.

Providers use email in order to coordinate and keep in touch with clients (and with other providers in the clients' home countries) throughout the process—as a means to reply to initial queries; as a way to communicate information about necessary medical, legal, or other procedural steps that need to be taken; to request and complete paperwork; to convey details about the success of egg retrievals, lab fertilizations, and surrogacy implantations; and for follow-up after the clients have returned back home. It also helps reduce some of the anxiety of maintaining a long-distance relationship with one's providers, particularly when third parties are involved and the intended parent wants to be updated with information about how an egg retrieval process has gone, or how a surrogate's pregnancy is proceeding.

Skype, too, has transformed the global fertility industry, particularly for intended parents who feel the need to be in close communication with the surrogate who is carrying their child. In the past, this was especially hard for those who lived in other countries, or thousands of miles away, who couldn't travel to visit frequently with her throughout the pregnancy. With Skype, they are able to schedule weekly appointments, not only to see how she is doing and if she needs anything, but to actually *see* her belly and her body transform as their child grows within her. Anne told a vivid story of a surrogate who brought her laptop in with her to her ultrasound appointment so that the intended parents could be virtually present.

> The doctor said "No way!" And [the surrogate] said, "No, no, no, they're in Russia! You know, it would mean the world." And the doctor, seeing this couple on Skype, and she showed them the baby, could see how extraordinary this was.

A virtual visit by way of Skype is not the same as being with the surrogate in person but, according to Anne, "It sure bridges a lot of gaps." Tammy, social worker at the same surrogacy agency as Anne, reiterated the importance of Skype in the relationship between intended parents and surrogate mothers because they can't "just pop over . . . , or pick up the phone and make a call that isn't such long distance. . . . These couples make appointments with their surrogates to talk to her every week at a certain time . . . to be as present as they can be." Besides visits between surrogates and intended parents, Skype also enables video communications between physicians and patients, between egg donor agencies and egg donors, and a number of other social interactions, including various parts of the screening process for egg donors, surrogates, and intended parents. For example, Tammy sometimes uses Skype to conduct psychological screenings with intended parents.

## PROCESSES AND TIMELINES

Along with communications, some of the processes involved with reproductive tourism also occur transnationally, in both the United States and in the intended parents' home countries. What distinguishes the international clients from domestic clients, according to Dr. Liu, San Francisco physician, is that "usually when they come here they are already in the process" of seeking fertility treatment and so he does not go through the same practice of meeting them and helping them talk through their decision-making. If they are already working with a clinic at home, Dr. Liu sends them documents his clinic has created in a variety of languages for them to bring to their local doctors.

Whereas local clients may rely upon one clinic for all of their fertility-related medical needs, international clients, in order to minimize costs and the amount of time they need to spend in the United States, may have their initial workups–including blood tests, hormonal screenings, and ultrasounds—conducted by medical providers at home. These may be physicians already known to or sought out by the clients, particularly if they have previously received fertility treatment at a local clinic, or with international colleagues that their United States providers have "hooked them up with" to start and monitor their cycle. According to Dr. Silverstein, his clinic "interface[s] with hundreds of local infertility centers, and we make arrangements for the patients to be monitored there. . . . It really enhances physician-physician interaction. Normally you would never talk to the physician. Here, we're good buddies, because we're taking care of the same patient."

In one of the Los Angeles clinics I visited, their outside laboratory developed a take-home blood kit for international patients. As Linda, the clinic administrator, explained, "Our Japanese patients literally take that kit home with them, and when it's time for them to do—for the husband to [test his blood]—he's able to do it in Japan and ship it here." A genetic counselor I interviewed also spoke of sending via Federal Express a testing kit to a client in Hong Kong who needed screening for cystic fibrosis, which he would then send back to her in New York. She laughed, and said, "With Fed-Ex, and telephone, and email, it's really not a big deal."

Although their time in the United States may be minimized by taking care of some medical processes at home, intended parents—no matter if they are getting IVF, purchasing eggs, or using the services of a surrogate—will have to spend at least a week in the United States, and many of them may have to come, depending on their particular situation, for additional visits. For egg donation, for example, Liz estimated that clients must be in New York for three to four weeks, even if they use clinics at home for "testing and cycle monitoring . . . and then come here for the last minute part of their cycle . . . through the donor cycle. Usually we would prefer that they're here right from day one of the donor stimulation, all the way through to maybe four days post-transfer." The woman who is providing the eggs may be hormonally simulated for two or three weeks before ova is retrieved. After retrieval, those eggs are fertilized *in vitro* in the laboratory, and transfer of fertilized eggs to the intended mother may not happen until three or five days later. Even after the retrieval, several more days may pass before she is able to return home if her physician advises bed rest.

The timeline varies somewhat depending on which clinics and agencies the intended parents are working with, even for the ostensibly same service, such as egg transfer. The timeline given by Megan of a Los Angeles egg donor agency was a bit shorter than that given by Liz. Megan estimated that her clients may need to spend only about a week in the United States for the egg retrieval and transfer. They begin their treatment receiving fertility shots and being monitored in their hometown, but "when they're getting close to their retrieval, they'll fly out here. . . . So they have to have the retrieval, then they have the transfer, and obviously you can't get on a plane—I believe it's five days—because you have to just lay still in bed after you've had that transfer. So they stay here, it happens, and then they fly home" to continue being monitored in their own country.

Fertility clinic doctors also offered slightly different timelines. Dr. Silverstein spoke of only needing patients to be in Los Angeles for seven days, as long as there is plenty of coordination among the providers in both countries. If he is performing surgery on an international patient, he may only actually meet her the day before the surgery, even though he has been communicating with her and her physicians by phone and email for several weeks prior. At Dr. Maynard's New York clinic, international patients receiving IVF must first make an in-person visit for an initial consultation, return home where they begin their cycle with and are monitored by a local doctor, and remain in contact with the United States clinic via phone. They return to New York for about ten days for the egg retrieval, fertilization, and transfer.

The process and timeline for surrogacy is somewhat different and more complex. Depending on the agencies, clinics, and firms they work with, and whether they are using their own gametes, the intended parents may need to come to the United States for in-person consultations, to undergo psychological screenings, for medical workups and procedures, to select and possibly meet with a surrogate, and to process legal items. Just as intended parents frequently undergo medical treatments and monitoring in their home countries as well as in the United States, when surrogacy is involved, attorneys must be consulted in both the United States and at home.

Michael, the family law attorney, explained that when he works with international clients, his firm must figure out "what sort of court judgment or birth certificate or both, will best assist them upon their return." Depending on the clients' home country's laws, and the sexual orientation and marital status of the intended parents, they may need to retain the surrogate mother's name on the birth certificate in order to avoid raising questions when they return home, or in some cases it is best to only include the names of the intended parents. Additionally, Michael advises them to consult family and/or immigration law attorneys "in their local region, and get prepared as early as possible." On the United States end of things, intended parents must, after obtaining a birth certificate, obtain a passport for the child in order to travel back home, and then begin the naturalization process in their own country. Even if the original birth certificate included the name of the surrogate mother and only the name of one intended parent, the state of California allows for the local birth certificate to be amended to add the second parent.

These examples of the transnational nature of securing assisted fertility services point to the way in which intended parents have become global biocitizens, frequently requiring medical and legal services in two countries, and thus subject to multiple nation-and region-specific medical and legal protocols. It also speaks to the complexity of reproduction, in that the steps to bringing home a biological child are vastly different from the steps to bringing home a manufactured consumer good from another country. Such a complex process demands rigorous and extensive coordination of net-worked actors using assorted tools of communication and transport, including phones, fax machines, email, Skype, and Federal Express.

## Challenges and Logistics

One of the biggest challenges that comes with working with clients from abroad is, as described previously, the coordination of medical treatment and legal services across large geographic distances, international borders, and time zones. Dr. Silverstein, based in Los Angeles, described a hypothetical scenario involving a woman from London:

> We have timed injections for all the things we do. You know, you take one shot, and 36 hours later you ovulate. So we'll say, "Okay, we want you to take that shot at 4 p.m." Well, 4 p.m. L.A. time, or 4 p.m. London time? And what if [the patient is] on an airplane traveling across? We say, "Set your watch right now to Los Angeles time, and don't change it back. And you look at your watch and take it at 4 p.m. Los Angeles." Well we've had it happen, they screw up. Because 4 p.m. Los Angeles means we do surgery at 10 o'clock in the morning. If they make a mistake, we're doing surgery at 3 o'clock in the morning. That's a huge problem.

Other providers also presented similar scenarios where coordinating testing and treatment is difficult because of time and distance, and there are so many points during the process of fertility treatment where something can go wrong. Dr. Bradley, for example, described the situation of a man coming to New York for a consultation and to freeze his sperm, who then plans to return home to his country. If his wife returns to New York for egg retrieval and transfer without him, and it turns out his "sperm doesn't work," the cycle is ruined, and the wife has wasted her trip. In order to miti-gate problems, some clinics have contingency plans. At Dr. Leveque's clinic, even when a heterosexual couple both plan to return to the United States for egg retrieval, fertilization, and transfer, they freeze a sperm sample "as a backup, just in case there are travel plan problems, or delays or anything, with the guy getting back here."

Even though international clients may come to the United States in part because of the perceived quality of services, providers acknowledge that the care they provide is often sped up when compared to the amount of time they spend with their local clients. This is due to the fact that providers are often trying to make the amount of time their international clients need to spend in the United States as short as possible. Even on the part of the providers this is seen as a reduction in care. According to Liz, international clients miss out on "face to face time" because they are not around as much as their local patients, who are able to attend classes on administering hormone shots, or to see one of the staff psychologists. Most of the support and consultations that the international clients wind up receiving is over the phone, unless they are able to fly into New York to receive them in person. Liz sounded a bit regretful about the care that these patients receive: "So, we always kind of feel a little bit like, oh, you know, we make ourselves available, but if the patients aren't here to take advantage of the services, then, you know—but I don't think that they have a *bad* experience. Maybe it's just me thinking that they should have more." Liz's colleague Jen, a genetic counselor, reiterated the "time crunch" that can occur with international patients. In the case of genetic testing, unlike local patients who she can send to a local lab or doctor with a prescription or have them come to walk-in hours at the clinic, she must wait for them to take the initiative on their own in their home countries.

Language is another challenge that providers face when working with international clients. Because of the typically elite status of many of their clients, many of them speak English, even those from non-English-speaking countries. Yet providers occasionally do have difficulty communicating with clients who do not speak any English, or who are unfamiliar with technical medical and legal terms, and thus they have to secure the services of interpreters and have documents translated into other languages. For some providers, being able to communicate in languages other than English actually serves as a marketing tool, and they are able to advertise the availability of people on staff who speak various languages. At Linda's clinic, staff members speak Spanish, Japanese, Armenian, and Korean. If a client speaking one of these languages needs services, "that means that we're taking out an employee for a whole day to interpret for these patients." In addition to language, the cultural competency of physicians was cited several times, as some intended parents prefer to work with physicians and other providers who not only speak Arabic, French, or Greek, but who have personal or familial knowledge of their culture.

To mitigate some of the challenges faced by international and other long-distance clients, providers in the United States may offer special services. These include translation and interpretation services, as mentioned above, but even go as far as helping clients arrange transportation, hotel accommodations, dining, and entertainment. Several providers mentioned having travel agents that they have their clients work with, and others go far beyond that. Dr. Silverstein's travel agent meets his clients at the airport and brings them to their hotel and to his office. Furthermore, his organization gives them free passes to a private magician's club, and "We give them a list of restaurants, and sort of help them get their feet on the ground. We help with Disneyland reservations. Everybody's got to go to Disneyland. A lot of them bring their kids in. . . . We sort of take them by the hand and try to get them here as easy as possible." These kinds of concierge-like services can also be found on the websites of fertility clinics and agencies. South Florida Institute for Reproductive Medicine, for example, has a special page for "International Patients," which states:

> Out-of-country patients are offered reduced rate accommodations at local hotels, as we have partnered with them to offer you a convenient and affordable stay while here in Florida for your treatment. . . . Services such as airport pickup and shuttle bus travel to-and-from our practice are just a small part of the convenience we've made available to you. Our multilingual staff will make you feel like you've found a home away from home.
>
> (South Florida Institute for Reproductive Medicine, 2013, para. 1)

As made clear by these websites and by conversations I had with providers, the fertility industry frequently offers far more than medical and legal services to its international clientele.


## CONCLUSION

On one of my first interviews, Dr. Gorman balked at the phrasing of several of my questions that used the term "fertility industry." "I don't look at it as an industry," he said to me. "I'm a physician, so I'm looking at it as a specialty area." It is easy to understand the reluctance of physicians, attorneys, social workers, and genetic counselors to view their work outside of the realm of the medical, legal, or psychological. Yet when it comes to working with international clients, these providers evoke other management skills, including marketing, networking, and communication, and outsourcing services to shipping companies, language interpreters, and even travel agents.

In this chapter, I have emphasized *process*. As a relatively new phenomenon, reproductive tourism is not widely known about. Although people may be familiar with the idea that some individuals use technology in order to help them have biological children, they are typically unfamiliar with the particulars of treatments and services. Likewise, people may be vaguely aware that some individuals travel to other countries for IVF, sex selection, egg donation, or surrogacy, but they are typically unfamiliar with just how this process works.

Transnational fertility services are not entirely different from domestic fertility services. No matter where the intended parents live, they need to find providers to work with, communicate and coordinate with them, and iron out logistical details. Everything gets more complex when international borders are crossed, however. Rather than depend upon clinicians, brokers, or attorneys where one lives, intended parents must instead rely upon other means to locate providers they want to work with. Thus, many wind up relying on the informal word of mouth recommendations from their friends who have gone through similar journeys, and/or formal referrals from their local physicians who have professional contacts in the United States. On the providers' side of things, even if they passively wait for referrals to come to them, there are still things they can do to make their program appeal to international clientele: a web presence that talks up their familiarity with serving patients from around the world, multilingual materials and access to interpreters, concierge services, and even a willingness to be flexible about timelines. More aggressively, providers network with other providers at international meetings, make trips to various countries to target potential clients, and publicize their services through press releases, interviews, and advertising.

Providers working with international clients are also more reliant upon communications technology than they are with their domestic clients. Working with clients thousands of miles away in different time zones can make communicating by phone incredibly difficult (and face to face sometimes impossible), and therefore email, fax machines, and Skype makes consultations, coordination, and answering questions much more manageable. In some cases this kind of distant communication can strain relationships between providers and clients because they have less of an in-person, real-time relationship. Yet it can also be preferable because email's lack of immediacy, for example, allows providers to be better prepared to provide answers to specific questions. The integration of Skype in interactions between and among providers, clients, and third parties has also allowed for some more intimacy, albeit digitally. The nature of relationships between providers is also amplified by reproductive tourism, as United States physicians and attorneys find themselves coordinating with their colleagues abroad about shared clients.

Finally, the temporal experience of intended parents coming from other countries may also vary. Providers spoke of a "time crunch" that happens with international clients, who often try to limit the frequency and duration of their visits to the United States. Domestic clients may work with one clinic throughout their experience, but international clients may work with one in their home country and another in the United States. Blood and genetic testing for domestic patients can take place on site, whereas international patients may have testing kits sent to them through the mail or Federal

Express. Likewise, in cases involving third party reproduction, attorneys may need to be consulted in both the home country and the United States.

What all of these differences in process underscore is the increased need for providers—in the United States and abroad—to manage and coordinate treatment and services transnationally. Tropes of globalization's reliance on technology infrastructure, transportation, digital communications, and the flow of people, capital, goods and services across borders are exemplified in these practices, making up a globalized reproductive bioeconomy. Waldby and Cooper have argued for a new understanding of the selling of eggs as "a very literal form of bodily, reproductive labour" now occurring "on a global scale," and we can surely extend this notion of reproductive labor to the renting of wombs (2008, p. 59). That reproductive labor is frequently obscured by the language of a gift economy does not reduce the work and effort involved in these "jobs." It is much easier to view the work of physicians, attorneys, social workers, genetic counselors, and brokers *as* work, even if we also tend to see this work through the rosy lenses of helping people have babies. Yet, just as reproductive tourism to countries where the sale of eggs and the renting of wombs is legal highlights the role of egg donors and surrogates as reproductive laborers, so too does reproductive tourism extend beyond supplying medical and legal services, underscoring the business acumen and management skills required of fertility industry providers.

## NOTE

1. From the initial 762 clinics cited, 438 URLs remained, after removing duplicates and broken links.

## REFERENCES

American Reproductive Centers. (2014). *ARC overview*. Retrieved from www.americanreproductivecenters.com/artificial-insemination-menu

American Society for Reproductive Medicine (ASRM). (2013). *Find a health professional*. Retrieved from https://www.asrm.org/euclid/detail.aspx?id=2328

Institute for Human Reproduction. (n.d.). *Egg donation*. Retrieved from www.infertilityihr.com/egg_donation.html

IVF Florida Reproductive Associates. (2014). *Information for long distance patients*. Retrieved from www.ivfflorida.com/long-distance-patients.asp

Reproductive Medicine Institute. (2011). *Reproductive Medicine Institute*. Retrieved from www.reproductivemedicineinstitute.com/

South Florida Institute for Reproductive Medicine. (2013). *International patients*. Retrieved from www.ivfmd.com/getting-started/international-patients

Waldby, C., & Cooper, M. (2008). The biopolitics of reproduction. *Australian Feminist Studies, 23*(55), 57–73.

# 5 Ethics, Professional Autonomy, and the United States Fertility Industry

Assisted reproductive technologies (ARTs) have been mired in controversy since at least the middle of the twentieth century, when researchers first began exploring ways to assist infertile couples that involved fertilization outside of the human body (Henig, 2004). Over time, ethics regarding these technologies have been codified and institutionalized in the form of government policies, religious decrees, and organizational mandates. Outside the United States, many nations restrict and regulate what types of reproductive technologies may be offered within their borders, and what types of people may have access to them. These restrictions and regulations, such as those outlawing surrogacy or sex selection, are largely based on a presumed set of collective or national ethics regarding matters of justice, life, and the sanctity of the human body, at least as they are framed by lawmakers, rather than by referendum. Federal regulations of ART in the United States, on the other hand, rather than articulating a stance on life or bodily integrity, deal primarily with laboratory and tissue handling procedures and the collection and publication of IVF success rates.

One can argue that placing a value on safety, consumer choice, and informed consent is also reflective of a particular ethical position, even if they do not rest upon deep-seated moral and religious questions about when life begins, what one can or cannot do with one's body for money, or what classes of people may partake of a medical procedure. This is not to say that those moral questions are settled in the United States, or are not fraught with politics. On the contrary, laws and policies regarding abortion, assisted suicide, and medical marijuana underscore the frequency with which the United States government takes a position on these weighty matters and, as it were, legislates both morality and medical practice. Regulation is not non-existent, but rather governance over these technologies is decentralized and fragmented, and primarily rests with states and more localized government bodies.

Many ethical questions are thus left open to interpretation by fertility industry professionals (Ehrich, Williams, Farsides, Sandall, & Scott, 2007; Frith, Jacoby, & Gabbay, 2011). One of the most contentious issues rife with various ethical interpretations is the matter of financial compensation for third-party gamete donors[1] and surrogates. Throughout much of the world where the fertility industry is operational, governments have drawn sharp lines around whether or not it is legal, ethical, or advisable for healthy women and men to sell their reprogenetic materials and labor as gamete "donors" (Leve, 2013; Waldby & Cooper, 2008), or for women to get paid to be impregnated, gestate, and give birth to a child to which she will have no legal claims (Markens, 2007; Munyon, 2003; Steinbock, 2004). In the United States, compensation for third-party reproduction is not a matter of federal government policy or regulation; it is left, for the most part, to the discretion of individuals who negotiate among themselves: medical practitioners, attorneys, brokers and recruiters, intended parents, and the third-party donors and surrogates. Compensation for surrogates and the legal recognition of surrogacy contracts varies from state to state, but the matter of compensation for egg and sperm donors is much clearer: aside from three states (Georgia, Louisiana, and Oklahoma), paying individuals for their gametes is legally permitted and almost entirely absent any regulation, at any level of government (Cone, 2012). Legislating how many embryos may be transferred during *in vitro fertilization* is another area in which practice in the United States is out of step with countries that have stronger regulations of the fertility industry.

Several fertility industry professionals expressed to me the idea that even with the decentralization and fragmentation of policies, there is still, in essence, an "American" style of ethics that guided their work. As one physician articulated as we sat in his office on the Upper East Side in Manhattan, there is a difference between "American" ethics and "European" ethics, namely that ethics in the United States center on the individual, whereas Europe focuses on the collective. He gave as an example the contrast in the free-market organization of health care in the United States as opposed to the socialized medical systems in many European nations. When the state is paying for the medical services of its citizens, it has more of a stake in determining what it is willing or unwilling to pay for. This point, one can argue, is one of the cudgels that American conservatives used in the recent health-care debates: any movement towards a more "socialist" form of health care, in which the government assumes a greater financial responsibility in paying for medical services, may lead to government overriding medical decisions made between physicians and their patients. In our current privatized system, it is more frequently employers and insurance companies who more often wield this power to override medical decisions.

Significantly, federal regulations in the United States are aimed at the medical and scientific professions, and not at the individuals who wish to obtain fertility services. This is quite contrary to policies that exist elsewhere that forbid, for example, an infertile couple from paying a woman to gestate and give birth to a child for them, or that demand that all gamete donors be registered in an accessible, national database. The individual in the United States is free to consume the services she desires, and, in a majority of states, to anonymously sell her gametes or rent her womb, but her embryologist, reproductive endocrinologist, and lab technician are bound by law and policy to follow certain procedures. When I began interviewing providers of fertility services—particularly physicians and others employed at clinics—I was surprised by how burdened many of them felt by the rules and regulations they were expected to comply with. Was not the United States, after all, one of the most laissez-faire of all countries when it comes to assisted fertility services? From the point of view of their East Asian or European counterparts, many of whom are not able to offer the same services that American providers can, the United States may seem like a free-for-all. But, from the American point of view, reproductive medical practice is guided by layers of bureaucracy—federal *and* state regulatory systems, professional guidelines, and health insurance policies.

All of the providers I interviewed—physicians, attorneys, office managers, social workers, egg and surrogate brokers—were aware of how ethically fraught the work they conduct is, on both a day-to-day basis and on a long-term, wide-ranging level. Although they may not be constantly mulling over philosophical problems in the course of their daily business, when asked about concerns they had with their industry, or questioned about which constituencies should have a voice in making policy, many expressed answers that reflected that they *had* considered these ethical questions and at times debated with their colleagues over them. Furthermore, given that this project is particularly focused on reproductive tourism, the providers I interviewed were also well aware that they are uniquely positioned to offer services to people who seek them out precisely because laws and cultural norms in their home countries have decreed these services to be unethical. Different patterns of regulations from country to country govern how the fertility industry works in those countries, but providers obviously do not always internalize externally imposed laws as professional or personal norms. Indeed, that providers in countries or states where certain ARTs are restricted or prohibited refer their clients to friendlier jurisdictions, as described in the previous chapter, makes it apparent that compatibility between laws and professional ethics do not necessarily coincide. Rather than view their own role in their clients' subversion of laws as a breach of normative ethics, the providers I interviewed saw their work with international clients as an extension of "American" ethics of choice, liberty, and autonomy.

## THE AMBIGUITY OF "DO NO HARM"

From the perspective of some providers, ethics and regulation are two separate issues. Whereas all of my informants agreed that their work is fraught with ethical issues, this did not necessarily translate into a belief that their field demands regulation or government oversight. On the contrary, many expressed the idea that ethics are either a personal matter to be reconciled by each individual, or that questions of right and wrong, when they have to do with medical procedures, should ultimately be left up to the medical profession. Regardless of their opinion on the role of government in legislating ethics (which will be explored further below), fertility industry professionals understand that significant ethical issues are at stake.

According to assisted fertility providers, their work demands special attention to ethical concerns because the nature of reproductive medicine and of the technology itself is imbued with risk and the potential for negative outcomes for intended parents, third-party donors and surrogates, offspring, and society at large. For example, artificial insemination, egg donation, and surrogacy put people at risk of contracting disease from infected tissue. As with blood transfusions and organ transfer, these technologies may put the person receiving the tissue (either an intended mother or a surrogate) at risk of infection. Additionally, the disease risk associated with reproductive technologies extends both bodily and temporally, in that any resultant offspring may also be at risk of contracting disease from infected tissue.

Reproductive medicine is unique in at least two respects: (1) It entails the *creation*, not merely the maintenance, of life, and (2) it involves *elective* procedures. These two distinctions contribute to the belief held by providers that assisted reproductive technologies are more risky, consequential, or in need of surveillance than other medical fields. Dr. Randolph discussed the potential pitfalls of his work as a fertility doctor:

> If you mess that up, you've got a . . . whole human life that is going to be affected. Yes, if you mess up the surgery [as] an orthopedic surgeon, you may have somebody who limps for the rest of their life, and that's pretty terrible, too, but you're not making baby after baby after baby.

Many of the physicians recognized the lifelong impact that their practice has on their patients and any offspring they have a hand in creating. This idea that they, unique among medical practitioners, are dealing with long-term issues of "creating life" leads many to conclude that their field requires some regulation or at the very least ethical reflection. The distinction between elective and non-elective medicine was made by Liz, egg donation coordinator at a large New York fertility clinic, who contrasted her work with other types of medical practice. Whereas she and her colleagues sometimes debate whether or not IVF is ethically, if not medically, valid in particular cases, she wondered if similar conversations took place among brain surgeons, for example. "I don't know if they have the same sort of discussions that we have about 'Should we even do it, or not, for this patient?'"

This feeling that reproductive technologies may be more risky or consequential than other fields was echoed by a number of fertility industry professionals. All medical procedures involve some measure of iatrogenic risk, but those risks are usually limited to the patient; likewise, all pregnancies also involve risks, but these risks are usually limited to the mother and fetus. In the case of third-party reproduction, the parties at risk extend beyond intended mothers and fetuses to include gamete donors and surrogates.[2] Anne, a surrogacy broker in Los Angeles, cited these expanded risks as a reason why ethics should be employed in screening potential clients who want to use her agency's services. Invoking the medical mandate to "Do no harm," Anne argued that her agency demands there be "a justifiable medical reason that somebody needs the help of a surrogate. It can't be because you're a famous actress. We're asking another [woman] to risk her life, perhaps voluntarily, but albeit, to risk her life, for somebody else's inability. It better be real. It better be for a real inability."

The principle to "Do no harm" came up, unprompted, in a number of interviews. Dr. Liu, a San Francisco fertility doctor, contemplated whether or not this principle was being honored. When asked about any concerns he had about his industry, he paused and, with eyebrows furrowed, verbally struggled to answer the question:

> Is it really "Do no harm" having somebody carry your children? Probably, but on the other hand, is that a benefit? . . . If you want to pay somebody, they can do that, pay $50,000, go to Harvard, recruit a nineteen-year-old girl. . . . But is it really right? Does that constitute egg *donation*, or is that coercion? Or is that just a friendly purchasing of human body parts?

"Are we doing the right thing?" Dr. Liu asked, rhetorically. Note how his point of view kept shifting, where it was not always clear whether or not "we" or "you" referred to himself and other doctors, to his patients, to me as the interviewer, or to an abstract interlocutor. "I guess that's the ultimate question: are we doing this, defying nature, or defying God. . . . As long as you pay you get whatever you want. Sometimes you think about it."

By invoking the ethical principle to "Do no harm," Anne and Dr. Liu highlighted one of the central ambiguities of third-party reproduction: who, exactly, are the doctor's patients? Are they the people who pay him to extract and handle other people's gametes, or are they the people whose gametes are being extracted and handled? Are they the people who plan to take home a baby, or the people whose bodies will carry and nurture that child for nine months? Is the doctor's patient the person who pays, or is it every person whose body is under his care? Without a clear understanding of who he is "treating," the principle of "Do no harm" is an insufficient guide that cannot reconcile the fact that all the parties involved—intended parents, donors, surrogates, and the physicians themselves—may have conflicting interests. Indeed, the situation demands that physicians not regard donors and surrogates as full patients. Given his conflicted feelings about egg donation and surrogacy as potentially coercive, if Dr. Liu viewed donors and surrogates as his primary patients, would he be obligated to advise them not to put their bodies at risk, effectively limiting a large source of his income? Medical professionals are not disinterested parties (Freidson, 1988).

This ambiguity exemplifies a problematic aspect of reproduction in the post-modern age, at once both medicalized and commodified. The medicalization of reproduction has transformed intended parents into *patients* requiring medical expertise (Jordan, 1993; Rothman, 2000). In the trajectory of infertility treatment, intended parents often begin their relationships with their physicians as patients to be examined, diagnosed, and then treated. This trajectory leads to more and more aggressive medical treatments, usually on the intended mothers' bodies, but may also extend beyond the initial patients' bodies into the bodies of others—sperm donors, egg donors, and surrogates (Becker, 2000; Franklin, 1997; Thompson, 2005).

Medical sociologists have described the process of medicalization as a form of social control (Conrad, 1992; Zola, 2009), or even, in Frank's (1997) terminology, colonization. The medicalization of reproduction shifts control over women's bodies from women themselves to physicians and other medical authorities (Ehrenreich & English, 2010; Jordan, 1993; Rothman, 2000). Even after physicians determine that more treatments would be fruitless, their patient's bodies are not decolonized. As long as they are still under counsel of physicians, intended parents do not cease being patients, even if other bodies are brought in as substitutes. They still fulfill the "sick role," diagnosed as incapable of a biological function, and requiring the care of a physician (Parsons, 1951). It is only when they exit the medical system, by turning to adoption, foster care, or resigning themselves to childlessness, that intended parents cease being patients.

Gamete donors and surrogates undergo a different kind of medicalization. While intended parents who are unable to procreate "naturally" either because of a biomedical condition or social status are regarded as deviant for their inability to be productive, the very productivity of gamete donors' and surrogates' bodies marks them as normative or even *super* normative. Their bodies are not colonized by the medical system because of a deviant status; rather, the colonization of their bodies results from the medicalization of *other people's bodies*, like so much collateral damage. Gamete donors and surrogates do not fulfill the sick role. Although their bodies, too, are palpated, examined, and operated on, patient status does not fully extend to them. Instead, their status is more ambiguous—it is somewhere in between patient, employee, and sole proprietor (Waldby, 2008).

This points to the second half of the medicalization/commodification equation. At the same time that procreation has become medicalized, transforming intended parents into patients, so have intended parents also been transformed into *consumers*. Although many may be loath to think of bodies or children in terms of commodities and markets, reproductive technology in the past thirty years has been remarkable for its fragmenting of the procreative process, enabling elements to be divided up and outsourced to various parties (Goodwin, 2010). Physician services, sperm and eggs, and the labor of women are all consumable products. Thus, bodies and body parts become commodities, physicians are also service providers, and donors and surrogates are employees/sole proprietors.

This tangle of roles and statuses is one source of the ambiguity raised by "Do no harm." In a simple one-to-one patient–physician relationship, the mandate of non-maleficence is not always unambiguous, which is why many medical practices convene ethics boards or committees to negotiate the complicated ethics of various medical treatments. Complicating matters even more, however, is that in the realm of reproductive medicine, the involvement of third parties muddles the patient–physician relationship. If physicians view donors and surrogates as *adjuncts* to procreation rather than as patients, whose risks do they prioritize?

The attorneys I interviewed understood that in cases involving third-party reproduction, they did not—and ethically *could* not, by the standards of their profession—represent intended parents *and* the third parties they contracted with, because this would be a clear conflict of interest. The waters got decidedly murkier among the non-medical and non-legal providers, however. Egg and surrogate brokering is not a "profession" in the same way that medicine or law are professions: they are not high-status occupations, are not highly organized, do not require special education, do not have closed or limited entry, and, in the United States, at least, are unlicensed and unregulated (Freidson, 1988). Neither is there any set of professional ethics that is particular to brokers—although, as Anne indicated, they may personally aim to uphold the "Do no harm" principle. A broker's role, which includes screening and matching suitable donors and surrogates, is intermediary and transactional. They have no professional duty to evaluate the merit of their clients' requests, but instead must rely on physicians and attorneys to insure that their clients' medical and legal needs are met.

Rebekah and Shelby, co-owners of a California surrogacy agency, described a client of theirs in Hong Kong whose surrogate was "unfortunately having a very difficult pregnancy." The client, a neonatologist, wanted the surrogate mother's doctor to use a particular steroid, but because of the difficulty communicating across time zones, used Rebekah and Shelby to convey the information to the doctor. In this conversation between the business partners, the interest of the client, rather than the distressed surrogate, seemed to be the biggest concern of the brokers:

*Shelby:*    He tells us, "Just make sure to check to see these are the steroids. There are two kinds of steroids they can give her." . . . He actually ended up saying it didn't matter, either one. But I didn't know that there are two kinds, and he wanted to know which one her doctor was going to give her. So my question, before he said it doesn't matter, was, well gee; let's find out which one.

*Rebekah:*    She's how many weeks pregnant now?

| | |
|---|---|
| *Shelby*: | 29. Getting there. |
| *Rebekah*: | And she has constant bleeding? |
| *Shelby*: | Constant bleeding. Now like minor contractions. And this is a surrogate who's carried twins to term. |
| *Rebekah*: | Would you use her again? |
| *Shelby*: | I probably would. I think it's just the way it implanted. |
| *Rebekah*: | Okay. Anyway. Sorry. |
| *Shelby*: | And she's being really good about it. She hasn't been a jerk, you know? |
| *Rebekah*: | She's getting paid, she doesn't care. |
| Shelby: | I know. |
| *Rebekah*: | I'm sorry. That's—she's one of those ones that's a little more mercenary, but I like her. |

In this snippet of conversation, we can see that the client in Hong Kong was regarded as a human being with desires and interests, whereas the "constantly bleeding" woman contracted as his surrogate was regarded by the brokers as a broken, but still usable, vessel. They also seemed to put the surrogate in an impossible position: if she complained about the fact that she is having a difficult pregnancy, this would have branded her as a "jerk," whereas not complaining was only proof that she did not value her own body and was only in it for the money. Rebekah's remarks at least acknowledged an awareness of her cynicism. The question about whether Shelby would "use" the surrogate again was also significant, because besides looking out for the clients who pay them handsomely, it is also in the brokers' interest to ensure that donors and surrogates have safe, fair, and pleasant experiences—if only to retain a pool of people willing to donate or carry a child again in the future. This is especially important given that donors and surrogates who have proven "successful" in the past garner a higher sum than first-time donors and surrogates.

Brokers have an ambiguous relationship with donors and surrogates, wherein they are not quite bosses or advocates but function more like headhunters or a temporary employment agency. As the mediator between the client and the donor-surrogate, the broker represents both parties, perhaps not always cognizant of the conflict of interest inherent in the nature of these relationships. Although some brokers spoke of wanting to protect "their" donors and surrogates, as I describe in detail below, they were more likely to express the need to protect their clients (i.e., the intended parents) from donors and surrogates who, in their opinion, are "mercenary" or sometimes overcharge for their services.

## BENEVOLENCE OR PRICE-SETTING?

In addition to the ambiguity of "Do no harm" is another situation of ethical uncertainty: compensation for egg donors. Globally, there are tiers of legality regarding egg donation and its compensation. Egg donation is outright prohibited in Germany, Italy, Norway, and Switzerland; in other nations, including Australia, Belgium, Canada, and France, altruistic egg donation is legal, but *commercial* egg donation, or selling eggs, is not (Jones, Cooke, Kempers, Brinsden, & Saunders, 2010). Similar prohibitions exist throughout the world regarding surrogacy—outright bans in some places, and bans on commercial surrogacy in others. One of the distinctive features—and competitive advantages—of the United States fertility industry is its lucrative market for ova and surrogates, and the lack of government intervention in regulating compensation structures. Absent government policy, the fertility industry self-regulates the egg donor and surrogacy markets. In 2007, the American Society for Reproductive Medicine (ASRM) Ethics Committee published a report outlining guidelines regarding informed consent procedures and financial compensation of oocyte donors (Ethics Committee of the ASRM, 2007). The report justifies the American practice of paying egg donors thousands of dollars as compensation for their "time, inconvenience, and discomfort," although providers themselves have varying opinions about it (Ethics Committee of the ASRM, 2007, p. 305). What is perhaps most interesting about these guidelines are two additional points: first, that physicians are to regard donors as "any other patients," which, as indicated above, is difficult to achieve in practice (Ethics Committee of the ASRM, 2007). Second, these 2007 guidelines attempt to set a price on a woman's eggs.

Others have written extensively about the problematics of egg "donation" and the commodification of body parts (Gimenez, 1991; Spar, 2006; Steinbock, 2004; Waldby & Cooper, 2008; Waldby, 2008). Although that is an important part of the conversation, we must also pay attention to the "disconnect" between the ethical justification made by the ASRM and views about compensation held by individual providers. Megan, a Los Angeles egg broker and former egg donor, emphasized how much *work* is involved: "If you've never been a donor before, you do have to do a lot of things. You have to go to doctor's visits, and you're injecting yourself with things, . . . and I think sometimes the question about why should she be paid so much, it's like, have you ever been through this? Do you even know what they have to go through?" Anne argued from a feminist perspective that it is inequitable and paternalistic to expect donors to supply their services altruistically, as they do in several European countries:

> Men have been paid to do things, but nobody blinks an eyelash. Nobody says, "Oh! The fire department's arrived to put out my burning house. You're doing this for free, though, right, 'cause I mean, you're saving my house and it's a good thing, right?" . . . Nobody questions that. . . . So why can't women be paid to donate their eggs?

Both Megan and Anne's statements lend credence to Waldby and Cooper's (2008) contention that the despite the language of donation and altruism, sale of eggs and other body parts should be regarded as *labor* (see also Almeling, 2011; Leve, 2013).

The ASRM guidelines do not reclassify egg "donors" as vendors or laborers, but by justifying substantial compensation for ova they at least acknowledge that egg donation takes place outside of a gift economy. Significantly, the guidelines name precise figures, in effect setting a price on the value of a woman's eggs: "Total payments to donors in excess of $5,000 require justification and sums above $10,000 are not appropriate" (Ethics Committee of the ASRM, 2007, p. 305). The guidelines acknowledge that paying for eggs may result in their commercialization, but rather than recommend a ban on paying donors, ASRM recommends caps on what it considers to be unreasonably high compensation. This is ostensibly to prevent coercion: too much money could "become undue inducements that will lead donors to discount risks," and is precisely why some of my informants expressed concerns about the compensation of egg donors (Ethics Committee of the ASRM, 2007, p. 308). Dr. Liu worried about coercion, and expressed discomfort about donating eggs "for obviously financial benefits." Tammy, a social worker employed by a surrogacy agency, also brought up "the coercion factor," which she sees as a particular issue for young women needing money for college. As she put it, "A lot of people would do a lot of things for $50,000, $100,000. I mean, how could you say no?"

In discussions about unreasonably high compensation, the primary issue appears to be that of coercion: if donors are offered huge sums of money for their ova, is this not an unethical inducement to young women to put their bodies at risk? Yet, the amounts of money that the ASRM finds reasonable and justified in the United States far exceed the more highly regulated amounts that have been legally established in other countries. The United Kingdom's Human Fertilisation and Embryology Authority (HFEA) maintains that sperm and egg donors should not be "paid" for their gametes; rather, they may be "reimbursed" for expenses for lost earnings (Human Fertilisation and Embryology Authority, 2011a). Recently, the compensation rate for egg donation cycles tripled from £250 (approximately US$430) to £750 (US$1,280) to improve recruitment rates and stem the country's egg shortages that lead intended parents to travel abroad to countries where donors are more highly compensated (Human Fertilisation and Embryology Authority, 2011b).

While similar concerns about coercion and commercialization may lead both the HFEA and the ASRM to cap donation cycles, the monetary differences (not to mention the enforcement capabilities) between those caps are striking. Debates about the merits and ethics of compensation assumes that egg donation *itself* is viewed as ethically justified, an assumption without merit in countries such as Italy and Germany, where the practice is completely banned. The market for ova, thriving throughout the world, not only shifts to those countries where the transfer of eggs from one woman to another is permitted, but the largest markets exist in those countries where *commercial* donation is permitted. As I describe in the next chapter, the global demand for American egg donors also hinges upon quasi-eugenic notions about the genetic quality of donors.

Aside from non-binding guidelines established by the ASRM, the United States does not regulate how much money an egg donor can receive per cycle, and rumors abound about Ivy League donors, for example, auctioning off their ova for the price of one year of tuition. Although paying a young woman $8,000 per cycle may seem excessive, coercive, or devaluing of human life, those high costs also create an incentive structure for young American women to sell their eggs that does not exist in places where they are less compensated. Women need to be paid enough to make the risks and inconveniences of extracting eggs worthwhile, but not so much that it becomes coercive. Whereas institutions on both sides of the Atlantic may frame egg "donation" as a form of altruism, clearly there are signs that it is actually a commercial transaction guided by market forces.

The individual providers I interviewed did not speak in altruistic terms. Rather, they described the *commercial* nature of their business, which renders the language of "donation" non-sensical. Dr. Leveque argued that without a market for eggs and surrogates, services would disappear in the United States, as they have in other nations: "If you want egg donation to exist, we've got to pay donors. If you want gestational carriers to exist, you've got to pay gestational carriers. And the market forces have established a price, which is a reasonable thing. It's a functional system. It works great." Another physician argued similarly that if commercial egg donation were to be banned in the United States, young women would no longer be willing to part with their eggs, leaving some infertile couples no longer able to have children. Rather dramatically, he stated, "[If] they pass a law saying we can't pay egg donors, that's just the end of it." Although both physicians used a language of compassion for infertile couples, they were not disinterested parties; after all, were the market for eggs to disappear, so too would their own industry shrink.

ASRM guidelines notwithstanding, without the force of law, prices can rise as high as the market will bear. Donors, intended parents, brokers, and clinics engage in a tug-of-war over who controls that market. Robin, director of an egg donor program, did not believe that young women should set their own rates. She thought it "insane" to allow a "twenty-some-odd year-old decide how much they're worth." When asked to elaborate, she explained that intended parents are vulnerable to being exploited by "the wrong kind of donors. I think it attracts donors who are just in it for, 'This is a great way of screwing a vulnerable person.' And, that's not right." Rebekah and Shelby also worried about "egg donation fees getting out of control," and the exploitation of intended parents by the donors. Shelby cited a client who paid a woman what she described as an outrageous sum of $25,000, on top of additional fees paid to the agency that coordinated the donation: "The truth is, some people don't care about what they're getting as long as it's healthy. . . . Would I pay 25,000? No, I think that's nuts." In this example, Shelby's primary concern was that this was the donor's first time selling her eggs. Experienced (or "proven") donors, in her point of view, merit higher compensation.

Despite Dr. Leveque's claim that market forces should determine the price of eggs, the ASRM and most providers actually argue *against* market-driven compensation rates. Concerns about market forces driving compensation are not about the commercialization of human life, however. Rather, arguments against the market are actually arguments against the control of the markets *by donors* rather than by fertility industry professionals. Dr. Bradley was one of the few physicians who argued that compensation rates should not be market-driven. Dr. Bradley was rather explicit about this, arguing that egg donation "shouldn't be market-driven by . . . the egg donor." He stated:

> Recipients have told me, "Oh, my egg donor's asking me for $25,000." I said to them, "Do you have running shoes? Put them on, turn around, and run away. As fast as you can." . . . *The minute you let the egg donors believe that they are running a market, then they're going to try to control the market.*
>
> (emphasis mine)

Were market forces and the laws of supply and demand truly used to determine compensation rates, young women would be able to charge as much for their oocytes as intended parents were willing to pay for them.

Despite the greater expenses, and the exponentially higher medical and legal risks associated with surrogacy, there are currently no ASRM guidelines about compensation or any industry-driven caps. The ASRM attempts to control the market for egg donation, but it currently offers no guidelines on caps for surrogates. According to Rebekah, surrogates control the market by communicating through Internet message boards about how much they charge for base fees, monthly allowances, maternity clothes, and C-sections. If word gets out that someone has raised their rates, "they all start talking, and the lawyers start negotiating." As a market-driven practice, surrogacy is competitive, much more so than egg donation. If a surrogate demanded $50,000, but the going rate is currently about $24,000, Rebekah explained that she would tell the surrogate: "You are *so* entitled to that amount of money. But let me tell you. There is somebody else that will do this for $22,000. And . . . if I were the intended parent, why would I choose you over somebody who'd do it for half the price? It's not that you don't deserve it, it's just it's not the market value."

In the language of the ASRM, caps on compensation for egg donation exist to reduce the coercive potential of exorbitant fees and to act as a check against the commercialization of human body parts. It is curious that there are currently no industry-driven caps on surrogacy based on concerns about exploitation, baby selling, or the commodification of women's bodies. As

I pointed out previously, the impetus for egg donation caps appears to be driven by market considerations, and thus one may conclude that market considerations also explain the lack of caps on surrogacy compensation. With such a small number of women willing to be surrogates, caps on compensation could further diminish the supply. Surrogates also have greater bargaining power, as they tend to be older and married and already have children, unlike the typically unmarried twenty-something women in college who sell their eggs.

The lack of caps on compensation rates for surrogacy diminishes the validity of the ethical justifications made by the ASRM for caps on the price of eggs. Capping compensation for egg donors appears to be more about attempts by the fertility industry to maintain control over their market position and reduce the bargaining power of donors (and the agencies that recruit them) than it is about reducing the potential for coercion or the commercialization of the human body. Unlike surrogacy, egg selling does not function as a free market; rather, this is industry-wide price-setting. Caps put control over the egg market in the hands of the fertility industry. These dynamics may be more explicit and crass when they involve the bodies of poor women in the Third World, but even when the lines of flight are from China to the United States rather than from France to India, similar sets of ethical questions must be raised. Thus the United States and a handful of other nations stand alone as places where it is considered ethical for women to be paid tens of thousands of dollars to sell their ova or gestate and give birth to a child with whom they will have no legal or social relationship. And, because so many countries in the world prohibit compensation to third-party donors and surrogates, the demand for donors and surrogates increasingly gets met by fertility industries in countries like the United States (and states like California), where compensation is permitted.

## EMBRYO TRANSFER AND "OCTOMOM"

Several European countries, including Belgium, the United Kingdom, Sweden, Finland, Norway, and Denmark, have adopted a policy known as eSET, or Elective Single Embryo Transfer, in order to reduce the rates of high-risk twin and other high-order multiple pregnancies (Cutting, Morroll, Roberts, Pickering, & Rutherford, 2008). Under eSET regulations, women who fit a particular set of criteria (such as being at risk of a twin or multiple pregnancy because of age and positive prognosis of conception via IVF) should have only a single embryo transferred during IVF rather than multiple embryos. One of the early drawbacks to using IVF was its correlation with twin and high-order multiple pregnancies, which place the birth mother and fetuses at risk. These multiple pregnancies resulted not only from the propensity of some transferred embryos to split (forming identical twins), but from the successful implantation of more than one embryo after transfer to the uterus (forming fraternal twins and other multiples).

The primary logic behind transferring multiple embryos during IVF is that not all embryos that are transferred into a woman's womb are necessarily viable, and therefore transferring more than one embryo increases the chances that at least one will implant and result in a pregnancy. Some argue that the propensity to transfer multiple embryos was exacerbated as an unintended consequence of the CDC's 1992 Fertility Clinic Success Rate and Certification Act that requires fertility clinics to keep track of and report statistics (Rogers, 2010). At a conference I attended that was organized by a national non-profit advocacy group for people wanting to have children through assisted fertility and adoption, I observed the founder and president of this group, surrounded by several members, stand up and passionately speak out against the repercussions of the 1992 Act. In her opinion, the Act may have been intended to protect consumers, but the end result was more harm. Because consumers could now search a database to identify how successful clinics were in terms of pregnancy and birth rates, there was a push from within clinics to boost these rates, and thus it was in clinics' interests to transfer multiple embryos to increase the likelihood of pregnancy.[3] This claim about physicians being incentivized to boost statistics was also anecdotally backed up by one of my informants. At Anne's surrogacy agency, they advocate for single embryo transfer, since the goal is "a happy, healthy baby. Not babies born a month early. Not babies because this doctor was so anxious to achieve a pregnancy, he put in too many embryos." Anne was angry that physicians could report multiple pregnancies as "successes" when they were not the ones who would have to deal with the subsequent problems, such as high medical bills or developmental delays resulting from premature births.

A third factor is on the demand side of the equation. Because IVF is quite expensive, consumers themselves may be willing to risk a twin or high-order multiple pregnancy by having more than one embryo transferred in order to increase the likelihood of a pregnancy during the first round or rounds of IVF. This problem is exacerbated for international patients, who have distance, in addition to costs, to contend with. As Dr. Randolph elaborated, he and his colleagues may transfer more than one embryo to patients who have traveled from long distances. If they lived nearby, he might advocate putting in one embryo, and having them come back the next month to try again if it did not work the first time. But this does not make sense for his international patients: "It's a lot harder to tell someone to fly from Australia every month for four months so you can have the one [embryo transfer]." Several of my informants supported the move within their profession towards reducing the rate of high-order multiple pregnancies by transferring fewer—or even single—embryos during IVF, and even urged their patients against multiple embryo transfer. Unfortunately, this does not always align with the desires of their patients, who are anxious to conceive and may be willing to take the risk.

No U.S. agencies have enacted regulations regarding embryo transfer, and the CDC has not changed the nature of statistics reporting to reflect the high rates of multiple pregnancies, but this area is another space where the ASRM offers professional guidance, perhaps to offset calls for the United States to adopt eSET policies similar to that of European countries. The Practice Committees of ASRM and SART argue that there must be flexibility in the number of embryos that may be transferred, in order to individualize treatment plans (Practice Committee of the ASRM and the Practice Committee of the SART, 2009). Their recommendations are similar to that of eSET policies, in that criteria weighing the woman's age and prognosis determine how many embryos should be transferred, with the recommendations erring on the side of caution to minimize high-order multiple pregnancies. Unlike eSET policies in other countries, however, the ASRM recommendations lack the teeth of law.

Not all providers I interviewed were supportive of the international move towards single embryo transfer. Dr. Gorman, who works extensively with women of advanced maternal age who have particularly difficult times conceiving even with IVF, derisively called the move towards eSET "ridiculous" and an "international obsession" that "every regulatory authority is jumping on." In his view, eSET does not make statistical sense, can raise rather than decrease cost, and reduce pregnancy rates. Dr. Randolph was similarly wary of government regulating embryo transfer because for him this would constitute the legislature being "in the business of practicing medicine. . . . When you start saying you know how many embryos to put back, you're practicing medicine, and they're not prepared to do that. I mean, they're not trained to do that." Even Anne, who advocated single embryo transfer for her surrogates, would rather that "experts," and not politicians, create these policies.

Looming like a specter in the background of these conversations about embryo transfer was a scandal that had rocked the fertility world (and the tabloid news circuit) only a few months before I began conducting interviews: On January 6, 2009, Nadya Suleman (dubbed "Octomom" by the media) gave birth to octuplets as a result of multiple embryo transfer during an IVF procedure (Archibold, 2009). Reports appeared over a year later (after my interviews had concluded) that her physician, Dr. Michael Kamrava, had actually transferred *twelve* embryos (Associated Press, 2010). That Suleman was only 33 years old, and had already successfully given birth to six children through previous IVF treatments, means that she was probably *not* a good candidate for having more than one or two embryos transferred. Had she resided in Sweden or the United Kingdom, official policy would have required only a single embryo transfer; and, while ASRM guidelines would have advised against transferring more than two embryos at a time, the transfer of twelve embryos was certainly not *illegal* in California. That is, Suleman's doctor may have gone against professional protocol, but he did not break any laws.

Although this might have been a freakish case perfectly enacted for our reality-television obsessed world, the Suleman scandal illustrates the problem of "renegade doctors" (as Robin, one of my subjects, put it), flouting the standards of medical practice. Is self-regulation by the industry enough to ensure that physicians act in the best interest of their patients? At the time of my interviews, Dr. Kamrava had yet to be brought before the California Medical Board. I was curious about what providers believed were the consequences for medical professionals who go against practice guidelines—not only Dr. Kamrava, but for any physician who flouts the conventions of his profession.

Dr. Bradley seemed unsure about any consequences for doctors who do not follow industry guidelines: "To be a member in good standing, you've got to conform to a certain kind of conduct. It's not just, you don't just send your check and do what you want to do. They could kick you out. Reprimand you. I don't know—that's a good question. I mean, this is America (*laughs*)." Robin wanted more serious repercussions for "unscrupulous doctors." She was aware of doctors who have injured egg donors but who are still "happily practicing." When I asked what the consequences should be, Robin replied that they should lose their medical license. This sentiment that the existing guidelines regarding embryo transfer and other protocols lacked "meat and bones" (as Michael put it), was iterated by many providers.

Yet, again, as with rules about compensation for donors and surrogates, several providers seemed both cynical about the enforcement of industry guidelines and wary of government intervention. Dr. Randolph would rather that renegades such as Dr. Kamrava be dealt with internally:

> The guy that made octuplets, the Octomom guy—people said, "Oh we gotta have rules, we gotta set rules. Fact of the matter is, there is a way to deal with this guy, and it's going to come from the medical board. . . . And the medical board will convene a team . . . to say, "Is this guy practicing outside the norm?" And we would all say yes, you don't transfer eight embryos into a woman 32 years of age. . . . There are rules already in place to deal with that.

Moreover, he disagreed with those who used Octomom as an example of why government standards for embryo transfer should be established. Rather than protect people, he believed that it would be especially harmful for those for whom conceiving is most difficult, guaranteeing that "they'll never get pregnant—ever, probably."

Providers may have expressed outrage at Dr. Kamrava—and at Suleman herself—yet this did not push them to demand more regulation of embryo transfer. Shelby, for example, stated that "something needs to be done. I don't want to see more Octomoms. That's outrageous to me. It's outrageous," but this did not lead her to conclude that limits should be placed on embryo transfer. Those sorts of limits would amount to what she calls "extreme right-wing regulation." Although most of the providers (with a few exceptions) that I interviewed viewed the actions of Dr. Kamrava as unethical, and demanded that he face repercussions such as being kicked out of ASRM and losing his medical license, very few used this case as grist for more regulation. Rather, most of them—even those who were cynical about how robustly industry standards are actually followed and enforced—circled the wagons even more closely, wanting to defend their business from outside scrutiny and deal with such problems internally. Octomom seemed to have hardened their belief that the government should not be in the business of regulating the fertility industry.

From the vantage point of European nations with eSET standards, the Octomom case might offer proof that more government intervention and regulation is necessary, and yet from the vantage point of American providers, even such an extreme flouting of medical standards is not enough to sway them from the ideology of professional autonomy and self-regulation. One set of ethics uses legislation and government decrees to protect women and fetuses from the risk of high-order multiple pregnancies, while the other set of ethics uses industry standards to protect the rights of doctors to practice medicine *and* the rights of individual patient-consumers to access the type of care they desire. The American set of ethics can be summed up by a particular interpretation of *choice* and *liberty* that holds the individual's right to make decisions about how they conduct business, how they may spend their money, and what they can do with their bodies, as sacrosanct.

The latter idea was expressed by Liam, CEO of a surrogacy agency, who was horrified by the Octomom case, but still supported Nadya Suleman's right to choose to have so many embryos transferred, and also to choose not to selectively reduce when she became pregnant with eight of them. He brought up the "fine line" and "slippery slope" argument, asking, "Is it the government's role to come in and tell people how they should reproduce, or not reproduce?" The question has personal resonance for him, as a gay man who fathered a child through surrogacy and egg donation, whose clients are primarily gay men, in a world where gay men and lesbians are often denied the right to form families. It also has professional relevance, as an American fertility industry professional who facilitates family formation for those living in countries where it is illegal for them to do so.

## FERTILITY PROFESSIONALS AS MORAL GATEKEEPERS

As providers reiterated, ethics are deeply embedded within their daily practice, and they take them seriously. Although the United States fertility industry is less regulated than many other nations, providers do not think this makes their country less ethical; rather, they believe that we organize our ethics differently here. Rather than have *government* create boundaries around what types of technologies and procedures may be offered, and to whom—as they do in Germany and Australia, for example—providers would prefer that these boundaries be established by physicians—and other fertility industry professionals—themselves.

Fertility industry professionals act, whether consciously or not, as moral gatekeepers (Ehrich et al., 2007). They repeatedly expressed that individuals have the right to make their own choices when it comes to procreative decision-making. Yet, they also voiced discomfort about clients who pushed them to do things they did not find medically necessary or who wanted assisted fertility services for the "wrong" reasons. When asked if they, as providers, have the right to turn down clients who want to do something they do not agree with, all responded in the affirmative. Personal autonomy gets trumped by *professional* autonomy (Freidson, 1988). Providers described clients they felt morally obligated to turn away, including people of advanced maternal or paternal age, a man who wanted to contract with three surrogates who would each simultaneously carry triplets, celebrities who did not want pregnancies to wreck their figures, and a couple in which one of the partners had AIDS. Dr. Randolph argued that it is a "given" that patients are responsible for deciding what is ethically right or wrong or morally permissible, but then immediately followed this statement with a reiteration of ethical principles from the standpoint of physicians rather than of patients.

Personal and professional ethics do not only apply to intended parents. Fertility industry providers also create rules that apply to donors and surrogates out of concern for their physical and psychological health. Anne stated that her agency puts a limit on how many times a woman may work with them as a surrogate, because "they're not machines. This isn't what they do for a living." Several agencies and clinics stated that young women may sell or donate eggs for no more than six cycles, and get angry when they find out that some donors have lied to them about previous cycles at other agencies.

Moreover, no one spoke of wanting to practice in a field that is just a free-for-all, where patients can get any type of services they want for any reason, or where providers act entirely on their own in decision-making; many spoke appreciatively of being able to consult with their colleagues (or with ethics committees, if their organizations had them) for help with tough ethical decisions. For the most part, providers told me that they appreciated the guidelines provided by their professional organizations and wanted there to be consequences when colleagues break the norms of their profession. Overall, many would like the benefits of policies developed by their *peers* without the interference of regulation developed by *lawmakers*. That is, the majority of the people I spoke with promote self-regulation, but not on the individual level; rather, they prefer regulation of the industry by the industry itself.

Even after articulating some of the pitfalls of their industry, such as rogue doctors, providers exhibited a deep mistrust of politicians to ameliorate things. For example, Tammy took an almost defeatist position about regulation, arguing, "It still is an industry that, put in the wrong hands, could cause harm to people. And has caused harm to people. But what can you do about that?" She believed that lawmakers who do not understand the science should not make policies that regulate it. Further, regulation would "confine people too much, and that could definitely hinder some couples in having the best chance for success." There was this continual tension within the provider testimonies about how to deal with the potential ethical lapses of their industry. Rebekah reflexively recognized the internal contradiction, and joked about being politically liberal on most issues, but not when it comes to the matter of regulation of the fertility industry:

> I said to myself, "Oh my god, I'm a Republican in that area!" I think there needs to be more self-regulation and governance from the professional organizations. I think they absolutely need to step in, because if they don't, the government's going to.

By keeping ethical debates and regulation of professional norms *within the industry itself*, with especial respect to the expert knowledge and authority of physicians, providers are able to act as "moral entrepreneurs," maintaining dominance over their field, above both political and religious authorities (Conrad & Schneider, 1992). It is physicians—and sometimes attorneys and other professionals—who are held up as the rational experts who can best negotiate the ethics of reproductive technologies. As Freidson writes, "[Professions] characteristically seek the freedom to manage their knowledge and work in their own way, protected from lay interference. Indeed, they celebrate the ideal of men who may be trusted to control their own affairs responsibly and in the public interest" (1988, p. xii). Self-regulation is a means for physicians and other professionals to maintain their authority and dominance over professional knowledge and practice.

Physicians and attorneys both have codes of professional ethics, but even those providers who serve more of a mediating or brokering role at egg donor and surrogacy agencies are able to latch onto or defer to the moral prestige and authority of their counterparts in the medical and legal professions. Providers do not want politicians to be moral gatekeepers, nor do they trust ethical norms to be led by religious adherents or the whims of society.

Medical sociologists have traced a gradual loss of authority by physicians within the United States (Clarke, Mamo, Fosket, Fishman, & Shim, 2010; Conrad, 2007; Light, 2009; McKinlay & Marceau, 2009). Doctors have become "proletarianized" as they have become employees of hospital corporations, burdened by HMOs that interfere with their medical decision-making, and must contend with the informed consumer who might question their medical expertise with their own knowledge gleaned from the

Internet, self-help groups, and direct-to-consumer advertising. However, because most fertility treatment is elective, several of these transformations of modern medicine do not apply to fertility doctors as severely as they do to, say, internists. Those fertility doctors associated with medical schools, for example, can reap huge salaries as some of the highest-paid faculty members (Lewin, 2009). Others work privately at their own clinics, hewing to the earlier model of the physician as small business owner. Fertility clinics may get overwhelmed by the paperwork required by health insurance and maintenance organizations, but given the high demand for their services, many consumers are willing to pay out of pocket for uncovered services; the high incomes of many of their clients means that they are perhaps not as constricted by Byzantine insurance requirements as colleagues in other fields. Serving an international clientele is especially appealing because the majority pay out of pocket, thus they do not have to deal with insurance companies at all.

Harnessing their expert knowledge and moral authority, providers compete with each other for clients. When consumers cannot get the services they want—because they are too expensive, prohibited, or any other reason—they may be empowered to search the Internet and query acquaintances in order to find these services elsewhere. The American fertility industry gains clients in this manner, but it also loses them for the same reason: when providers turn down a client's request for treatment, that client retains the option to find someone who will fulfill their desire. This, again, occurs partially as a result of the ambiguous role of the patient as consumer, wherein a tension exists between two clichés: "Doctors Know Best" and "The Customer Is Always Right." With only personal and professional ethics to guide them, and not government regulation, providers can be more flexible about what desires they will or will not fulfill. By acting as a safe haven for intended parents around the world who are prohibited from consuming services that their home cultures find ethically troubling, if not morally repugnant, the United States fertility industry increases its *global* market share, all the while paying lip service to the *national* ideals of freedom, rights, liberty, and personal (and professional) autonomy. These national ideals—contrasted with the alternative ethics that emphasize the collective good—are employed as a "competitive advantage" in the global fertility marketplace.

## ETHICS AND AUTONOMIES

Providers' animosity towards government regulation is part of their general discomfort with politics determining either medical ethics *or* family building. They do not generally espouse a strict libertarian ethos heralding the supreme right of the individual, as displayed by their arguments against a free market for eggs. Rather, their political orientation weighs more towards a neoliberal regard for privatization. The collective narrative that emerges from my interviews aligns with a liberal interpretation of medicine and the family as private, self-enclosed spheres that should be shielded by the vagaries of government, religion, and other social institutions. Allowing doctors to be free to practice medicine (professional autonomy) converges with the desire for intended parents to be free to form families (reproductive autonomy). This ethical orientation links the sanctity of the physician-patient relationship with the privacy of the family.

Reproductive autonomy is conceptually linked and overlaps with bodily autonomy, but they are distinct rights. That is, we tend to see the right to self-determination over procreative decision-making as a subset of the right to self-determination over one's body. This is surely the case when it comes to contraception, abortion, and even many forms of fertility treatment. Although they place their own professional autonomy at the top of their personal moral hierarchy, fertility industry providers champion both the *reproductive* autonomy of intended parents to build families using the resources of technology and medicine, and the *bodily* autonomy of donors and surrogates to sell their reproductive labor and body parts. Fertility providers frame themselves as professionals who enable intended parents and third parties to achieve their wants, needs, and desires, in the face of cultural norms or overt policies that tell them that they *do not have this right* or that *it is ethically wrong*. In this respect, providers are champions of a different form of reproductive autonomy that emphasizes not only the right to do with one's body as one wishes, but to the right to procreate and build families in the way that one chooses—with the use of another person's body, for example.

The premise for the legality of surrogacy within the United States (albeit not in all fifty states), for example, is that women should retain the right of self-determination and ownership of their bodies (Andrews, 1999). The language of autonomy as it is applied to assisted reproductive technologies is not without its detractors, however. It presents a particular conundrum for feminists who may be troubled by situations where one person's reproductive autonomy is premised on the manipulation of someone else's body, which may very well be a corruption of the notion of "autonomy" itself. Just as feminists have historically been divided over whether sex work is a display of autonomy or exploitation, so too do arguments occur about the relative autonomy of women who choose to become surrogates or sell their eggs. This split between championing women's bodily autonomy and protecting women against the corruption of bodily integrity is exemplified by the different directions that New York and California have taken in regard to surrogacy: commercial surrogacy is de facto illegal in New York, whereas California's laws have made that state a haven for surrogacy (Markens, 2007).

This intranational split between New York and California is instructive. Although national policies regarding the body, population, sexuality, and reproduction may be attempts by elected officials and technocrats to translate *collective ethics* into law—a neat illustration of Foucault's (2007) concept of "governmentality"—this does not erase conflicts between sub-national regions, in which case the very notion of "collective ethics" may begin to break down into smaller and smaller units. Government bodies are not the only type of "collectives," either. Other stakeholders may have their own set of ethics that align or conflict with policy, including fertility industry providers, intended parents, third-party donors and surrogates, the offspring of assisted reproductive technologies, religious institutions, reproductive rights organizations, insurance companies, employers, and bioethicists, among others.

And yet, even though fertility industry professionals are aware that different regions within the United States have different laws and policies, that some conservative and religious groups, for example, disapprove of their meddling with the creation of human life, and that, on a micro level, each individual brings to the table his or her own personal set of ethics, some fertility industry professionals express a belief that there is something particularly "American" about how the fertility industry operates. This ethic is rooted in those classical liberal tropes of autonomy, liberty, and choice. Dr. Gorman, whom I cited at the beginning of this chapter for articulating a difference between "American" and "European" ethics, shed more light on what he saw as the American emphasis on the individual over the collective:

> I think in principle, at least here in America, we believe that we have a right to decide how we want to live our lives, how we want to create our families. . . . We are . . . coming from a tradition of self-determination. . . . And some of our strongest clashes, especially in our specialty meetings with European colleagues . . . have been on that subject, because they are much more driven by what they perceive to be good for everybody. . . . We here in the United States have a lot of tolerance for individual rights. Our European colleagues have much less.

Such language articulates a belief in the supremacy of individual rights over the collective, and frames American fertility industry professionals as enabling their clients—even non-Americans—to assume these rights. Imagining a unique set of ethics with the autonomous, rights-bearing individual at its apex fits neatly into narratives of American exceptionalism and moral righteousness.

## CONCLUSION

Reproductive technologies are highly regulated in many nations, with restrictions about what services may be offered within their borders, who may access them, and how. These restrictions and regulations are largely based on a presumed or imagined, in the Andersonian sense, set of collective or national ethics—about what one can or cannot do with one's body, about the sanctity of human life, about who is considered fit for parenting (Anderson, 1991). Despite lacking the kind of regulations regarding reproductive technologies that exist in most other Western nations, ethics are deeply woven into the practices of the American fertility industry. In this chapter I highlighted how those who are involved with providing or brokering assisted fertility services navigate murky terrain in which laws, professional guidelines, religious doctrines, and personal morality frequently do not align. Even though they are not guided by federal law, ethics still get institutionalized in the ways that providers deal with such issues as "Do no harm" principles, compensation for third parties, and embryo transfer.

Fertility industry professionals, including but not limited to physicians, repeatedly invoked the principle of non-maleficence as an ethical guidepost for their practice. Yet, as I argued, the mandate to "Do No Harm" is made ambiguous because it is not always clear—even to the providers themselves—which individuals count as patients or clients. That is, medicalization and the commodification of reproductive body parts makes ambiguous the status of third-party gamete donors and surrogates as *quasi* patients. Were providers to view intended parents and third parties as patients or clients, they would have to give equal weight to the medical and legal risks and benefits for *all* parties involved, without regard for who is footing the bill for assisted fertility services.

The ambiguous status of third-party donors and surrogates as independent contractors, entrepreneurs, or even employees, rather than as patients/clients, undergirds the widespread practice in the United States of paying women for eggs and for their gestational labor. Viewing donors and surrogates as adjuncts to procreation rather than as patients or clients allows them to encourage young women to take medical and legal risks and reduce their bargaining power. Compensating women for eggs or for their labors as surrogates is prohibited in many countries because of fears that it is coercive or contributes to the commodification of the human body but remains legal (if ambiguously so) in most regions of the United States. Professional guidelines regarding compensation for egg donors attempt to address the coercion issue by establishing caps on how much donors may earn for their eggs, yet the same sort of caps to payments for surrogacy are not advised, despite the far greater medical risks.

Professional guidelines also exist that recommend limiting the number of embryos that should be transferred during IVF, and yet these lack the regulatory teeth of eSET policies in many European nations. Even with outrageous cases such as Octomom, providers still argued that embryo transfer should not be regulated but should remain in the realm of doctor-patient negotiation. This stance of retaining professional autonomy free from the heavy hand of government was articulated by providers who rely upon the norms of their profession in their practice.

In their quest to maintain their position as moral gatekeepers, acting as the experts who can best determine what services that intended parents should have access to, providers expressed a desire for professional autonomy that is above politics. This desire for professional autonomy—linking up with their clients' desire for reproductive autonomy—is conceptually aligned with an imagined American propensity towards civil liberty, freedom, and individual rights. By contrasting their practice with that of their colleagues in other nations, American fertility industry professionals construct a narrative about the "Americanness" of the United States fertility industry, and imagine a national ethic rooted in classical liberalism. That these tropes also align with free market ideologies—when it is profitable—is not a coincidence. The liberal orientation of the United States fertility industry offers them a competitive advantage in the global marketplace for reproductive technologies. United States providers are thus able to envision the country as a liberal beacon for those global biocitizens who believe that they are being prevented from enacting their reproductive autonomy.

## NOTES

1. Throughout this chapter, I mimic the language of the fertility industry by describing men and women who sell their gametes as "donors" rather than vendors, and the process of gamete selling as "donation," yet what I wish to stress in this chapter—and throughout this book—is that in the United States this is a *market* transaction, not a gift economy. Quotation marks are implied with each iteration of "donor" and "donation."
2. This kind of risk is also present, of course, for other procedures involving tissue and organ donation.
3. Field notes. (See also Rogers, 2010; Schieve & Reynolds, 2004.)

## REFERENCES

Almeling, R. (2011). *Sex cells: The medical market for eggs and sperm.* Berkeley: University of California Press.

Anderson, B. (1991). *Imagined communities* (Rev. ed.). London: Verso.

Andrews, L. B. (1999). Reproductive technology comes of age. *Whittier Law Review,* 21(2), 375–389.

Archibold, R. C. (2009, February 3). Octuplets, 6 siblings, and many questions. *New York Times.* Retrieved from www.nytimes.com/2009/02/04/us/04octuplets.html?ref=nadyasuleman

Associated Press. (2010, October 19). California: Hearing begins for doctor in octuplet births. *New York Times.* Retrieved from www.nytimes.com/2010/10/19/us/19brfs-HEARINGBEGIN_BRF.html?ref=nadyasuleman

Becker, G. (2000). *The elusive embryo: How women and men approach new reproductive technologies.* Berkeley: University of California Press.

Clarke, A. E., Mamo, L., Fosket, J. R., Fishman, J. R., & Shim, J. K. (Eds.). (2010). *Biomedicalization: Technoscience, health, and illness in the U.S.* Durham, NC: Duke University Press.

Cone, K. L. (2012). Family law—Egg donation and stem cell research—Eggs for sale: The scrambled state of legislation in the human egg market. *UALR Law Review*, 35, 189–226.

Conrad, P. (1992). Medicalization and social control. *Annual Review of Sociology*, 18, 209–232.

Conrad, P. (2007). *The medicalization of society: On the transformation of human conditions into treatable disorders*. Baltimore, MD: Johns Hopkins University Press.

Conrad, P., & Schneider, J. W. (1992). *Deviance and medicalization: From badness to sickness*. Philadelphia, PA: Temple University Press.

Cutting, R., Morroll, D., Roberts, S. A., Pickering, S., & Rutherford, A. (2008). Elective single embryo transfer: Guidelines for practice British Fertility Society and Association of Clinical Embryologists. *Human Fertility*, 11(3), 131–146.

Ehrenreich, B., & English, D. (2010). *Witches, midwives, and nurses: A history of women healers* (2nd ed.). New York: The Feminist Press at CUNY.

Ehrich, K., Williams, C., Farsides, B., Sandall, J., & Scott, R. (2007). Choosing embryos: Ethical complexity and relational autonomy in staff accounts of PGD. *Sociology of Health & Illness*, 29(7), 1091–1106.

Ethics Committee of the ASRM. (2007). Financial compensation of oocyte donors. *Fertility and Sterility*, 88(2), 305–309. doi:10.1016/j.fertnstert.2007.01.104

Foucault, M. (2007). *Security, territory, population: Lectures at the Collège de France, 1977–1978*. New York: Picador.

Frank, A. W. (1997). *The wounded storyteller: Body, illness, and ethics*. Chicago, IL: University of Chicago Press.

Franklin, S. (1997). *Embodied progress: A cultural account of assisted conception*. New York: Routledge.

Freidson, E. (1988). *Profession of medicine: A study of the sociology of applied knowledge*. Chicago: University of Chicago Press.

Frith, L., Jacoby, A., & Gabbay, M. (2011). Ethical boundary-work in the infertility clinic. *Sociology of Health & Illness*, 33(4), 570–585. doi:10.1111/j.1467-9566.2010.01308.x

Gimenez, M. E. (1991). The mode of reproduction in transition. *Gender & Society*, 5(3), 334–350.

Goodwin, M. B. (2010). *Baby markets: Money and the new politics of creating families*. Cambridge: Cambridge University Press.

Henig, R. M. (2004). *Pandora's baby: How the first test tube babies sparked the reproductive revolution*. Boston, MA: Houghton Mifflin Harcourt.

Human Fertilisation and Embryology Authority. (2011a). *Donor compensation, reimbursement and benefits in kind*. Retrieved from www.hfea.gov.uk/6177. html#policy

Human Fertilisation and Embryology Authority. (2011b, October 19). *HFEA agrees new policies to improve sperm and egg donation services*. Retrieved from www. hfea.gov.uk/6700.html

Jones, H. W., Jr., Cooke, I., Kempers, R., Brinsden, P., & Saunders, D. (2010). IFFS surveillance 2010. *Fertility and Sterility*. Retrieved from www.iffs-reproduction. org/documents/IFFS_Surveillance_2010.pdf

Jordan, B. (1993). *Birth in four cultures: A crosscultural investigation of childbirth in Yucatan, Holland, Sweden, and the United States*. Long Grove, IL: Waveland Press.

Leve, M. (2013). Reproductive bodies and bits: Exploring dilemmas of egg donation under neoliberalism. *Studies in Gender and Sexuality*, 14(4), 277–288. doi:10. 1080/15240657.2013.848319

Lewin, T. (2009, February 23). Many specialists at private universities earn more than presidents. *New York Times*. Retrieved from www.nytimes.com/2009/02/23/education/23pay.html

Light, D. (2009). Countervailing power: The changing character of the medical profession in the United States. In P. Conrad (Ed.), *The sociology of health and illness* (8th ed., pp. 239–248). New York: Worth.

Markens, S. (2007). *Surrogate motherhood and the politics of reproduction*. Berkeley: University of California Press.

McKinlay, J.B., & Marceau, L.D. (2009). The end of the golden age of doctoring. In P. Conrad (Ed.), *The sociology of health and illness: Critical perspectives* (pp. 213–239). New York: Worth.

Munyon, J.H. (2003). Protectionism and freedom of contract: The erosion of female autonomy in surrogacy decisions. *Suffolk University Law Review, 36*(3), 717–744.

Parsons, T. (1951). *The social system*. New York: Free Press.

Practice Committee of the ASRM and the Practice Committee of the SART. (2009). Guidelines on number of embryos transferred. *Fertility and Sterility, 92*(5), 1518–1519.

Rogers, J. (2010, September 16). Assisted Reproductive Technology: Let's focus on one healthy baby at a time. *RHRealityCheck.org.* Retrieved from www.rhreality check.org/blog/2010/09/16/one-healthy-baby-at-a-time

Rothman, B.K. (2000). *Recreating motherhood*. New Brunswick, NJ: Rutgers University Press.

Schieve, L.A., & Reynolds, M.A. (2004). What is the most relevant standard of success in assisted reproduction? *Human Reproduction, 19*(4), 778–782.

Spar, D. (2006). *The baby business: How money, science, and politics drive the commerce of conception*. Boston, MA: Harvard Business School Press.

Steinbock, B. (2004). Payment for egg donation and surrogacy. *The Mount Sinai Journal of Medicine, New York, 71*(4), 255–265.

Thompson, C. (2005). *Making parents: The ontological choreography of reproductive technologies*. Cambridge, MA: The MIT Press.

Waldby, C. (2008). Oocyte markets: Women's reproductive work in embryonic stem cell research. *New Genetics and Society, 27*(1), 19–31.

Waldby, C., & Cooper, M. (2008). The biopolitics of reproduction. *Australian Feminist Studies, 23*(55), 57–73.

Zola, I.K. (2009). Medicine as an institution of social control. In P. Conrad (Ed.), *The sociology of health and illness: Critical perspectives* (8th ed., pp. 470–480). New York: Worth.

# 6    Genetic Imperatives and Selective Technologies in the Global Landscape

My interview with Robin, the owner of an egg donor agency in Los Angeles, had concluded, so I turned off the tape recorder. Robin had an eager expression on her face, as if there was something she had been dying to ask me. As I began to pack up my things and put my legal pad of notes away in my bag, she sat back in her chair, looked at me, and said, "And why haven't *you* donated your eggs yet?" I was, to say the least, taken back a bit. I had been under the naïve impression that it was I, the researcher, who was doing the observing, the scrutinizing, the evaluating. Of course, this is a false notion, but it had not quite occurred to me that the entire time I was interviewing Robin, she, in turn, had been assessing me. That was her job, after all—as the owner of an egg donor agency, she spends much of her time recruiting young women to sell their eggs, screening them thoroughly to determine whether or not they would make good candidates, and matching them with the eager intended parents who entrust her to find them a suitable donor. And here I was, a seemingly perfect specimen: at the time a fresh-faced PhD candidate, of average height, slim, and racially ambiguous enough to pass for numerous ethnicities. Flustered, I made light of Robin 's question. "Oh, my eggs are too old, "I told her. When I admitted that I was in my thirties, she replied, "Yeah, that is too old. Too bad. "I reflexively placed my hands on my lower abdomen, over my ovaries with their no-longer-good-enough eggs.

Genetic thinking permeates our lives. Stories involving genetics abound in the mainstream press; we are continually confronted with reports about controversies or breakthroughs around cloning, stem-cell research, animal-human hybrids, "designer babies," breast-cancer genes, or yet another man on death row freed after DNA testing proves his innocence (Nelkin & Lindee, 1995; Reilly, 2006; Roberts, 2011; Rothman, 2001). As the term "designer babies" indicates, popular understandings about genetics are wrapped up in many assisted fertility practices, leaving some with the impression that the science fiction world of *Gattaca* is not too far from becoming reality, or that these possibilities of genetic design already exist.

As I have articulated in the previous chapters, restrictive public policies lead some intended parents to go outside their countries' borders in search of desired services, and these include ones that may be used for selective purposes. Internationally, gamete donation, sex selection, and preimplantation genetic diagnosis (PGD), are widely restricted or regulated, driving reproductive tourism to more permissive countries (Blyth, 2010; Gupta, 2012; Jones, Cooke, Kempers, Brinsden, & Saunders, 2010; Whittaker, 2010, 2011). A lack of restrictions, combined with other advantageous factors such as an abundance of fertility programs,[1] high success rates, and state-of-the-art facilities draw intended parents worldwide to regional hubs in the United States, despite the high costs of treatment (Blyth, 2010; Markens, 2012; Twine, 2011). Specifically, a more permissive orientation toward ARTs, including selective technologies, makes the United States a favorable place for intended parents from anywhere in the world who wish to access egg donation, preimplantation genetic diagnosis, and sex selection. The availability of these technologies, and the ways in which they can be used as tools for selective purposes, make U.S. clinics and programs competitive on a global stage.

In this chapter, I explore the role of genetic thinking within the fertility industry. I begin with a brief overview of how the history of eugenics has shaped reproductive politics in the United States and elsewhere. Next, I explore how this history has also left an imprint on the development of reproductive technologies, imbuing its consumers and producers with ideas about the genetic imperative and the possibilities of genetic determinism and selection. I consider the relationship between attitudes of providers in the United States and popular understandings of genetics that transcend national laws and policy.

## EUGENICS, REPRODUCTIVE TECHNOLOGIES, AND THE GENETIC IMPERATIVE

The average producer or consumer of assisted fertility services would probably balk at the idea that there is a relationship, however tentative, between nineteenth- and twentieth-century eugenics and more recent strands of genetic determinism. The term *eugenics* evokes compulsory sterilization laws and population control programs, Hitler's genocidal Nazi regime, marriage laws, and the institutionalization of people with physical and mental disabilities, all of which aimed to limit or eliminate a person's or an entire people's reproductive capacities based on a metric of "fitness." Eugenics was a practice of socially engineering populations through policy and technology in order to propagate good genes (positive eugenics) and eliminate bad genetic strains (negative eugenics). As poor and institutionalized women in the 1920s and 1930s were sterilized to prevent them from having children, affluent white women were targeted with propaganda urging them to procreate (Gordon, 1976; Haller, 1963; Kevles, 1995; Moreno, 2011). As a technique of *biopower*, the function of eugenics in the late nineteenth and early twentieth centuries was not merely social engineering but also discipline and regulation of the individual and social body (Foucault, 1978).

In the first decades of the twentieth century, policymakers, social workers, birth-control advocates, and other eugenicists lamented the number of babies being born to poor, immigrant, and non-white women. Affluent white women, in turn, were accused of committing "race suicide" by practicing birth control and limiting the numbers of children they bore; the fate of the American population rested in their wombs (Gordon, 1976). Although one may seem more benign than the other, both positive and negative eugenics are grounded in the same ideology that labels some members of the population worthy of reproduction, and others worthy of elimination; they are two sides of the same coin, shaping such modern-day practices as sperm banking and genetic testing, and other areas of reproductive medicine (Duster, 2003; Moore, 2007; Parthasarathy, 2004; Rothschild, 2005).

Eugenics exemplifies a convergence of science, technology, race, and sexuality through embodied practices. The popularity of eugenics and its most repressive tactics faded in the wake of World War II and developments in the social and biological sciences, but eugenics has never really left us; rather, it has manifested in new and subtler forms. In Troy Duster's terminology, eugenics now enters through the back door (Duster, 2003). Contemporary debates about genetic screening, euthanasia, disability rights, and welfare reform may point us towards the ways that fears of a eugenic reprisal linger in our consciousness. The history of eugenics has surely influenced many of the policies outside of the United States that ban or highly regulate particular assisted fertility services such as PGD and sex selection.

Affluent and middle-class women at the turn of the twenty-first century are sometimes accused of being selfish for putting their careers first and delaying childbirth. Yet, what science has contributed to our modern-day Cult of True Womanhood is the ability for motherhood to transcend the limits of biology and the aging body: through the wonders of reproductive technology, a woman can rise in the ranks of her profession and still be able to experience the (medical) miracle of childbirth. As Angela Davis writes,

> The new reproductive medicine sends out a message to those who are capable of receiving it: motherhood lies just beyond the next technology. The consequence is an ideological compulsion toward a palpable goal: a child one creates either via one's own reproductive activity or via someone else's.
>
> (1993, p. 360)

Many reproductive technologies are linked to this power to facilitate the birth of children to certain classes of women—and thus its arguable linkage with new forms of positive eugenics. See, for example, the recent string of *New York Times Magazine* first-person narratives written by upper- and upper-middle-class white women relying on costly IVF and third-party reproduction in their struggles against infertility (Kuczynski, 2008; Orenstein, 2007; Thernstrom, 2010).

In many respects, reproductive technologies are seemingly innocuous practices that help the infertile to have biological children, with no concrete relationship to last century's state-sanctioned eugenics movement involving large populations. They involve market-oriented transactions, mediated not by the state but by private agencies and medical clinics, in order to facilitate the birth of individual children, what sociologist Barbara Katz Rothman (2001) calls "microeugenics." These differences notwithstanding, we can trace a lingering ideological and discursive thread from twentieth-century eugenic practices to twenty-first-century forms of reproductive and genetic technologies. This lingering thread is *heritability,* which attempts to account for the variance within a given population by inherited genetic traits (Duster, 2003; Kevles, 1995). In decades past, traits such as intelligence, promiscuity, poverty, and criminality were believed to be heritable qualities passed down through one's genes; this belief was linked with biological determinism and the idea that biology is destiny. The ideological backdrop of biological determinism and Social Darwinism served to justify the sterilization and institutionalization of tens of thousands of people in the United States—and the mass murder of millions in Europe—in the first half of the twentieth century. If heritability of traits was the theory, eugenics was the practice.

Theories of biological determinism did not disappear with the demise of the popular eugenics movement; rather, they have continued to flourish in new ways, conjoined with advances in science and technology. It is through technology, some would argue, that we can finally wrest destiny out of the hands of biology. New projects in the fields of science and medicine have similar—though clearly less sinister—goals, as did eugenic programs from the previous century; scientists aim to learn what our genes have to tell us, and with that knowledge, to gain power over our destiny and over life itself. Thus, when reproductive scientists screen embryos and fetuses for genetic defects, or fertility clinics advertise the stellar qualities of their egg donors, implicit in these practices is the idea that our genetic material is ripe with useful and identifiable knowledge that can be manipulated to alter and improve us.

Donna Haraway identifies a "gene fetishism" within contemporary bioscience and biotechnology, wherein the gene is valued as a thing in and of itself, separate from the body and its processes (1997, pp. 141–148). We do not have to take too far a leap to see how easily a woman's ova—bundles of genetic material in themselves—can become fetishized and commodified. The value of her eggs may be explicitly tied to the value of her genetic material—the "goodness" of her heritable traits. Yet, how does one quantify the value of a woman's genetic material, the fitness of her oocytes? If her ova have a story to tell about ancestral history and genetic destiny, then we need a feasible way to decipher what those gametes are telling us. At the same time the gene is fetishized as a thing in and of itself—the part standing in for, and apart from, the whole—it is the woman *in her totality*, a sort of reverse metonymy, that also comes to stand in for the eggs she carries. Similarly, preimplantation genetic diagnosis allows technicians to peek microscopically at the genetic information of embryos, one step in a process that will determine the fate of that embryo.

The marketing, provision, and consumption of assisted reproductive technologies do not exist within a vacuum. Rather, practices such as surrogacy tourism, egg donation and egg freezing, and sex selection are overdetermined by a number of structural, technological, and ideological factors. These independent variables include the contemporary manifestations of global capitalism and neoliberalism, scientific advancement and innovation, the biomedicalization of reproduction, and what I refer to here as the "genetic imperative." What is it that drives the extraordinary financial, geographic, and technological ends that individuals undergo to get pregnant, give birth to or take home a child?

By "genetic imperative" I mean both the individual drive *and* the cultural mandate to have genetically related children, to "reproduce" oneself, regardless of whether that desire is evolutionarily hard-wired or culturally produced (cf. Cronk & Gerkey, 2007; Dawkins, 2006; Freedman, 1979; Haraway, 1991; Lancaster, 2003; Wilson, 2000). Another way to frame the genetic imperative beyond the nature/culture debate is as an ideology or discourse. That is, what are the social or discursive effects of this line of genetic thinking? Who is espousing it? To what ends is this discourse used? Who profits from it? Who is burdened by it? What are the power relations embedded within it? In this sense, it does not matter if the genetic imperative is a result of instinct, socialization, or some combination of the two.

From a sociological standpoint, the genetic imperative has meaningful consequences for our senses of self, the choices we make, and our ideas about what is or is not possible and purposeful. As French sociologist Pierre Bourdieu (1984) might put it, the genetic imperative is a "structuring structure," framing and molding our habits, our desires, and our actions in culturally distinct ways. For example, not being able to reproduce "naturally" can be a source of stigma in societies that view having biologically related children as a necessary and desirable life process in the path to full adulthood. This is especially so for women who, feminists have argued, have been both *biologically* and *morally* tied to reproductive roles. In her classic feminist polemic, Shulamith Firestone (1970) argues that patriarchal societies use the biological fact of women's bodies and capacities for reproduction as a means to shackle them into roles as breeders and mothers. Adrienne Rich speaks of the moral imperatives attached to mothering, and condemns the idea that motherhood is a "sacred calling" for women (1986, p. 42). Both authors contribute to a wide feminist literature on the nature of compulsory motherhood, the idea that procreation is not a choice made by each individual woman, but that it is an ideology prescribed and compelled.

At the same time, given histories of eugenics and reproductive control, it is impossible to state that motherhood is mandatory for *all* women; rather, women's reproductive choices have long been defined by wider societal goals and actors. Indeed, history bears out that motherhood is only valued (or indeed compulsory) for certain classes of women, and that for some, the drive to reproduce must be stamped out or disincentivized (Collins, 2000; Flavin, 2008; Gordon, 1976; Roberts, 1997; Smith-Rosenberg, 1986; Solinger, 2000). Eugenics and Social Darwinism, after all, were movements that expressed fears of any innate genetic imperative that would lead people to "selfishly" reproduce themselves regardless of their contribution to the human gene pool.

Apart from the feasibility of some evolutionary drive, compulsory motherhood and the genetic imperative are culturally prescribed and reinforced by family pressures, the media, and institutional and political barriers to alternative family formation. If one is a member of a class compelled or encouraged to have biological children, but is in the situation of not being able to reproduce via heterosexual intercourse, either because of a biomedical condition (i.e. infertility), or because of one's relationship status (i.e. single or in a same-sex relationship), assisted reproductive technologies (ART) may help one fulfill that mandate. The fertility industry operates to support and uphold the genetic imperative for certain classes of people, and in the process both relieves and reinforces the stigma of childlessness and infertility.

As a "structuring structure," the genetic imperative produces a normative mode of parenting that reifies the genetic relatedness between parent and child over other relations of kinship (L. J. Martin, 2010). Those who are infertile, single, and/or gay may be stigmatized for not being able to fulfill this genetic imperative. Prior to the widening awareness and availability of reproductive technologies, these categories of people may have experienced a legitimate "out" or "excuse" for their inability to have genetically related children without medical intervention (Mamo, 2007). Today, the genetic imperative even holds for those individuals whose parenting is typically marginalized by their relationship status or sexual orientation, such that if single people or lesbian or gay couples strive to have children, assisted reproductive technologies allow them to fulfill this goal without resorting to adoption. In this respect, we see the co-constructive relationship between reproductive technologies and the genetic imperative. Scientists and physicians have innovated reproductive technologies to enable the infertile, single people, lesbians, and gay men to have genetically related children. The development of these technologies is in direct response to the genetic imperative and the desire/drive to continue the genetic line of at least one of the intended parents.

Once the technology exists, those who previously might have resigned themselves to childlessness or who would have become parents through other means such as adoption are now no longer absolved from the genetic imperative. The technology itself becomes prescriptive, even as it remains financially out of reach for many. This is not to be technologically determinist, but to point out how technology is both laden with and creates norms and values. The co-construction of technology and ideology problematizes norms about "natural" parenting. Although reproductive technologies such as IVF faced much public backlash when they were initially developed and successfully implemented, they have entered the public consciousness as available means of parenting and procreation, at least for those who can afford it or whose insurance covers it (Henig, 2004).[2] Furthermore, if the genetic imperative—that is, the drive to have genetically related children—is described as something "only natural," then the use of artificial means to achieve this imperative also becomes bound up with the natural. Isn't it "only natural" that a parent would want to be genetically related to his or her offspring? What is more natural than a family with shared DNA?

The genetic imperative to have a genetically related child is related to, but distinct from, the biological imperative to have a biologically related child. Assisted reproductive technologies enable intended parents to achieve one, if not both, of these demands. For men, either imperative is genetically based, but for women, this biological imperative speaks to a relation born of DNA *or* blood; it is about inheritance *or* nurturance (Rothman, 2000). Prior to the advent of reproductive technologies, there was no need to separate out these two aspects of biological relatedness. For women, to have a biological child was to nurture a child *in utero* that was implicitly "your own." Today, women who cannot "naturally" conceive and/or gestate a child have a number of options that enable their biological motherhood. Ideas about the possibility of parenting via technology are transmitted to and known even by those living in countries that forbid this use of technology.

## Race, Nation, and the Genetic Imperative

The drive for genetic continuity is not merely an individualized phenomenon, but is bound up with notions of nationhood, culture, race, ethnicity, and religion. In Benedict Anderson's (1991) famous formulation, there is an "imagined" quality to people's conceptions of themselves as members of nations and other communities, and part of the mythmaking involved in the creation of nationalist sentiments is about the relatedness of its people. We can point to many instances throughout history and today, of pronatalist policies in Israel, for example, that urge Jewish Israeli citizens to procreate at the behest of their nation (Kahn, 1998), or of rape being used as a tool of genocide in civil conflicts (Das, 1995; Sharlach, 2000). In these cases we see the commingling of nationalist and racialized ideologies of *blood* and *genes*.

These examples point to another aspect of the genetic imperative that goes beyond the evolutionary perspective that this "drive" to reproduce oneself is part of natural selection; this is the idea that contained within the strands of DNA are bits of information that not only bind parent to offspring, of nation to citizen, but that will determine the outcome of that child. Built into the genetic imperative is the ideology of genetic determinism. When it comes to assisted reproductive technologies, the latter ideology may at times substitute for the first. For example, in the case of egg donation, the genetic imperative on the individual female line is obviously not being fulfilled, since it is the genetic code of the egg donor that will be passed on. Yet, genetic determinism becomes a substitute for the genetic imperative, shaping how a particular donor is chosen. As I describe below, those traits are often coded in terms of race, ethnicity, and nation, in addition to phenotypic markers of appearance.

The genetic imperative is not always about passing on one's *own* genetic material. Sometimes it is about passing on the genetic material of one who is racially, ethnically, or phenotypically similar. Packed within the genetic imperative is the idea that genes *matter*, that they are *knowable, racialized*, and *transferable*. If one can't pass on one's own genetic material, the next best thing is, perhaps, to have some control over whose genes *will* be passed on. Whether one uses one's own gametes or that of a donor, the ideology of the genetic imperative is that genetics is destiny, that we can make an educated guess about a potential child's appearance, temperament, abilities, behavior, health, size, intelligence, and so on, by two routes: either by assessing the individuals whose gametes are to mingle (*in vivo* or *in vitro*), or by screening the DNA of embryos.

Egg donation and PGD share many worrisome similarities with old fashioned eugenic practices: both encourage and enable elite women to become mothers and raise children; seek to produce children with desirable and superior qualities while screening out less than desirable traits—and inform us about just what constitutes that fitness or desirability; share the belief that both desirable and undesirable traits can be transmitted through one's genes; and use science and technology as both the instrument and justification for the practice. Both also have an unmistakable racialized and classed narrative, in which the "fittest" genes are frequently those that belong to the white and the privileged.

In the marketplace for selective technologies, the biology-as-destiny equation that drove earlier eugenic practices still lingers, as does the desire to manipulate that equation through the uses of money and technology. We should not minimize the emotions and imperatives that drive the demand for assisted fertility services, but we must also take care not to minimize its potential eugenic implications in socially engineering populations. The use of assisted reproductive technologies is driven in part by reproductive and genetic imperatives, both of which are means to mitigate risk and maintain control. There is, obviously, no way to *know* what a baby is going to be like or how it is going to turn out. It is, therefore, a risk people take when they decide to parent, whether that be through "natural" reproduction, assisted fertility, or fostering/adoption. There is always an element of the unknown.

Technologies today, however, attempt to mitigate those risks, to give the consumers of the technology, that is, the intended parents, some modicum of control over the "product." That can be by either using one's own genetic material, intense screening of donors' genetic material, and/or the manipulation of genetic material by assessing, ranking, and selecting the quality of gametes and embryos. This screening and assessing is taking place on a global scale, enabled by reproductive tourism for selective purposes.

## THE GLOBAL REGULATORY LANDSCAPE

Policies that regulate, restrict, limit, or ban reproductive technologies act as push factors for reproductive tourism. Such policies include restrictions on types of services, bans or limits on compensation for third parties, and guidelines regarding age, sexual orientation, and marital status of intended parents. Sperm and egg donation are widely regulated worldwide, and in some countries banned (Jones et al., 2010, pp. 43–62). A number of nations have statutes or guidelines forbidding paying donors, require that donors' information be kept in registries, restrict how many offspring or donation cycles are allowed per donor, and/or prohibit anonymous gamete donation. Such restrictions on gamete donation correlate with donor shortages in those countries (Jones et al., 2010, pp. 43–62).

Preimplantation genetic diagnosis (PGD), which involves screening *in vitro* embryos for the absence or presence of specific genetic traits, is not globally accepted as an ethical practice (Pavone & Arias, 2012). Some countries ban PGD outright, others regulate its use as a means to screen for chromosomal abnormalities, allow PGD only to screen for specific diseases, or prohibit its use for sex selective purposes (Jones et al., 2010, pp. 95–106). PGD enables carriers of sex-linked genetic diseases, such as hemophilia or fragile-X syndrome, to select for girls because they are far less likely to be affected (WHO Genomic resource centre, 2011). A socially ambiguous use of sex selection is for the so-called "gender balancing" of one's offspring (McGowan & Sharp, 2012; Sharp et al., 2010). Even more controversial is sex selection as a mere matter of preference, indicated by the global tendency to select *for* boys and *against* girls (Guilmoto, 2007; Hvistendahl, 2011; Sen, 2003). Austria, New Zealand, and South Korea ban sex selection for any purpose, and several other countries, including Germany, France, and the United Kingdom, ban any "social" uses of sex selection, including gender balancing (BioPolicyWiki, 2009). In addition to PGD, several countries ban the use of sperm-sorting technology for sex-selective purposes (Jones et al., 2010, pp. 127–131).

The United States government does not ban or limit gamete donation, PGD, or sex selection, but the Food and Drug Administration (FDA) and Centers for Disease Control and Prevention (CDC) have established guidelines regarding informed consent and the prevention of the spread of disease via human tissue transfer. Individual states may have their own sets of regulations or restrictions, or Department of Health guidelines. Additionally, providers may follow professional guidelines established by organizations such as the American Society for Reproductive Medicine (ASRM). In this relatively permissive regulatory climate, U.S. providers may offer selective technologies and services to domestic consumers as well as to those intended parents who live in more restrictive countries. Countries have a variety of reasons for instituting bans and restrictions on reproductive technologies. Such factors include religious doctrines about the moral status of embryos or when life begins, ethical orientations informed by histories of eugenics, attitudes about the commodification of human bodies and body parts, the rights of offspring to know about their genetic origins, and medico-scientific protocols regarding informed consent and laboratory procedures. Despite the presence of nation-wide prohibitions or regulations, all residents and citizens of a given country (including intended parents and fertility industry providers) may not personally agree with the normative principles underlying bans and regulations—or with the absence of bans and regulations.

Despite other nations' laws and policies, ideologies supportive of the use of selective technologies do not end at the United States' borders, and the globalization of communications, media, and transportation technologies enable their spread. Larger themes of genetic heritability and consumer choice are embedded in the U.S. fertility industry and transformed into marketing tools broadcast to appeal to foreign nationals unable to acquire the technologies, services, and reproductive materials they desire and demand. Understanding and analyzing attitudes of fertility industry providers in the United States matters because they work in a particular ethical context where they serve international clients who choose their services precisely because their own country's laws hinder their desire to use reproductive technologies as a means to select particular traits for their future offspring.

## SELECTIVE USES OF TECHNOLOGY IN THE UNITED STATES

In addition to a growing literature on reproductive tourism, several ethnographies have explored attitudes of the primary agents involved in the buying and selling of fertility services, including fertility industry providers, intended parents, surrogates, and gamete donors. Researchers provide accounts from the perspectives of surrogates (Pande, 2012; Ragone, 1994; Teman, 2010), gamete donors (Almeling, 2011), and intended parents who used or considered using various technologies, including prenatal testing (Rapp, 2000; Rothman, 1993), sex selection (McGowan & Sharp, 2012; Sharp et al., 2010), surrogacy (Teman, 2010), IVF (Becker, 2000; Franklin, 1997; Thompson, 2005), and PGD (Franklin & Roberts, 2006). Attitudes of fertility clinic providers regarding reproductive technologies and genetic counseling have also been extensively studied. Almeling (2011), for example, studied the selling of gametes by interviewing sperm and egg donors and people who work in clinics, egg agencies, and sperm banks. She found gendered differences in the recruiting practices of agencies and banks, requiring, for example, more "altruistic" motives on the part of women than of men (Almeling, 2011, pp. 36–37).

Scholars in the United Kingdom also studied the attitudes of clinicians and genetic counselors offering PGD, sex selection, and other assisted fertility services (Ehrich, Farsides, Williams, & Scott, 2007; Ehrich, Williams, Farsides, Sandall, & Scott, 2007; Franklin & Roberts, 2006; Frith, Jacoby, & Gabbay, 2011; Frith, 2009). Ehrich, Williams, et al (2007) found that clinic workers experience dilemmas around such "gray areas" as when parents using PGD inadvertently learn the sex of their embryos and want to use this knowledge to select for sex; although workers want to present intended parents with information and options, this imperative does not always align with their personal ethics regarding sex selection (nor with the U.K. prohibition of sex selection for non-medical purposes). In another study, researchers found that many clinic workers see PGD as a good alternative to prenatal diagnosis to the benefit of intended parents *and* to the workers themselves, as workers experience less moral ambivalence about the destruction of embryos than with the termination of a fetus with genetic abnormalities (Ehrich, Farsides, et al., 2007). This orientation regarding the moral status of embryos aligns clinic workers in the United Kingdom with those in Israel, but not necessarily those in Germany (Hashiloni-Dolev & Weiner, 2008). As Hashiloni-Dolev and Weiner (2008) argue in their comparative study, differences in the history, culture, religion, and politics of Germany and Israel lead to differences in the ethical orientation of clinic workers concerning the status of the embryo as an autonomous rights-bearing being or as an entity that is not independent of its relational status to its family (see also Habermas, 2003; Jasanoff, 2005).

Building on the argument made by Hashiloni-Dolev and Weiner about clinic workers in Israel and Germany, I draw on provider interviews to show evidence for a shared American cultural and ethical perspective. The shared perspective of U.S. providers not only shapes their industry but it also impacts the global reach of American attitudes and ethics regarding reproductive technologies. By focusing on the attitudes of U.S. providers regarding the use of selective reproductive technologies by domestic and international clientele, this chapter combines several streams of literature, including analyses of reproductive tourism, ethnographies of assisted fertility, and studies (largely outside the U.S.) about the attitudes of clinic workers. Although my informants express a variety of beliefs about the ethics of using genetic diagnosis to select for sex or other traits, most are supportive of using selective criteria, including race and status markers, to recruit, screen, and match egg donors. Further, the providers largely accept the lack of federal regulation of ARTs.

Technologies and practices that enable intended parents to "select" traits in future offspring—egg donation, sex selection, and PGD—are highly regulated if not banned in many countries, leading many of my informants' international clients to seek their services.

Providers discussed their experiences working with both domestic and international clientele. When asked what percentage of their clients come from abroad, answers varied greatly, from a mere 1%–2% for a physician in San Francisco to a claim of 60% by a Los Angeles doctor, with an overall average of 25%.[3] According to my informants, many of their international clients seek services such as egg donation, gestational surrogacy, and sex selection that are illegal or difficult to obtain in their own countries.

Fertility industry providers in the United States are able to capitalize on the restrictions on gamete donation that exist worldwide. Unlike countries where selling ova is outlawed, egg "donation" in the United States is largely a commercial enterprise, not an altruistic one. In the U.S. egg market, young women may legally sell their ova for any agreed-upon price, with the current market rate set at approximately $8,000 per cycle. They are recruited by fertility clinics and egg donation agencies, and may also market themselves directly to intended parents. The egg market is heterogeneous, reflecting the size and diversity of the United States. However, all ova are not equal or equally desired: prospective donors are assessed by clinics, agencies, and intended parents. Although egg donation may have begun as a primarily *assistive* technology, in the context of the U.S. fertility industry it has also transformed into a *selective* technology (Spar, 2006, p. 42).

The genetic imperative as it relates to genetic determinism is invoked by a common practice in which gamete donors are extensively screened for their physical and mental health, educational background, artistic and athletic talents, and ethnicity. The power of genetics is also invoked in screening practices of PGD, in which genetic traits are selected or, more commonly, screened out prior to implantation. In both cases, an emphasis is placed on using science to select for particular traits seen as transmissible through DNA, rather than rely on narratives about the fate of children resulting from the luck of the draw or cultural rearing.

Brokers recruit young women via college newspapers, Craigslist, and their own websites, frequently specifying desired qualities such as SAT scores, hair color, talents, and race/ethnicity. Robin, owner of a Los Angeles agency, spoke in her interview about the need to be "always recruiting donors to provide the best available out there for [clients]." Megan, marketing director of an L.A. egg donation agency, acknowledged recruiting specific ethnic populations in order to appeal to intended parents of that particular background: "Like, oh, we don't have any Armenian donors. I need to get us some Armenian donors."

Not all applicants for donation are accepted. Applicants over thirty years old are often rejected outright because of age-related decline in ova quality, as are smokers and overweight donors. Egg brokers typically meet prospective donors in person or via Skype, and at some programs and clinics, the screening may extend to physical exams, bloodwork, genetic screening, psychological evaluations, and collection of family histories regarding alcoholism and mental disorders. Clinics and agencies emphasize a *marketability* approach to their donor recruitment and selection. As Megan informed me, "A lot of the times [intended parents] want somebody who's bright. And we work with a lot of models and actresses, and they get chosen all the time. So basically, *we look for candidates that people would really choose*" (emphasis added). When asked why clients—especially those coming from abroad—choose to work with them, several providers remarked upon the "quality" of their donors, implying that they or their agencies are particularly adept at assessing and evaluating the genetic potential of young women.

Prospective egg donors are subjected to a holistic process in which agencies and clinics create a biography that includes physical description, social history, medical history, family background, and race/ethnicity. In creating an individual biography of each egg donor, the screening process surveils, objectifies, documents, and codifies each donor as an individual "case" (Foucault, 1995). As a result, fertility brokers exercise power as they seek to gain knowledge about and judge the potential egg donor, ultimately producing a normative subject whose biography can be marketed and consumed. Because they cannot ascertain the adequacy of each donor's eggs by merely looking at her, they use the application to assess the intimate details of her genetic, social, familial, and medical biography. This information is presented to intended parents by fertility clinics and agencies through donor directories that typically include photographs and detailed descriptions. Intended parents who live abroad do not need to visit a clinic or agency in person to select a donor, since most of this information is catalogued and available to them over the Internet, free of charge. Catalogues and advertisements remarking on sterling qualities of egg donors only feed into the desires of prospective parents to breed a certain caliber of child. Demand for donors with advanced degrees, musical ability, and Ivy League pedigrees implies that these markers of class and rearing are genetically transmissible; *cultural* capital is thus a manifestation of, and shorthand for, *genetic* capital. Egg donors' genetic capital becomes a marketable commodity, with their cultural capital as convenient shorthand.

Those who work for these organizations are not ignorant of the implications of ranking donors by intelligence, grade point averages, or subjective criteria such as beauty. Megan explained the large number of egg donor agencies in Los Angeles with the presence of so many aspiring actresses who turn to egg donation to supplement their income. These beautiful, ambitious donors, she said, are likely to be chosen: "Kind of the creepy thing about egg donation is that a lot of people will just choose a beautiful donor." Whereas some of Megan's clients care less about physical appearance than they do about how "nice" the donor is, others, who she described as "Ivy Leaguers," enquire about donors' test scores and degrees. This is not, of course, limited only to international clients; rather, the qualities highlighted by egg donation programs and demanded by clients take on an almost flattened, universal appeal.

Research on gamete donation in the United States shows how particular traits, such as race, are used to select egg and sperm donors, but what I wish to highlight is how this kind of selection extends beyond American consumers (e.g. Almeling, 2011; Moore, 2007; Roberts, 2011). Globalization enables U.S. providers to market the quality of their donors to intended parents worldwide. This marketing is evident on many fertility program websites, such as Donor Concierge (Donor Concierge, 2013), based in California, which has a special page for "International Services," advertising their ability to help "intended parents from around the world find an egg donor and/or surrogate in the United States to help create their family. . . . We have access to more U.S. egg donor and surrogate databases than anyone in the world. Donor Concierge is your best bet for finding the donor or surrogate who most closely fits your requirements." The website of a fertility clinic in Florida (another destination for reproduction tourism), lists "unique benefits for patients from other countries" including the "ability to provide an anonymous egg donor where the patients can view photos and extensive background profiles. Many countries limit the information available to patients. In addition, we have a large pool of egg donors because in Florida donors can be compensated for their time and efforts" (Fertility Center & Applied Genetics of Florida, n.d., para. 4). By traveling to the United States for gamete donors, international clientele have a much larger and more "elite" pool of donors to select from.

The donor matching process in the United States was also touted as a competitive advantage by providers. Intended parents are not matched willy-nilly with whichever donor is next in line; rather, as I describe below, the biographical data compiled about each prospective donor is used to *individually select* the donor deemed most appropriate, which my informants saw as an advantage compared to programs in other countries. This individual selection is particularly interesting given that every provider involved in egg donation mentioned the same criteria used to match donors with intended parents: race/ethnicity and resemblance. Race/ethnicity is a primary factor, according to Liz, egg donor coordinator at a clinic in New York City: "So if we have someone who's Caucasian, and Italian, or Mediterranean or something, we'd go that way, and if they're Western European, or if they're Russian, or Northern European . . . we try to stick to the demographics." By choosing a program in the United States, international clientele have access to a diverse roster of egg donors, as indicated on the Donor Concierge (2013) page, which boasts the ability to find donors with "the ethnic background that will fit your family" and "have the physical characteristics that you are looking for." As Liz succinctly put it, "[Coming] to the United States, you have every possibility of finding someone that looks like you." Anne, employee of a Los Angeles surrogacy agency, was even more blunt; although India is a popular destination in the surrogacy market, the pluralism of the United States gives it greater potential to tap into the egg donor market. If people go to India for assisted fertility and they "need an egg donor, you've got one kind. It's called Indian."

Race/ethnicity matching assumes that there is some genetic basis of race and ethnicity, or that by matching intended parents with donors of similar ancestral background, the gametes purchased will come from a similar gene pool (Roberts, 2011). Matching by race or ethnicity in some cases serves as a weak proxy for selecting egg donors who resemble the intended mother. Rather than advertise for a donor with olive skin and dark hair, recruiters may state that they are seeking a donor of "Italian" or "Mediterranean" descent, as if all Italians have those same physical characteristics.

Providers offer this approximate matching as a cover for people wishing to hide their use of an egg donor, or to facilitate offspring being able to better "blend in" with the rest of the family. Robin, for example, said "I find that the women a lot of times want to pretend that they never did this. And, they just don't want to think about what they had to do to get here. This is their child, and the rest of it is just magic." Robin spoke about "women" in general, not differentiating between her domestic and international clients. However, this kind of dissemblance is less possible in countries that ban anonymous donation, require donor registries, and uphold the right of offspring to know about their genetic parentage. Regardless of the clients' country of origin, this sort of matching by resemblance, even if it is not accompanied by magical thinking or deception, ultimately is an attempt to create physical continuity within a family, to approximate, as closely as possible, a genetic child. We are not replaceable, but we can come as close as possible by purchasing the gametes of our doppelgangers. According to Megan, clients "will look for people who look similar to them. You know, 'Here's pictures of all my family. Find somebody who looks just like this!'" Her coworker, who Megan described as having "a Rolodex in her mind," helps clients choose donors by suggesting ones with similar bone structure or other similarities. In addition to matching by race/ethnicity and appearance (hair and eye color, height and weight, facial features, etc.), some providers attempt to match personality and accomplishments. Liz and her team match by "shape, size, color, . . . body type, . . . skin tone and, I mean there are just a million little factors, and things, and you can tell personality, mannerisms, sometimes."

This matching process—one donor for one client—sets American clinics and agencies apart from their international competitors, and providers have come to normalize the practice without any policy mandate. In comparison, in Spain legislation requires gamete donor anonymity and confidentiality, does not allow for personal selection of donors, and stresses that donors selected by clinics should approximate intended mothers phenotypically and immunologically (European Society of Human Reproduction and

Embryology, 2006). Several informants expressed concern and even bafflement over rumors about how donors are matched with recipients in other countries. Liz's interpretation of a clinic in Spain was that, "Basically, they constantly stimulate [ovulation in] donors. They just don't stop. So they . . . have however many donors stimulating at the same time, and then the patients just kind of come in and, I don't think there's much matching that goes on." This is quite different from her own clinic and similar programs in the United States where "We match one recipient to one donor. It's just kind of like, [in Spain] they're constantly stimulating the donors, so whoever's next in line gets their oocytes. . . . It just seemed to me, the next person who walked in got the next donor's eggs that were retrieved, regardless of what they looked like."

Dr. Randolph spoke about the "bizarre" process that existed in Italy, before egg donation was banned: "Patients came back to this country who told me they had been there, and it was very bizarre to me. They would call them up and say, 'Okay, we have some eggs here. Come on down,' and then they'd say, 'Oh well, maybe these eggs aren't right,' you know, and you just wonder, what's the criteria for picking eggs, and what's the criteria for maintaining records, or knowing that this is a safe situation. You just really are concerned." Furthermore, he mused about the relative importance of selecting an egg from a particular donor:

> I guess if you go somewhere and they say, "Well, we're just going to give you an egg, and you'll get a baby," and you have no choice . . . maybe it doesn't matter. Who cares whether it came from one woman or a different woman? All you were going over there for was to get some eggs and hopefully have a baby. You had no say-so in who it was anyway. So maybe just shut up.

He contrasted this kind of matching process with how his and other clinics operate: "Here, in California, when you get an egg donor, the specific eggs you get belong to you. . . . They don't just take a random egg or any egg is okay."

Megan similarly expressed both concerns and ambivalence about selection practices in other countries. "It would be pretty nerve-wracking to be a recipient in the United Kingdom, because you don't know what egg you're getting. And it might not be a good one, and you've put your hopes into thinking it will work. And, you don't know if the woman that you're getting it from is in her 40s too." She equivocated, however, when she imagined herself as an intended parent: "I mean, personally, I wouldn't care, it could be kind of fun if you don't know what she looks like. You just get whatever you get! Which is great, but I think a lot of people struggle with the fact that they're not going to be able to have their own kids that they can pass their own self onto." Of course, by using an egg donor, the intended mother is not passing on any of her "genetic" self, but the mere act of having control over selecting a donor (particularly one who resembles the intended mother), rather than using a "random" egg, somehow helps compensate for that.

Even if providers did not know the precise laws about gamete donor matching in other countries, their perceptions of how clinics operate abroad informed how they viewed their own practice. Statements by Liz, Dr. Randolph, and Megan reveal how providers, most familiar with how practices are done in their region, justify their way as the best way. They also show how providers are not absolutely rigid about these methods, and when given space and time to think deeply about their practice, they can imagine other possibilities and justifications. Yet rather than adjust their process to align with practices in other parts of the world, providers heralded the American style of matching one donor to one recipient as an asset. What makes the United States exceptional in the fertility industry becomes a competitive advantage in the global marketplace. Eggs from U.S. donors cost much more than eggs in the United Kingdom, for example (approximately $8,000 versus $1,200 per cycle), but this higher price tag brings greater consumer choice over the "commodity" being purchased. Additionally, paying thousands of dollars to an American egg donor may symbolically indicate that recipients are purchasing high-quality ova.

Egg donation and other selective technologies are matters of "consumer sovereignty," in which consumers enjoy "freedom in the form of personal liberty" to which institutions must adjust to remain competitive (Slater, 1997, p. 35). The desire for a child (and, by proxy, an egg donor) who resembles the intended parents in appearance, educational background, personality, or hobbies, is not unique to Americans. Strathern, (1992) writing about the context of assisted reproduction in the United Kingdom, describes a "phantasia of options" in a British and European "Enterprise Culture" (p. 33): "One will no longer think one can do nothing about the sex of one's children, about birth abnormalities and the characteristics they will inherit, any more than one will be able to regard one's own endowment as a matter of fate. One's fate will be to put up with the results of other persons' enterprises" (Strathern, 1992, p. 40). Intended parents come to the United States to work with agencies and clinics that cater to desires for a particular kind of child/donor—desires that many government and clinic policies regarding egg donation abroad make difficult to fulfill.

In addition to the availability of egg donation as a selective technology, the United States is also a destination for PGD and sex selection. Formal laws and informal professional guidelines regulating PGD and sex selection do not necessarily stifle demand for the practice; instead, the market for them shifts to more favorable legal and political climates. Several informants cited sex selection as one of the primary reasons that they received inquiries from international clients. A physician at a Los Angeles clinic, for example, estimated about 60% of his clients were from overseas, and the majority of them (about 80%) were coming to him precisely for sex selection: "It's illegal everywhere, it's legal here, they come in."

PGD and sex selection are both legal in the United States, but every fertility program does not offer these services. As a largely unregulated industry, professionals maintain the right to determine whether or not they will provide any service, deciding on a case-by-case basis or by blanket policy. What providers identify as normative practice is also subject to shifts over time. For example, Dr. Gorman, a New York physician, spoke of the influence of his professional organization in shifting the acceptance of sex selection for non-medical reasons within the industry:

> They really raised the whole issue of gender selection in our profession by issuing a policy that for the first time raised the concept of elective gender selection for family balancing purposes as an ethically acceptable option. Until then, the broad mainstream of us in the specialty thought, nobody wanted to deal with gender selection. It was actually the organization that raised it.

As the professional norms regarding PGD and sex selection change, so may the attitudes of providers.

## PROVIDERS' ATTITUDES TOWARDS SELECTION

The generally permissive attitude of the United States federal government towards assisted reproduction makes it amenable to intended parents worldwide who seek selective technologies to increase their chances of having (or avoiding having) children with particular genetic qualities or traits by way of egg donation and/or PGD. As described previously, it is standard practice in the United States to use selective criteria to recruit, screen, and match egg donors. Most informants did not express any major problem or concern with this practice, and had reservations about other nations' abilities to match donors.

Egg donation in the United States is imbued with a certain *genetic* understanding of kinship (Harrington, Becker, & Nachtigall, 2008). Egg donation breaks the genetic line between intended mother and child, yet fertility industry professionals work to make this break as invisible as possible by matching intended mothers with donors who resemble them or have similar ethnic backgrounds. Even when this kind of matching is not the explicit goal, the recruiting and selecting process uses criteria that filter, sort, and rank egg donors by desirable traits and behaviors that are not necessarily genetic or heritable, but are at the very least marketable. By promoting the superior qualities of their donors and/or matching their domestic and international clients with donors who are superficially similar, clinics and brokers reify genetic determinist ideas about heritability.

Yet, people employed within the fertility industry are not ignorant of the probabilistic nature of genetics, or the influence of environmental factors.

This is evident in how they described cases where their clients assumed direct correlation between traits they desired in their children and traits they demanded of their egg donors. Deirdre, a San Francisco family law attorney with a social work background, described how she tries to educate her clients about the realities of assisted fertility and genetics: "We talk about . . . what they're really looking for. If they're looking for a clone of themselves, there's usually a detour to discuss that, and to discuss expectations of what a child produced will be." Deirdre saw it as part of her job to convey to intended parents that having children always involves risk, and that technology cannot be used to completely control the process or to create "an idealized person."

> You're not using "master gametes," so to speak, to make the person you have in your mind. [They should] recognize that this child, no matter what gametes are used, and what the attributes are of the genetic materials of the people that have contributed to them, . . . may still be the black sheep of the family. . . . What if this kid is just typical and normal? "Oh my god. I wanted a boy, because I wanted him to be six foot tall, like John Wayne, and you're only five-ten. And you have red hair for god's sakes. How did that happen?"

Megan also worried about clients who assumed that an egg donor's traits would automatically be passed down to offspring. Couples sometimes demanded that donors have blue eyes and a certain type of nose, for example, or refused any donor that had acne or braces as a child. Like Deirdre, Megan was concerned about what would happen to children who do not turn out to be what the parents imagined they were creating. Megan found it "crazy" when people were "freakishly picky": "Are you going to love them less because they have green eyes, or brown eyes?" So concerned was she that she described the "slippery slope" from PGD to "genetically engineering a baby to look just the way they want," which "seems really Nazi to me."

Providers conveyed that their professional experience makes them more knowledgeable than their clients about the science behind reproductive technologies. This knowledge gap presents an opportunity to educate their clients. Liz, for example, articulated that if you educate those clients who walk in saying, "I want to do this and I want to do that," they would eventually back down and "self-regulate." Other informants, however, expressed frustration with unrealistic expectations. Selecting a particular donor does not automatically result in trait selection for one's child, but, as Rebekah put it, it is merely a matter of "upping your odds." As her business partner Shelby continued with the gambling metaphor, "By the roll of the dice, your [child's] DNA may end up with [those qualities] or not." It is a contradiction when brokers market the qualities of their donors to clients, as if it is these qualities themselves, and not the base genetic material, that is the product being sold to them, yet get upset when their clients think that they can design their own children.

In addition to some wary but contradictory attitudes towards egg donation as a selective technology, a number of providers disapproved of sex selection, particularly for non-medical reasons. Liz described a case where a potential client wanted to use IVF and PGD for sex selection even though there was no other medical indication for this treatment. The ethics committee turned her down because they believed the risks of surgery (which include compromising her fertility or even death) outweighed the desire for a child of a particular sex. Several others also expressed reservations about sex selection. New York physician Dr. Bradley, for example, said he is against people choosing to terminate a pregnancy because the fetus is of the "wrong sex," and has qualms against PGD being used for sex-selective purposes because it may bring about a gender imbalance in society. Robin also brought up "unfortunate" gender ratios:

> I think if you want a baby, you want a baby. Period. And to say, "I don't want a girl baby, I don't want a boy baby," or vice versa, you know—it hasn't worked out so well in China, has it? . . . It's all disproportionate. Oh, geez, surprise! We could have predicted that twenty years ago.

Even those providers with personal reservations about sex selection or non-medical uses of PGD did not want to see a ban imposed in the United States, however; they would rather leave it up to individual providers to decide whether or not to accept those clients. Providers viewed the provision and consumption of new reproductive technologies as something that should be negotiated between individuals—provider and client—rather than by legislation. As Rebekah put it, "The way it is now, if you're not able to get services in one place, you go somewhere else. That's what people are doing internationally. They're coming here. So, there's always that availability. For us, at this time, we self-regulate ourselves." Clients (domestic or international) who are turned down at one clinic can always take their business elsewhere. Drs. Leveque and Randolph, both working out of the same fertility clinic in California, in separate interviews expressed reservations about using technology to select traits such as deafness or to help a woman over the age of sixty-five to have a child, but both also applauded the "pluralistic" nature of the United States that allows them to refuse to provide services without completely closing off those patients' options.

Rather than merely turn clients away, some providers saw these cases as opportunities to steer clients towards choices they find more "appropriate." Dr. Maynard, a New York physician, stated:

> If the patient comes in and says, 'I'm interested in doing PGD because I want a boy and I have three girls already,' well, as a physician, you have to explain to the patient what are the cons of doing that. And you

have to guide the patient . . . in terms of what's right, what's wrong, and again, the patient has the right to choose what she wants to do or not.

Linda was more blunt about her disdain for sex selection for non-medical reasons:

> I'm sorry, you know, you don't need PGD. PGD is meant for testing for genetic issues that might come up for your ultimate goal, which is to have a baby. . . . It doesn't matter if it's a boy or a girl. . . . I have very strong issues with that.

She maintained that she tries to guide her clients to what she considers a more "moral" decision. Linda described a recent incident in which a couple inquired about sex selection: "I just blurted—usually I don't do that—I said, 'You don't even want to go there. You'll be lucky to have one biological healthy child, and that should be your goal right now.'" Providers did not universally disdain sex selection, however, even for non-medical reasons. Three providers informed me that they used sex-selective PGD when they had their own children.

More broadly, providers were accepting of PGD for medical reasons. Tammy, a social worker who consults for a California surrogacy agency, described PGD as an "invaluable invention" that "has a very important role in terms of ruling out horrible genetic disorders." Yet, similar to egg donation and sex selection, there is a line that some providers contend should not be crossed. Although PGD is largely used to reduce the risk of genetic disease, it may also be used to select *for* traits. Dr. Maynard was explicit about distinguishing between the two, stating, "We don't do PGD for special traits, we do PGD to detect genetic mutations." Many informants disapproved of its use by those who would use the technology to increase the likelihood of a child with "special traits" or by those who would select for embryos that carry a genetic trait for deafness or dwarfism. Similar to egg donation, providers expressed frustration—and sometimes amusement—about what their clients expect from technology. Jen, a genetic counselor at a New York clinic, laughed at the idea that reproductive scientists can create "designer babies":

> There are some things that people can choose to test for, certain conditions, whether it's screening for Down Syndrome, maybe eye color, things like that—sure. But . . . there's a lot of things that are really out of people's control, and I think that the technology will show us that. As more tests become available, . . . we'll learn more the limitations of what we still can't test for. And that we can't really play God, although that's what people think we are doing (*laughs*).

Without any regulations against the uses of PGD within the United States for non-medical reasons, market forces help determine the types of services that clinics offer. Dr. Silverstein of Los Angeles claimed that his clinic had developed technology to determine eye and hair color. However, after releasing this information to the media,

> The world went berserk. My publicist in New York called me up and said, "Doctor, the pope's talking about you." . . . So we said, okay, the world's not ready for this, and we just withdrew it. A huge media thing, designer babies. . . . Okay, fine, forget it.

As consumer demand increases, however—including the demand from overseas clients—Dr. Silverstein and others are prepared to offer these selective services.

## CONCLUSION: EUGENICS, MARKETING AND CONSUMER CHOICE

During the eugenics movement of the late nineteenth and early twentieth centuries, the "fitness" of individuals determined whether or not they were worthy of propagating their gene pool through reproduction. This belief about the fitness of individuals—and of entire populations—influenced by scientific and pseudoscientific theories about heredity, determined the course of positive and negative eugenic practices. In 1963, before the advent of IVF and most new reproductive technologies, historian Mark Haller wrote of the ways in which advances in the study of genetics was leading to a revived interest in eugenics: "[While] eugenists generally recognize that their movement currently has only minor influence and importance, they look forward to the day when man can, by bringing his genetic future under control, do much to make human life healthier and happier" (Haller, 1963, p. 189). Terms such as "homemade eugenics" (Kevles, 1995), "populist market eugenics" (Daniels & Golden, 2004), "microeugenics" (Rothman, 2001), and "backdoor eugenics" (Duster, 2003) indicate how contemporary genetic and reproductive technologies have introduced modified forms of eugenics. Genetic screening, prenatal sex selection, and egg donation all share characteristics of positive and negative eugenics: screening *out* the unfit, and selecting *for* desirable traits.

As a neo-eugenic practice, it is important to make note of how contemporary practices differ from earlier eugenic strategies. Egg donation, PGD, and sex selection are not compulsory, nor are they enforced by the state; in the United States, at least, they are largely unregulated market transactions. A laissez-faire approach is still an ideological approach, however, as noted by philosopher and ethicist Guido Pennings: "Neutrality of the state is impossible here. A nation without legislation on bioethical issues supports the liberal position that every citizen should decide according to his or her moral convictions" (2005, p. 121). Because it is not explicit social policy, the effect of these technologies is not overt manipulation or regulation of the social body. As quite expensive infertility treatments, they are available only to the few who can afford it. The material consequences of these selective reproductive technologies, even as a neo-eugenic practice, are not nearly as widespread as the popular eugenics campaigns of the first half of the twentieth century. However, the discursive and ideological consequences are just as rampant. It expands the categories of people who can now fulfill the personal drive and cultural imperative to have biological children at the same time its high price tag excludes others.

In the age of globalization, intended parents of means and privilege are not limited by culture or policy. Enterprise Culture, which Strathern (1992) describes as a consumerist orientation to procreation and kinship, is not regionally bound, and those intended parents who wish to enact this particular orientation regarding procreation may search for providers—in whatever country—who will help them on that path. Intended parents may express a desire for control over the reproductive process, hoping that their children's genetic outcomes can be determined or predicted through technology. However, these desires are not universally accepted, and the trend in many industrialized nations has been to clamp down on commercialization through regulations that prohibit or limit the ability of intended parents to pay for bodily materials or technologies that enable them to select or influence traits in future offspring. Those who reside in countries that forbid or highly regulate egg donation and PGD must put their own desires ahead of their countries' laws, and travel to less regulated jurisdictions to find brokers and clinics that will meet their needs.

Whether one uses one's own gametes or that of a donor, the ideologies of genetic determinism and consumer sovereignty converge in these selective technologies. Providers in the United States welcome international "consumers" to obtain selective technologies at their programs, and may simultaneously wrestle with the implications of these same technologies. Egg donors are recruited and selected by providers on the basis of what is believed to be most marketable to intended parents. At the same time, providers described how egg donor compensation or selection in other countries is frequently prohibited, leading to wait lists, shortages, and lack of variety in what they consider to be the "quality" of egg donors. The screening and matching process used by U.S. programs implies a correlation between an egg donor's qualities and the outcome of her genetic offspring's appearance, temperament, abilities, and behavior. Despite this implication of their marketing of egg donor qualities and selection, providers in the United States expressed frustration with clients who demanded particular traits in their donors as if these traits would automatically be regenerated in their offspring.

Providers also had a complex relationship with PGD which, unlike egg donation, is used more definitively to diagnose the DNA of embryos to screen out or select for sex or particular genetic conditions. PGD is frequently regulated, prohibited, or limited in other nations, particularly for sex-selective purposes. Most frequently, providers found unacceptable the use of PGD when it is not medically indicated, but this was not the case across the board, even for sex selection. Whereas some providers were completely against sex selection, others marketed it internationally or used the technology themselves.

Most interestingly, even if providers personally found the use of technology for selective purposes to be morally repugnant, they still appreciated that the United States fertility industry could offer services that are forbidden elsewhere. This attitude promotes the American fertility industry, because as long as the laws remain favorable towards technologies that other countries ban or highly regulate, the United States maintains an advantage as a destination for intended parents wanting to wager on selective technologies. A roster of "high quality" donors and access to PGD and sex selection are desired services that U.S. providers offer intended parents even though they cannot guarantee—and in fact often object to—fulfilling every demand that intended parents request.

By emphasizing the individual right of the consumer (regardless of residence or citizenship) to negotiate with an individual provider about what services will or will not be offered, my informants emphasized the *market* relationship between provider and client, and deemphasized the role of the state in governing that relationship. In contrast with how they viewed the regulatory landscape in their international clients' home countries, providers presented the United States fertility industry as a free marketplace that can meet the desires of intended parents worldwide. A market relationship is two sided, however. In its promotion of the quality of donors and the availability of selective technologies, the U.S. fertility industry not only meets global demand, it also shapes it.

## NOTES

An earlier version of this chapter appears in *Science, Technology & Human Values* 39(3): 432–455 (L. J. Martin, 2014).

1. The International Federation of Fertility Societies estimate that there are approximately 450 to 480 fertility centers in the United States (Jones et al., 2010). The American Society for Reproductive Medicine database of healthcare providers contains over 3500 entries (ASRM, "Find a Health Professional," 2013). These numbers do not include egg donor agencies, sperm banks, surrogacy agencies, or legal professionals who specialize in assisted reproduction.
2. See, for example, the growing number of Hollywood movies featuring assisted reproduction, such as *Baby Mama, The Kids Are All Right,* and *Then She Found Me,* and the tabloid stories about celebrities who have had children through the use of surrogates.
3. These were estimates made by informants during the interviews based on their personal recollections and may not match up precisely with official data collected by their programs.

# REFERENCES

Almeling, R. (2011). *Sex cells: The medical market for eggs and sperm.* Berkeley: University of California Press.

American Society for Reproductive Medicine (ASRM). (2013). *Find a health professional.* Retrieved from https://www.asrm.org/euclid/detail.aspx?id=2328

Anderson, B. (1991). *Imagined communities* (Rev. ed.). London: Verso.

Becker, G. (2000). *The elusive embryo: How women and men approach new reproductive technologies.* Berkeley: University of California Press.

BioPolicyWiki. (2009). Sex selection. *BioPolicyWiki.* Retrieved from www.biopolicy wiki.org/index.php?title=Sex_selection

Blyth, E. (2010). Fertility patients' experiences of cross-border reproductive care. *Fertility and Sterility, 94*(1), e11–e15.

Bourdieu, P. (1984). *Distinction: A social critique of the judgement of taste.* Cambridge, MA: Harvard University Press.

Collins, P. H. (2000). *Black feminist thought: Knowledge, consciousness, and the politics of empowerment.* New York: Routledge.

Cronk, L., & Gerkey, D. (2007). Kinship and descent. In R.I.M. Dunbar & L. Barrett (Eds.), *The Oxford handbook of evolutionary psychology* (pp. 463–478). Oxford: Oxford University Press.

Daniels, C. R., & Golden, J. (2004). Procreative compounds: Popular eugenics, artificial insemination and the rise of the American sperm banking industry. *Journal of Social History, 38*(1), 5–28.

Das, V. (1995). National honor and practical kinship: Unwanted women and children. In F. D. Ginsburg & R. Rapp (Eds.), *Conceiving the new world order: The global politics of reproduction* (pp. 212–233). Berkeley: University of California Press.

Davis, A. Y. (1993). Outcast mothers and surrogates: Racism and reproductive rights in the nineties. In L. S. Kauffman (Ed.), *American feminist thought at century's end: A reader* (pp. 355–366). Cambridge: Wiley-Blackwell.

Dawkins, R. (2006). *The selfish gene.* Oxford: Oxford University Press.

Donor Concierge. (2013). *International services.* Retrieved from www.donorconcierge. com/international/international-services/

Duster, T. (2003). *Backdoor to eugenics.* New York: Routledge.

Ehrich, K., Farsides, B., Williams, C., & Scott, R. (2007). Testing the embryo, testing the fetus. *Clinical Ethics, 2*(4), 181–186.

Ehrich, K., Williams, C., Farsides, B., Sandall, J., & Scott, R. (2007). Choosing embryos: Ethical complexity and relational autonomy in staff accounts of PGD. *Sociology of Health & Illness, 29*(7), 1091–1106.

European Society of Human Reproduction and Embryology. (2006). *Spanish legislation: Donor anonymity.* Retrieved from www.eshre.eu/ESHRE/English/Guidelines-Legal/Legal-documentation/Spain/Donor-anonymity/page.aspx/188

Fertility Center & Applied Genetics of Florida. (n.d.). *International patients.* Retrieved from www.geneticsandfertility.com/international-patients/

Firestone, S. (1970). *The dialectic of sex: The case for feminist revolution.* New York: Morrow.

Flavin, J. (2008). *Our bodies, our crimes: The policing of women's reproduction in America.* New York: New York University Press.

Foucault, M. (1978). *The history of sexuality: An introduction. Vol. 1.* New York: Vintage.

Foucault, M. (1995). *Discipline and punish: The birth of the prison.* New York: Vintage.

Franklin, S. (1997). *Embodied progress: A cultural account of assisted conception.* New York: Routledge.

Franklin, S., & Roberts, C. (2006). *Born and made: An ethnography of preimplantation genetic diagnosis.* Princeton, NJ: Princeton University Press.

Freedman, D. G. (1979). *Human sociobiology: A holistic approach.* New York: Free Press.

Frith, L. (2009). Process and consensus: Ethical decision-making in the infertility clinic—A qualitative study. *Journal of Medical Ethics, 35*(11), 662–667.

Frith, L., Jacoby, A., & Gabbay, M. (2011). Ethical boundary-work in the infertility clinic. *Sociology of Health & Illness, 33*(4), 570–585.

Gordon, L. (1976). *Woman's body, woman's right: A social history of birth control in America.* New York: Penguin Books.

Guilmoto, C. Z. (2007). *Sex-ratio imbalance in Asia: Trends, consequences and policy responses.* Hyderabad, India: UNFPA. Retrieved from www.unfpa.org/gender/case_studies.htm

Gupta, J. A. (2012). Reproductive biocrossings: Indian egg donors and surrogates in the globalized fertility market. *International Journal of Feminist Approaches to Bioethics, 5*(1), 25–51.

Habermas, J. (2003). *The future of human nature.* Cambridge: Polity Press.

Haller, M. H. (1963). *Eugenics: Hereditarian attitudes in American thought.* New Brunswick, NJ: Rutgers University Press.

Haraway, D. J. (1991). *Simians, cyborgs, and women: The reinvention of nature.* New York: Routledge.

Haraway, D. J. (1997). *Modest- witness@ second- Millennium. FemaleMan- Meets- OncoMouse: Feminism and technoscience.* New York: Routledge.

Harrington, J., Becker, G., & Nachtigall, R. (2008). Nonreproductive technologies: Remediating kin structure with donor gametes. *Science, Technology & Human Values, 33*(3), 393–418.

Hashiloni-Dolev, Y., & Weiner, N. (2008). New reproductive technologies, genetic counselling and the standing of the fetus: Views from Germany and Israel. *Sociology of Health & Illness, 30*(7), 1055–1069.

Henig, R. M. (2004). *Pandora's baby: How the first test tube babies sparked the reproductive revolution.* Boston, MA: Houghton Mifflin Harcourt.

Hvistendahl, M. (2011). *Unnatural selection: Choosing boys over girls, and the consequences of a world full of men.* New York: Public Affairs.

Jasanoff, S. (2005). *Designs on nature: Science and democracy in Europe and the United States.* Princeton, NJ: Princeton University Press.

Jones, H. W., Jr., Cooke, I., Kempers, R., Brinsden, P., & Saunders, D. (2010). IFFS surveillance 2010. *Fertility and Sterility.* Retrieved from www.iffs-reproduction.org/documents/IFFS_Surveillance_2010.pdf

Kahn, S. M. (1998). Putting Jewish wombs to work: Israelis confront new reproductive technologies. *Lilith, 23*, 30.

Kevles, D. J. (1995). *In the name of eugenics: Genetics and the uses of human heredity.* Cambridge, MA: Harvard University Press.

Kuczynski, A. (2008, November 30). Her body, my baby. *The New York Times.* Retrieved from www.nytimes.com/2008/11/30/magazine/30Surrogate-t.html?pagewanted=all

Lancaster, R. N. (2003). *The trouble with nature: Sex in science and popular culture.* Berkeley: University of California Press.

Mamo, L. (2007). *Queering reproduction: Achieving pregnancy in the age of technoscience.* Durham, NC: Duke University Press.

Markens, S. (2012). The global reproductive health market: U.S. media framings and public discourses about transnational surrogacy. *Social Science & Medicine (1982), 74*(11), 1745–1753.

Martin, L. J. (2010). Anticipating infertility: Egg freezing, genetic preservation, and risk. *Gender & Society, 24*(4), 526–545.

Martin, L. J. (2014). The world's not ready for this globalizing selective technologies. *Science, Technology & Human Values, 39*(3), 432–455. doi:10.1177/0162243913516014

McGowan, M. L., & Sharp, R. R. (2012). Justice in the context of family balancing. *Science, Technology & Human Values, 38*(2), 271–293.

Moore, L. J. (2007). *Sperm counts: Overcome by man's most precious fluid.* New York: New York University Press.

Moreno, J. D. (2011). *The body politic: The battle over science in America.* New York: Bellevue Literary Press.

Nelkin, D., & Lindee, M. S. (1995). *The DNA mystique: The gene as a cultural icon.* New York: Freeman.

Orenstein, P. (2007, July 15). Your gamete, myself. *New York Times.* Retrieved from www.nytimes.com/2007/07/15/magazine/15egg-t.html?scp=2&sq=peggy+orenstein&st=nyt&gwh=3F3CD232BDDA935FA42483207DA599C4

Pande, A. (2012). "It may be her eggs but it's my blood": Surrogates and everyday forms of kinship in India. *Qualitative Sociology, 32*(4), 379–397.

Parthasarathy, S. (2004). Regulating risk: Defining genetic privacy in the United States and Britain. *Science, Technology & Human Values, 29*(3), 332–352. doi:10.1177/0162243904264485

Pavone, V., & Arias, F. (2012). Beyond the geneticization thesis: The political economy of PGD/PGS in Spain. *Science, Technology & Human Values, 37*(3), 235–261.

Pennings, G. (2005). Legal harmonization and reproductive tourism in Europe. *Reproductive Health Matters, 13*(25), 120–128.

Ragone, H. (1994). *Surrogate motherhood: Conception in the heart.* Boulder, CO: Westview Press.

Rapp, R. (2000). *Testing women, testing the fetus: The social impact of amniocentesis in America.* New York: Routledge.

Reilly, P. (2006). *The strongest boy in the world.* Cold Spring Harbor, NY: Cold Spring Harbor Laboratory Press.

Rich, A. (1986). *Of woman born: Motherhood as experience and institution.* New York: W. W. Norton.

Roberts, D. (1997). *Killing the black body: Race, reproduction, and the meaning of liberty.* New York: Vintage Books.

Roberts, D. (2011). *Fatal invention: How science, politics, and big business re-create race in the twenty-first century.* New York: The New Press.

Rothman, B. K. (1993). *The tentative pregnancy: How amniocentesis changes the experience of motherhood.* New York: W. W. Norton.

Rothman, B. K. (2000). *Recreating motherhood.* New Brunswick, NJ: Rutgers University Press.

Rothman, B. K. (2001). *The book of life: A personal and ethical guide to race, normality, and the implications of the human genome project.* Boston, MA: Beacon Press.

Rothschild, J. (2005). *The dream of the perfect child.* Bloomington: Indiana University Press.

Sen, A. (2003). Missing women—Revisited. *BMJ: British Medical Journal, 327*(7427), 1297–1298.

Sharlach, L. (2000). Rape as genocide: Bangladesh, the former Yugoslavia, and Rwanda. *New Political Science, 22*(1), 89–102. doi:10.1080/073931400113549

Sharp, R. R., McGowan, M. L., Verma, J. A., Landy, D. C., McAdoo, S., Carson, S. A. et al. (2010). Moral attitudes and beliefs among couples pursuing PGD for sex selection. *Reproductive Biomedicine Online, 21*(7), 838.

Slater, D. (1997). *Consumer culture and modernity.* Cambridge, UK: Polity.

Smith-Rosenberg, C. (1986). *Disorderly conduct: Visions of gender in Victorian America.* New York: Oxford University Press.

Solinger, R. (2000). *Wake up little Susie: Single pregnancy and race before Roe v. Wade*. New York: Routledge.

Spar, D. (2006). *The baby business: How money, science, and politics drive the commerce of conception*. Boston, MA: Harvard Business School Press.

Strathern, M. (1992). *Reproducing the future: Essays on anthropology, kinship and the new reproductive technologies*. New York: Routledge.

Teman, E. (2010). *Birthing a mother*. Berkeley: University of California Press.

Thernstrom, M. (2010, December 29). Meet the Twiblings. *New York Times*. Retrieved from www.nytimes.com/2011/01/02/magazine/02babymaking-t.html? ref=todayspaper

Thompson, C. (2005). *Making parents: The ontological choreography of reproductive technologies*. Cambridge, MA: The MIT Press.

Twine, F. W. (2011). *Outsourcing the womb: Race, class and gestational surrogacy in a global market*. New York: Routledge.

Whittaker, A. (2010). Challenges of medical travel to global regulation: A case study of reproductive travel in Asia. *Global Social Policy, 10*(3), 396–415.

Whittaker, A. (2011). Reproduction opportunists in the new global sex trade: PGD and non-medical sex selection. *Reproductive BioMedicine Online, 23*(5), 609–617.

WHO Genomic Resource Centre. (2011). *Gender and genetics*. Retrieved from www.who.int/genomics/gender/en/index.html

Wilson, E. O. (2000). *Sociobiology: The new synthesis*. Cambridge, MA: Harvard University Press.

# Conclusion
## Setting Regional and Global Standards

My concern is, there is not currently an international standard . . . that would say that no matter where you went in the world, you'll get [the same kind of treatment]. . . . But, in essence that's not even true in the United States, because although we have regulations, we have SART, and they publish guidelines and stuff, practice may be different in different places. So I don't know that it makes all that much of a difference where you go, whether you go across state lines or whether you leave the country. Where you're going to end up is very important, relative to how good of a clinic are they, how ethical are they, how much money are you going to end up spending, that kind of thing.

(Dr. Randolph, San Francisco)

Dr. Randolph, like other participants in this study, recognized the difficulty in standardizing the practice of reproductive medicine and family formation nationally, let alone internationally, because even when policies and professional norms exist, individual providers, clinics, and organizations do not necessarily adhere to or follow them to the letter or in the same exact way. As discussed in Chapter 3, providers in the United States were not opposed to all forms of regulation of their industry, yet they typically preferred that it come from within the industry itself, rather than imposed by legislative bodies. Even so, many claimed that professional guidelines made by ASRM and SART lack any significant power. Violating professional guidelines may result in getting labeled a rogue practitioner, but it will not necessarily stop the behavior. For example, guidelines about how much young women should be compensated for their oocytes may exist, but that does not prevent companies or clinics from offering amounts far above those suggested limits.

Professional organizations have begun to offer guidelines around reproductive tourism. In 2013, the Ethics Committee of the ASRM published an opinion on cross-border reproductive care, which discussed the driving factors, ethical concerns, and some guidance for how to ameliorate those ethical dilemmas (Ethics Committee of the ASRM, 2013). Interestingly, the guidelines mostly apply to situations in which individuals go *outside of* the United States for fertility services. Three suggestions deal primarily with what the opinion describes as "Departure Country Physicians," and include: a duty to disclose to patients who ask about opportunities to obtain services abroad accurate information that will help them make an informed decision; to inform them about the risks and benefits about going abroad for care; and to continue seeing the patient after she or he returns from abroad after having sought treatment (Ethics Committee of the ASRM, 2013, pp. 648–649). In another section of the opinion, the ethics committee determines that "Destination Country Physicians" do not have an obligation to disclose legal or practical information to their patients if the services requested are illegal in the patients' home countries:

> A physician's duty to provide high-quality medical care and accurate treatment information does not include a duty to investigate or disclose nonmedical information over which the physician has no control and from which the physician derives no personal benefit. Destination country physicians have no duty to act as a patient's legal advisor, and in fact doing so carries a risk of engaging in the unlawful practice of law.
>
> (Ethics Committee of the ASRM, 2013, p. 649)

According to the ASRM, physicians should be held to the standards of their own jurisdictions, and not of the jurisdictions from which the patients are arriving. Adherence to ASRM guidelines, then, maintains a system of wildly divergent practices worldwide.

In Europe, the equivalent professional organization ESHRE (European Society of Human Reproduction and Embryology) has more thorough guidelines regarding cross-border reproductive care (Shenfield, Pennings, Mouzon, Ferraretti, & Goossens, 2011). These include equity for local and foreign patients in terms of minimizing differences in costs, protocols, information, and support; comparable care for donors and patients,[1] and comparable compensation and recruitment criteria for local and foreign donors; informed consent for patients and donors; establishment of national registries of gamete donors; minimization of risks of abuse and trafficking of donors; single embryo transfer for surrogates; and shared responsibility among all providers in sending and receiving countries. Because ESHRE is an institution of providers from numerous countries, adhering to these standards leads to a regionalization of care. It still does not bring us to a *global* standard, however.

The fact that regulations currently vary widely throughout the world does not mean that convergence in policy will not happen at some point in the future, possibly beginning with regional federations such as the European Union. The European Parliament and the European Union Council, in fact, approved a Human Tissues and Cells Directive on March 31, 2004, "on setting standards of quality and safety for the donation, procurement, testing, processing, preservation, storage and distribution of human tissues and cells" (European Union, 2004, p. 48). Although it strives to set a regional standard, the Directive does not diminish the sovereignty of Member States. It stresses European cultural universals such as protection of human rights and human dignity, safety, and informed consent, but the section on Implementation specifically states that Member States may choose to enact more stringent guidelines (Article 4, p. 52). It is therefore not a universalization of Member States' policies, but is instead a baseline of minimal regulation.

For example, the Directive speaks of anonymity and compensation for donation of human tissues and cells. "As a matter of principle," states Paragraph 18, donation should be voluntary, unpaid, anonymous, and altruistic, and therefore, "Member States are urged to take steps to encourage a strong public and non-profit sector involvement in the provision of tissue and cell application services and the related research and development" (European Union, 2004, p. 49). Note that this paragraph does not *order* Member States to forbid compensation or anonymity for donors, but rather *urges* them to do so. In fact, Article 12 states "Member States define the conditions under which compensation may be granted" (European Union, 2004, p. 54). In 2006, a Commissioning Directive was approved by the same body, implementing the 2004 Tissue Directive "as regards traceability requirements, notification of serious adverse reactions and events and certain technical requirements for the coding, processing, preservation, storage and distribution of human tissues and cells" (European Union, 2006, p. 32).

As this example illustrates, the Directive of the European Parliament and Council of the European Union provides regional quality and safety standards, as well as ideals for Member States to strive for, but it leaves room for individuality in Member States' policies. In this respect, aspects of the Directive are less stringent than the Council of Europe's 1997 Oviedo Convention on Human Rights and Medicine. This Convention, which as of 2008 has been ratified by only 21 out of 47 Member States, outright forbids sex selection for social purposes (Article 14), and prohibits financial gain arising from the disposal of the human body or body parts (Article 21) (Council of Europe, 1997).

The Human Tissues and Cells Directive has already had an influence on how the United Kingdom's Human Fertilisation and Embryology Authority (HFEA) deals with reproductive tourism. If people wish to import donated sperm, eggs, or embryos from another country within the European Union, that country must have implemented the standards outlined in the Directive, the donated materials must be screened in accordance with the HFEA's own requirements, and foreign donors, like British ones, must be identifiable and receive compensation only for reasonable expenses. For sperm, eggs, and embryos donated from countries not part of the E.U., the patients' clinic must apply to the HFEA for a Special Direction, and again, adhere to the HFEA's guidelines (Human Fertilisation and Embryology Authority, 2009a). While the HFEA and the E.U. Tissues and Cells Directive have consequences for the importation of reproductive commodities, they do *not* prevent British reproductive tourists from traveling abroad themselves in search of services (Human Fertilisation and Embryology Authority, 2009b). By universalizing some procedures, regional standards such as the Human Tissues and Cells Directive may reduce some forms of reproductive tourism *within* the European Union, but may actually increase the practice of reproductive tourism by European citizens to non-E.U. states.

Intergovernmental and non-governmental organizations may be another source of global standards. For example, the World Health Organization (WHO), United Nations Educational, Scientific and Cultural Organization (UNESCO), and World Medical Association (WMA) have each released statements addressing global bioethical standards for reproductive technologies and infertility treatment (United Nations Educational, Scientific and Cultural Organization [UNESCO], 2005; Vayena, Rowe, & Griffin, 2002; World Medical Association [WMA], 2006). Yet each statement provides only a baseline of ethical practice, rather than a convergence or harmonization of regulations. Declarations by UNESCO, the WHO, or the World Medical Association do not preclude the possibility of countries violating their terms. As with any "universal declaration," the universality of global standards may prove to be stratified, in which some states act as signatories and/or enforcers, while others flagrantly abuse them. Furthermore, maverick physicians and scientists may continue to practice in ways that their colleagues or their governments disapprove of, and if restricted from practicing in one locality, have the possibility of offshoring, and moving where the same regulations do not apply.

Another model of convergence that nations may want to consider is the Hague Convention on the Protection of Children and Co-Operation in Respect of Intercountry Adoption (more familiarly known as the Hague Adoption Convention), a multilateral agreement monitoring transnational adoption practices among over seventy nations. This international law sets baseline, universal standards for adoptions occurring between participating countries to ensure that full, informed consent has been freely given, and that the best interests of the child are met. The Convention also includes provisions mandating that countries establish a Central Authority to keep records, enforce rules, accredit service providers, and communicate with its international counterparts (Hague Conference on Private International Law, 1993).

The Adoption Convention, which already acknowledges the reality of the transnationalization of reproduction, may be a potential model for dealing with reproductive tourism. Both transnational adoption and reproductive tourism reveal the geographic ends to which people will go in order to form families, and both are rife with ethical dilemmas and potentials for abuse and exploitation. At the very least, the Hague Adoption Convention acknowledges that as long as intercountry adoption is a reality, international regulations may help to stem abuses such as kidnapping or the trafficking of children.

Applying international law to reproductive tourism may be a way to ensure that the exercising of one person's right to use technology to have children does not infringe on another's health and well-being. Provisions mandating the establishment of a central authority in each signing country may presage the formation or identification of a national regulatory body in those countries that currently lack one. Although a Convention on Reproductive Tourism would probably encounter backlash from the fertility industry in laissez-faire countries such as the United States, it may still be in those countries' interest to sign in order to continue to attract fertility clinic patients from other signing countries. At the very least, it may begin a conversation about whether adoption of national policies regarding reproductive technologies is warranted or even constitutional.[2]

Even if international standards are adopted, it is doubtful that reproductive tourism will disappear. Although some practices such as multiple embryo transfers, exorbitant compensation for egg donation, or sex selection could conceivably be banned by international law, the global marketplace and the demand for reproductive technologies already exists. Furthermore, the pace of scientific innovation may prove to be a step ahead of regulation, with new procedures and services arising as older techniques are banned or standardized. While international standards may not stem reproductive tourism, nor modify the stratified nature of it, they may at the very least ameliorate some of the potentials for abuse and exploitation associated with reproductive technologies. Something like a Hague Convention on Reproductive Tourism would acknowledge the twin forces of technology and globalization that have utterly transformed procreation.

## FINAL THOUGHTS

Analysis of the relationship between providers, clients, and the global fertility market points to the competitive advantages that the United States fertility industry has to offer, but also speaks to the larger, macro implications of globalization. There are abundant and diverse types of services available worldwide for medically assisted conception, and providers compete on a global stage for consumers of those services. This book argues that the United States fertility market is uniquely positioned to capitalize on a complex combination of push and pull factors driving reproductive tourism. Fertility industry providers help meet the desires of those individuals willing to travel hundreds or thousands of miles, across oceans and time zones, in order to have biological children. The providers interviewed for this book subjectively described to me the world of reproductive tourism from their very particular point of view, which may, of course, differ from that of the clients they work with. Providers create and sustain the thriving fertility industry, market their services to an international consumer base, and join professional organizations that lobby for the continued laissez-faire climate regarding reproductive technologies.

Those who, like the providers interviewed in this book, defend reproductive tourism, may use the language of reproductive freedom and rights, couched in universalism. If one has the "right" to have a child by any means possible, is it not also one's right to travel elsewhere as an act of civil disobedience to become a procreative outlaw? Is this not their duty as liberal global biocitizens? Or is this an example, as Aihwa Ong (2007) may put it, merely another "neoliberal exception" and "self-responsibilization" (p. 172)? As Ong writes,

American neoliberalization is now articulated by the Bush administration as "every citizen an agent of his or her own destiny." American liberty is tweaked to mean freedom *from* state protection and freedom to respond autonomously to the turbulence of global markets.

(2007, p. 172)

Are reproductive tourists, as global biocitizens, using ideals of American liberty to express their reproductive destiny on the global marketplace?

Globalization and the ease of movement across borders by global elites adds another dimension to this equation, in that the self-responsibilization articulated by Ong applies not only to American citizens but also to any global elite who can afford to take part in neoliberal American dreams of unfettered business and consumerism. Notions of American liberty and freedom from state protection are value-adding marketable selling points aimed at global elites to consume the goods and services of American industries and corporations. Much like small island nations marketing their offshore tax havens and export processing zones, or like the Netherlands marketing its liberal drug and prostitution laws, the United States markets its neoliberal biopolitics and positions itself globally as a Mother Country, as a creator of families and a producer of babies for a global citizenry.

## NOTES

1. Note that ESHRE implies that "patient" refers to the intended parents, and not to the third-party donors.
2. It appears that such conversations are indeed occurring. In August 2014, an International Forum on Intercountry Adoption & Global Surrogacy took place in The Hague, Netherlands (International Institute of Social Studies in The Hague, 2014).

## REFERENCES

Council of Europe. (1997). *Convention for the protection of human rights and dignity of the human being with regard to the application of biology and medicine: Convention on Human Rights and Biomedicine.* Oviedo. Retrieved from http://conventions.coe.int/Treaty/en/Treaties/html/164.htm

Ethics Committee of the ASRM. (2013). Cross-border reproductive care: A committee opinion. *Fertility and Sterility, 100*(3), 645–650. doi:10.1016/j.fertnstert.2013.02.051

European Union. (2004). Directive 2004/23/EC of the European Parliament and of the Council of 31 March 2004 on setting standards of quality and safety for the donation, procurement, testing, processing, preservation, storage and distribution of human tissues and cells. *Official Journal of the European Union, L102*, 48–58.

European Union. (2006). Commission directive 2006/86/EC of 24 October 2006 implementing Directive 2004/23/EC of the European Parliament and of the Council as regards traceability requirements, notification of serious adverse reactions and events and certain technical requirements for the coding, processing, preservation, storage and distribution of human tissues and cells. *Official Journal of the European Union, L294*, 32–50.

Hague Conference on Private International Law. (1993, May 29). *Convention on protection of children and co-operation in respect of intercountry adoption.* Retrieved from www.hcch.net/index_en.php?act=conventions.text&cid=69

Human Fertilisation and Embryology Authority. (2009a, August 28). *Importing sperm, eggs or embryos from abroad—IVF FAQs.* Retrieved from www.hfea.gov.uk/patient-questions-importing.html

Human Fertilisation and Embryology Authority. (2009b, August 28). *IVF treatment abroad: Issues and risks.* Retrieved from www.hfea.gov.uk/fertility-clinics-treatment-abroad.html

International Institute of Social Studies in The Hague. (2014). *International forum on intercountry adoption & global surrogacy.* Retrieved from www.iss.nl/research/conferences_and_seminars/periodic_conferences_debates_and_seminars/international_forum_on_intercountry_adoption_global_surrogacy/

Ong, A. (2007). *Neoliberalism as exception: Mutations in citizenship and sovereignty* (2nd printing). Durham, NC: Duke University Press.

Shenfield, F., Pennings, G., Mouzon, J.D., Ferraretti, A.P., & Goossens, V. (2011). ESHRE's good practice guide for cross-border reproductive care for centers and practitioners. *Human Reproduction, 26*(7), 1625–1627. doi:10.1093/humrep/der090

United Nations Educational, Scientific and Cultural Organization (UNESCO). (2005, October 19). *Universal declaration on bioethics and human rights.* Retrieved from http://portal.unesco.org/en/ev.php-URL_ID=31058&URL_DO=DO_TOPIC&URL_SECTION=201.html

Vayena, E., Rowe, P.J., & Griffin, P.D. (2002). *Current practices and controversies in assisted reproduction.* Geneva: World Health Organization.

World Medical Association (WMA). (2006, October). *WMA statement on assisted reproductive technologies.* Retrieved from www.wma.net/en/30publications/10policies/r3/index.html

# Appendix
## Notes on Methodology and Sampling

### PARTICIPANT OBSERVATION

I conducted unobtrusive participant observation at public events in New York City and San Francisco that were sponsored by fertility clinics, programs, and a non-profit advocacy group. The events fell in three categories: "Open House" seminars, special topic seminars, and conferences. At Open House seminars ($n = 5$), fertility clinic staff members (usually physicians and other medical staff) presented educational information about infertility and infertility treatments, informed potential clients about their services, and often gave tours of the facilities. The special topic seminars ($n = 3$) were narrower in scope than the Open Houses, featuring formal presentations (also by physicians and other professionals) and moderated discussion about such topics as egg freezing, fertility preservation, and infertility prevention. Two of these seminars occurred on site at clinics, but the third, as described below, took place at a nail salon. Both the Open House and special topic seminars typically lasted 1.5 to 2 hours, whereas the conferences ($n = 2$) were daylong events. The latter, both organized by the same non-profit organization but co-sponsored by fertility clinics, pharmaceutical organizations, and other corporate and non-profit entities, took place at conference centers and consisted of series of panels and workshops led by physicians, attorneys, and social workers on a variety of topics.

Participation at most events seemed to be evenly split between whites and people of color. Two of the special topic seminars were billed as "women only" events, but the other events had a mix of solitary women, heterosexual couples, and friend pairs. A wide range of ages were represented, with most participants appearing to be in their thirties. I did not record any identifying information about participants or their infertility status if they disclosed it.

### IN-DEPTH INTERVIEWS: SAMPLING AND RECRUITMENT

I sampled and recruited providers in New York City, Los Angeles, and the San Francisco Bay Area (see Table A.1). These regions are three of the most popular destinations for reproductive tourism within the United States.

Selection and recruitment of subjects was made through the use of public records (including websites), participant observation at public events, and a minor bit of snowball sampling. I found providers to contact to inquire about interviews via several sources, including the SART (Society for Assisted Reproductive Technology) online national database of clinics and fertility doctors, ASRM's (American Society for Reproductive Medicine) published list of approved egg donor agencies, and print and online directories of fertility professionals from the non-profit advocacy groups RESOLVE and the American Fertility Association (AFA). I also conducted Internet searches via Google, using such keywords as "New York egg donor," "California surrogacy," and "sex selection fertility clinic." Additionally, some providers I contacted were people I had met while conducting participant observation at public events. Some minor snowball sampling yielded interviews with co-workers or colleagues at other clinics. I contacted a total of 126 providers via email, which ultimately yielded twenty interviews, a response rate of almost 16% (see Table A.2).

*Table A.1*   Recruitment

| City | Number of providers contacted | Number of interviews scheduled | Response rate |
|---|---|---|---|
| New York City | 50 | 6 | 12% |
| Los Angeles | 38 | 8 | 21% |
| San Francisco | 38 | 6 | 15.7% |
| Total | 126 | 20 | 15.8% |

*Table A.2*   Providers Interviewed

| Name[1] | City | Occupation[2] | Type of program | Executive? |
|---|---|---|---|---|
| Dr. Gorman | NYC | Physician | Clinic | X |
| Dr. Bradley | NYC | Physician | Clinic | X |
| Dr. Helos | NYC | Physician | Clinic | X |
| Dr. Maynard | NYC | Physician | Clinic | |
| Liz | NYC | Broker | Clinic (egg donation program) | |
| Jen | NYC | Genetic Counselor | Clinic | |
| Robin | LA | Broker | Egg Donor Agency | X |
| Michael | LA | Attorney | Law Firm | |
| Linda | LA | Administrator | Clinic | |
| Anne | LA | Broker | Surrogacy Agency | |
| Liam | LA | Broker | Donor and Surrogacy Agency | X |
| Rebekah | LA | Broker | Donor and Surrogacy Agency | X |
| Shelby | LA | Broker | Donor and Surrogacy Agency | X |

*Table A.2* (continued)

| Name[1] | City | Occupation[2] | Type of program | Executive? |
|---|---|---|---|---|
| Dr. Silverstein | LA | Physician | Clinic | X |
| Megan | LA | Broker | Egg Donor Agency | |
| Dr. Liu | SF | Physician | Clinic | |
| Deirdre | SF | Attorney | Law Firm | X |
| Tammy | SF | Social Worker | Surrogacy Agency | |
| Dr. Leveque | SF | Physician | Clinic | |
| Dr. Randolph | SF | Physician | Clinic | X |

[1] Although some providers consented to using their real names, several requested a pseudonym. In order to be consistent, I have changed the names of all people I spoke with.

[2] These "occupations" are not necessarily the providers' official titles, but I have placed them within these general categories.

## IN-DEPTH INTERVIEWS: STRUCTURE AND ANALYSIS

Each interview lasted approximately one to one-and-a-half hours each. I created an interview protocol with open-ended questions to guide the conversation, but I also allowed space for tangents and other questions to emerge organically. The approximate arc of the interview protocol was as follows:

1. Warm-up questions about career and organization
2. The state of the fertility industry
3. The organization of reproductive medicine
4. Demographics of clients
5. Interactions with clients
6. Reproductive tourism—process, challenges
7. How policy affects their practice
8. Perspectives on regulation

More specifically, some sample questions were:

Do you have any concerns about the state of the field of reproductive medicine either nationally or globally?

What do you think are the factors that go into your clients' decisions to work with your particular organization?

Can you tell me how exactly the process [of reproductive tourism] works—that is, how is the process different for your international clients than from your local clients?

Can you describe for me how, if at all, public polices and regulations affect your practice?

Given the recent debates about health care in the United States, do you foresee any changes in the regulation of reproductive medicine?

With one exception (Dr. Helos), providers consented to having their conversations digitally recorded. For Dr. Helos' interview, I took notes by hand.

Interview transcripts were coded with qualitative analysis software Atlas.ti, using grounded theory techniques. As Charmaz and Mitchell (2001, p. 165) put it, these codes "arise *from* analyzing data, rather than from applying concepts from earlier works *to* data. When coding, researchers take an active stance toward their data. . . . They must ask questions of these data." While I may have had some preliminary ideas about themes prior to conducting the interviews, it is the data that I collected that pushed the subsequent analysis. Some examples of emergent themes and categories that I coded for included: "Challenges of Reproductive Tourism," "Ethics," "How Patients Choose," "Liberalism," "Market Driven," and "Why USA." Whereas "Ethics" is a generic category I coded for when conversation veered to a discussion concerning ethical matters or professional norms, the code for "Market Driven" emerged when I noticed a *pattern* in which providers described, challenged, or supported the idea that aspects of their work involve commercial transactions.

## REFERENCE

Charmaz, K., & Mitchell, R. (2001). Grounded theory in ethnography. In P. Atkinson, A. Coffey, S. Delamont, J. Lofland, & L. Lofland (Eds.), *Handbook of ethnography* (pp. 160–176). London: Sage.

# Index

For Product Safety Concerns and Information please contact our EU
representative GPSR@taylorandfrancis.com Taylor & Francis Verlag GmbH,
Kaufingerstraße 24, 80331 München, Germany


Printed and bound by CPI Group (UK) Ltd, Croydon, CR0 4YY

01/05/2025

01858438-0002